In the night between Wednesday 6 and Thursday 7
of December 1978, the security guard Pier Fortunato
Zanfretta of the Institute of Private Security
Val Bisagno in Genoa, Italy, was found
in a state of shock and terror-stricken
near the country house *Casa Nostra* (Our House)
placed in Marzano of Torriglia,
a village up in the hills of Genoa.
When he woke up, Zanfretta told shaking that
he saw "a very big alien, three meters (118.11 inches) tall,
with a fat and corrugated gray skin, like it was a flabby suit,"
who few minutes later fly away
"aboard a giant bright light triangular shaped,
with small little lights of different colors in the upper side."
During regressive hypnosis, the night adventure was
borne out by the man, and he told was dragged inside
the "spaceship" where four monstrous aliens
examined him in great details.
An investigation by Carabinieri, the Italian military police,
verified that 52 people saw a very big flying bright saucer
at that time in the Torriglia sky. Besides, in the meadow
where the others' security guards found Zanfretta,
Carabinieri found out a three meters mark,
horseshoe shaped.
The people were still thinking to that mysterious encounter
of the third kind, that twenty days later it happened again.
This time Carabinieri found out footprints 50 centimeters
long (19.69 inches) near the security guard's car.
The Zanfretta case was just beginning.

THE ZANFRETTA CASE

Chronicle of an Incredible True Story

by
Rino Di Stefano

First International English Edition

Originally published as
Luci nella Notte – UFO: il caso Zanfretta (1984)

This first international English edition of *The Zanfretta Case* has been
registered at the U.S. Copyright Office on January 16, 2015 with the
number TX8-061-575.

The original Italian edition of this book, entitled *Luci nella Notte –
UFO: il caso Zanfretta,* has been registered at the U.S. Copyright
Office on March 3, 1992 with the number PA577211 and cataloged
in the Library of Congress with the Control Number (LCCN)
93230974.

On the cover:
One of the footprint (dotted line) found near Zanfretta's car up in the
hill in proximity to the village of Rossi (Genoa, Italy) compared with
the shoe no. 10 of brigadier Antonio Nucchi.
(Photo by Luciano Zeggio)

Author Website: www.rinodistefano.com

ISBN-10: 1-5056-5009-7
ISBN-13: 978-1-5056-5009-9

Published in December 2014

Available on Kindle and online stores

Printed by CreateSpace
www.createspace.com

To Lory and Daniel

CONTENTS

INTRODUCTION
An Incredible True Story

The Zanfretta Case was first published in Italy in 1984. It is currently in its sixth edition. This is the first international English language edition. The book rights have been bought even by Hikaruland Publishing Co. Ltd. in Tokyo. The success of the book may be due to the fact that it is based on newspaper reporting, chronicling a story that actually happened. As a reporter, I did an investigation lasting two years, from 1978 to 1980, while the story was ongoing.

The protagonist of this incredible story, Pier Fortunato Zanfretta, was a security guard who during that time had contact with giant 'aliens' at least six times. The backdrop to this event was the town of Torriglia on the hilltops of the Ligurian Apennine mountains. The Carabinieri, the Italian military police force, opened a judicial inquiry into these inexplicable episodes, which was later transferred to the Genoa Magistrate's Court. The case was archived on December 31, 1979 for 'lack of criminal evidence.' We are not talking about an approximation or a story that was hearsay. What you will read in this book is a faithful recounting and reporting of what actually happened while it was still happening. There are no comments or interpretations, just a chronicle of the events. The most baffling thing is that Zanfretta was not the only witness to the events narrated. Dozens and dozens of people, among whom some of his colleagues, saw with their own eyes a large flying disk in the same places and at the same time that Zanfretta was being mysteriously abducted. For only his first encounter, the Carabinieri identified 52 eyewitnesses. Moreover, during the second encounter, footprints 50 centimeters long (approximately 20 inches) were found all around Zanfretta's car.

According to Zanfretta's story, the 'aliens' gave him a mysterious ball that still today, he guards carefully. This detail sparked the interest of an American millionaire from Arizona who in 1991 got in touch with Zanfretta, offering him a great sum of money in exchange for the sphere. But Zanfretta refused the offer. Because of the buzz that his story generated, Zanfretta lost his family (he is the father of four children), his job and his peace of mind. Today he lives on his pension in a small apartment in the center of Genoa.

What follows here is his story, the facts of an incredible true story. Any reference to facts and people is absolutely real and true, and the information contained in this book has been verified by me personally. The judgment about what actually happened is instead completely up to you, who are now reading this story.

December 2014

Rino Di Stefano

FOREWORD

Rino Di Stefano

and

The Zanfretta Case

Rino Di Stefano was the first Italian journalist to take serious interest in and to begin a serious investigation into the case of UFO contact with a Uniformed Security Guard and his patrol car in the Vicinity of Genoa, Italy.

I found the case so effectively reported and so exciting that I invited Rino Di Stefano to come to my *First World UFO Congress* in Tucson, Arizona, in 1991, bringing Pier Fortunato Zanfretta with him, and paid their travel and expenses.

They were a hit and the audience voted them one of my top presentations that year.

This is one of the most informative cases of UFO contact, and who they are and why are they here on record, thanks to Rino Di Stefano.

A must read book.

Wendelle C. Stevens
Lt. Col. USAF (Ret.)

PREFACE

A Book To Read Twice

This is a book that you need to read twice.

The first time, you have no choice after the first few pages, when the reader finds himself engrossed in an adventure that is just as compelling as a classic 'mystery novel'...

The curiosity to know 'how is it going to end...' will bring you to devour chapter after chapter, and deceive you into thinking or even hoping that you will find a surprise ending. But there is none, because there can be none, in that this is a careful chronicle and not a literary invention.

So then there comes the impetus to re-read it, reading between the lines, trying to understand and interpret situations that seem too far away from our usual knowledge and understanding; we want to put away and pigeonhole everything we are wiling to accept.

And it is in this second approach that we can fully appreciate the author's talent, such a scrupulous journalist, so faithful to his professional commitment that he doesn't even exploit the voluminous or, if you want, sensational material that he gathered in order "to build a story." He prefers the role of the anonymous narrator to that of protagonist.

Rino Di Stefano thus offers a substantial contribution to the study of mysterious phenomena, exactly through the deliberate choice not to intervene in the affair that he narrates with comments or personal interpretations.

And in any case, he is not a detached narrator, because he tries to understand the origins, motives and developments of every detail, going to research the eyewitness accounts and then compare them with what he has already acquired in his store of knowledge.

He verges on nitpicking sometimes, but this is the risk that a journalist runs when he wants to be precise and exhaustive. That is to say, if he wants to be a real reporter.

And Rino Di Stefano is just that, a full-blooded reporter and he shows it in this work.

To create this book he also paid the price of emotions, describing the protagonist's affairs in this chronicle without ever letting himself get caught in attitudes that could be construed as shared or sentimental or emotional or critical.

It cannot have been easy, because Fortunato Zanfretta is the ideal character to let yourself get involved, one way or another, either in total adoption or total rejection of the story and its protagonist.

We will say no more about Fortunato Zanfretta, the security guard who maintains that he had numerous tormented encounters with extraterrestrials, also because there is nothing to add to the detailed essay reported here and that you are about to read.

It is singular, if anything, that we are speaking of UFOs, that is to say unidentified objects, in a book that in its concreteness is anything but a UFO.

Alfredo Provenzali
President of
The Group of Ligurian Reporters

The Zanfretta Case

Any reference to facts or people
is not absolutely by chance
This book is just the detailed report
of an incredible and astonishing true story

1978 – 1980
THE STORY

CHAPTER 1

Flying Saucers in Torriglia

The morning of Friday, December 8, 1978, things were bustling in the newsroom at the Genoese evening newspaper *Corriere Mercantile*. The newsroom was abuzz with the report of a sighting of a bright flying saucer in a little town on the hilltops above Genoa, Torriglia. It had been spotted by a night watchman, Fortunato Zanfretta, 26 years old, married with two children, who worked for the *Istituto di Vigilanza* "Val Bisagno," a security patrol company.

Everybody was talking about it. Especially the *Secolo XIX*, the most widely read newspaper in the region of Liguria, which had run a six-column article. The title was telling: "Close Encounters in Torriglia..."

There were chuckles, comments and some wisecracks, and no one was taking the watchman's nighttime adventure seriously. Mimmo Angeli, who at the time was the chief reporter and who today is the editor-in-chief at the *Corriere Mercantile* described it as bullshit. Other editors echoed his sentiments with biting comments.

After all, it wasn't easy to take what they had written about Zanfretta in the *Secolo XIX* as being the truth. The journalist Enzo Bonifazi, sticking rigorously to simply reporting the facts, said that the guard was in shock for having met, during a routine inspection of a villa in Marzano di Torriglia, *a huge being, about 3 meters tall, with wavy skin as if it were fat or a loose sweatsuit and gray in any case. Right after that, the extra-terrestrial supposedly flew away in a giant light, triangular shape topped by little lights of different colors.*

Even if it was a figment of someone's imagination, there were however a few details that gave one pause. In fact, according to the report of the Carabinieri of Torriglia, who were informed immediately by the directors of the security patrol company "Val Bisagno", other people also confirmed the presence of a great light in the sky over Torriglia that night exactly in those same hours during which the episode that Zanfretta described took place, and for which he was the casual protagonist.

I decided that the case interested me. First I asked Angeli for permission to go to the place with our press photographer Luciano Zeggio, to get a feel for the place.

At first, Angeli didn't want me to, saying it was a waste of time. Then, realizing I intended to go in the afternoon after work, he told me he had no objections.

Among my colleagues there was one, Alfredo Passadore, who showed a certain curiosity about the night watchman's incident. Obviously, since flying saucers were involved, he didn't want to seem too keen. Also because when talking about UFOs, in some journalistic circles at least, not to compromise yourself, you have to laugh it off.

But this time, even he – having read the report of what had gone on in Torriglia – was curious.

Zanfretta was in shock. We asked ourselves: is it possible that a security guard known as a responsible and courageous person, could come to the point that he trembles with fear for having seen an *extraterrestrial and his flying saucer?*

So when I asked Passadore if he wanted to come with Zeggio and me to Torriglia, he accepted with just a slight reservation.

We left at about 3:30 p.m. with the fire engine red Alfa Sud that Passadore had bought just a few days earlier.

We traveled without problems up to the Scoffera Pass where the tunnel that connects to the road for Torriglia starts. Just out of the tunnel, however, everything changed. It was as if we had passed from one season to the next in a second. The road was icy, snow had piled up on the sides, the landscape had taken on that typical wintery gray.

Finding the turn-off that leads to Marzano from State Road 45 was not hard. We found it to the left, just before the town of Torriglia. Almost crawling, we started up the little street. All in all, there are about 20 houses scattered on the top of a hill.

When we arrived in a little square, which we found out later was the center of the village, a farmer indicated the road to take to the place that interested us. According to the Carabinieri's report (they had opened an investigation on the sighting), Zanfretta had alleged that he'd seen a UFO rising into the sky near the Villa Casa Nostra which belonged to a Genoese dentist, Ettore Righi.

The monstrous and enormous *martian* had been in the garden of the very same villa.

From the path, we saw the villa right away: it was a nice freestanding home, two-story, with a sloping roof and stucco walls.

After having parked on the side of the road, we started toward the house. The cold was biting. The vegetation around the villa was

20

completely covered in frost.

Apparently, from what we could see from a first inspection, there was nothing to make us think that in that same place, 48 hours earlier, something so exceptional had happened. Only the panorama had something gloomy, almost ghost-like. The house faced onto a valley and the reddish and tenuous light of winter made it seem like a bottomless coffin.

The mountaintops on the other side of the valley were surrounded by a reddish halo broken by the deepening blue of the evening to come.

Passadore wandered around the garden near the gate. Zeggio and I inspected the frozen front yard where Zanfretta had been found by his colleagues.

The sign that the Carabinieri had described as the *mark left by a helicopter or something large* that *had landed on the yard next to the house* was on the other side, toward the mountains.

By now however, it was hardly visible. But we were flabbergasted when we saw a very clearly drawn, distinct semicircle about 3 meters in diameter exactly in the center of the lawn where we were standing.

The thickness of the semicircle was about 15 centimeters and formed a very precise design, having pressed down the frozen grass about 3 centimeters deep.

At that point, even if no conclusion could be drawn, it was clear that something, whatever it was, had landed on that field.

On the way back, we decided to stop by Torriglia to talk with the commander of the local Carabinieri station.

Brigadier Antonio Nucchi welcomed us in a friendly manner. He told us right away that he had met Zanfretta some years before when the guard was still working as a bartender in Sampierdarena, the first district to the west of Genoa.

He gave us an interview that I then published in the Monday edition on December 11, 1978. This is what was written:

"When we learned of the fact, we went immediately to the place," says Brigadier Nucchi. "Zanfretta at first did not even want to come with us. He was scared to death. Which is a strange thing because I've known him for years and I can assure you that he is a very decisive fellow who on various occasions has even had to shoot, when that was necessary. So he's not the type of person who scares easily. I would say the exact opposite. He has always been someone who reflects on things, he never had strange thoughts in his head.

"That day however, he was afraid to go back to the villa. Then we convinced him and we went. The strange thing is that his behavior changed as soon as we were in sight of the house.

"First he was normal, and we made small talk without any problem. Then suddenly he started to stutter. He was remembering what had happened and was frightened.

"In any case, he brought us to the place and showed us the exact area. There, in the open space right behind the villa, we found a deep mark in the ground, shaped like a horseshoe. It was also pretty clear: about a span thick, two and a half meters wide extending about three meters.

"It seemed as though an object of that shape, rather heavy, had been laid on the grass. The vegetation, in fact, looked clearly flattened.

"On the other hand I think that something like what Zanfretta described actually did happen there that Thursday in Marzano. There are too many clues that confirm the hypothesis of a UFO.

"When the word got out that someone had seen a flying object in that area, some people got courageous and told us that phenomena of that type were not uncommon in that area.

"There were two women in a nearby village that confirmed having seen around 9 p.m., from the terrace of their home, a bright aircraft heading for the area where the villa is.

"Someone else, from Marzano this time, said they had seen a UFO hovering in that area more than once. They never spoke about it, they explained, because they were afraid of being laughed at.

"I believe, therefore, that in this instance we can reasonably speak of a phenomenon that in any case has something to do with UFOs. The fact is that now I have to write a report and try to find who is responsible for the incident. You tell me, who do I charge?"

The Carabinieri have a manual containing all the procedures needed in case of a call on site. They added a page to this manual, 92 *bis*, where they speak expressly of UFOs.

What is written is that, in case of a sighting, the station chief has to immediately report all the details to Headquarters, including the details of any possible witness.

On page 92 *bis* it also says that there is an office at the Department of Defense in Rome that exclusively takes care of UFO sightings that happen on Italian soil.

Nucchi told us later on that during his investigation a good 52 people saw a large bright object over Marzano that night.

Among others, there is the testimony of the Brigadier of the Finanza (Italian Finance Police), Salvatore Esposito, who was terrified. He was near the garage of his house, trying to pull up the roller-door. All of a sudden, the sky lit up like daytime. Thinking that the friend who was waiting for him in the car had turned on the high beams, he told him, annoyed, to turn them off.

But when he turned around, he saw that the car's headlights were off, and that his friend's eyes were popping out of his head as he looked toward the sky. Above them was a huge flying saucer, completely still, that was projecting an intense white light toward the ground.

The Brigadier was paralyzed with fear. He started to feel like himself again only after a few seconds, when the saucer leaped forward and took off. Neither of them said anything to anyone else, with the exception of Nucchi.

This is when the Zanfretta case started for me. There were too many eyewitness reports from reliable and disinterested people for the night watchman's adventure not to be, at least in part, believable.

Passadore did not share my opinion entirely. Reluctant to expose himself more than necessary, he published with me only the report that appeared in the *Gazzetta del Lunedì* (the Monday edition), but did not want to be on the case anymore. Our collaboration ended there.

I, instead, went on. I wanted to meet Zanfretta in person, to talk to him and especially to see what kind of man he was.

Among other things, to confirm Zanfretta's incident, another UFO sighting took place the very next day, on Saturday, December 9, 1978, this time in Barletta, in the region of Puglia. As reported by the *Secolo XIX* in the Sunday edition of December 10, 1978 in an article by Pino Aprile, a squad car of the Carabinieri and four young men who were traveling by car, were literally dazzled by a big flying saucer that was spinning on itself and giving off a blinding light. In their fear, the boys' car went off the road, and one of them, Cosimo Nero, was hospitalized for shock.

The flying saucer had even landed. "On the place of the sightings", the article says, "once the UFOs had disappeared, a horse-shoe shaped print was discovered, with a diameter over 2 meters wide." Well, one could talk about coincidences, but it was evident that the two episodes, even if separated by distance, really had some things in common.

When I called "Val Bisagno" to have an appointment, I was told that I first had to speak with Lieutenant Giovanni Cassiba. The director, Gianfranco Tutti, had delegated to him the task of taking care of those curious people who wanted to know more about what had happened.

Cassiba welcomed me in his 10th floor office in the skyscraper on Via Ceccardi where the radio command center of the security patrol agency is located. A stern man, without mincing words, he told me right off that they did not want a lot of noise made about their employee.

I explained that I had no intention of making Zanfretta appear ridiculous, if that was what he meant, but in fact wanted to speak to him and get an idea of what actually happened during the incident that night.

I think my sincerity was perceptible. Cassiba proved to be very polite and authorized me to speak both with Zanfretta and the telephone operator who was on duty the night of the *encounter*, and with the same colleagues who found him after.

When I met him, I realized he was very shy. You had to pull the words out of his mouth. With a little bit of good will, I showed him that I didn't intend to distort any of the facts that he was telling me and I earned his trust. What follows is the story he told me and that I published in an article in the weekly magazine *Gente*, on January 20, 1979.

"Wednesday, December 6, around 11:30 p.m.," the night watchman says, "I went to Marzano for the usual round. When I got nearby the Villa Casa Nostra my car suddenly stopped, with its electrical system out of order. In the distance then I saw four lights that were moving on the lawn next to the villa. Right away I thought of robbers, and tried to call headquarters with the radio to tell them about it, but even the radio had gone mysteriously silent.

"At the time I thought of a breakdown and I didn't really give it too much thought. I got out of the car, and with my gun in my hand, I went toward the villa. In my other hand I had my flashlight, which was obviously off. All I could think of at the moment was to catch the thieves, there's no time for being afraid or anything of the sort.

"Near the villa I saw that the gate was open and the front door was wide open. So I went in and got close to the wall, so that I could eventually jump out from there and arrest the robbers. Just then,"

Zanfretta continues, "I was pushed and I turned around quickly with my gun drawn and flashlight on. There, a few centimeters from where I was standing, I saw something that gave me goose-bumps. It was a monstrous being, frightening, and very tall. To look at it in the face, I had to turn the flashlight upward and I calculated that it couldn't be less than 3 meters tall. I was so scared I dropped the flashlight. I picked it up and fled. While running, all of a sudden I felt an enormous light behind me. I turned around and I was somewhat blinded by an aircraft, triangular in shape but very flat, that was lifting up from behind the villa with a hiss. It was very bright and bigger than the house itself. The light was so bright I had to cover my eyes with my arm. It had gotten very warm all around me."

This version of the facts was confirmed to me also by Carlo Toccalino, the operator who that night was on duty at the radio command center. "I received the first call," Toccalino was remembering, "around a quarter past midnight. Zanfretta was shouting and kept saying, 'Oh my God, is that ugly!' So I asked him if he was being assaulted, and he replied, 'No, they're not men, they're not men.' At this point, the connection was interrupted and I informed Lieutenant Cassiba."

He added further details to the story. He told me that he immediately dispatched the guards Luna and Mascia to find Zanfretta and that they found him only around 1:15 a.m., face down on the ground in the front yard of the villa. That is, in the same place that Zeggio, the photojournalist, and I had noticed the semi-circular mark on the ground.

"When he saw them, he jumped up with his gun in one hand and the flashlight which was on in the other," Cassiba told me in front of Zanfretta, who almost as if feeling guilty, was sitting very quietly in a corner. "He didn't recognize them and his eyes were popping out of his head. They told him to put the gun down, but he didn't even seem to understand. In the end, they had to jump on him and disarm him. What is strange is that his clothes were warm despite the biting cold, as it often gets in that area. Moreover, both the gate and the door to the villa were closed as they always are. The signs of a landing of a UFO were clearly visible."

Talking to those people, I realized that there had to be something true in this whole story. It's not as if I believed straight away that UFOs existed, or that I really took what was being told to me as being the truth. Nothing of the sort. I was quite surprised on the other hand by the fact that this story involved so many common people, people with a normal existence who in such circumstances found themselves completely out of place. And in any case, ill at ease.

It didn't take long for the Zanfretta case to interest UFO specialists. There was one among them, Luciano Boccone, who both for his personality and background could be considered rather impartial. Boccone, who died prematurely four years later, was President of the UFO research group of Arenzano *(a seaside village 30 km west of Genoa)* and I had already met him a year earlier when I had written an article about UFO sightings in Liguria for the *Gazzetta del Lunedì*.

Boccone's group kept records on this type of phenomena and I got a lot of interesting data from him. I have to say that we did not agree on many things. From my point of view, Boccone was too abstract and even if he and his collaborators used complex scientific equipment for their research, he tended to give an almost paranormal or mystical explanation to the UFO phenomenon. The idea that unidentified flying objects could be very sophisticated machines led by intelligent beings never occurred to him.

In any case, he was a nice person, educated and fun to be around. So when he called me and proposed asking "Val Bisagno" to have Zanfretta undergo hypnosis to have him go back in time and have him relive those moments, it had me thinking a while. No doubt I was curious and the temptation to know more about that night stimulated me.

To begin with, even before talking with Zanfretta's bosses, a hypnotist had to be found. The person who would have had to perform hypnosis had to be qualified and above all trustworthy. The name came out when I spoke about it with a friend, Alfredo Ferraro, a writer of parapsychology and spiritism, author of various books. Ferraro gave me the name of Dr. Mauro Moretti without hesitation. He was a medical doctor specialized in hypnosis with his office at no. 15, Via San Sebastiano in Genoa.

I got in touch with him by phone. Ferraro had told me he was a young doctor, very serious and very good. Counting on this reference, I told him all about the story and asked if he would be willing to put Zanfretta under hypnosis. He answered that he would do it if the person who was directly involved gave his consent.

Safe in the knowledge that I had found the right person for the task, this time I turned to Gianfranco Tutti. The director of "Val Bisagno" told me that Fortunato Zanfretta's story left him somewhat perplexed and he didn't know what to think of it. Zanfretta, he said, had always been a good employee and a night watchman worthy of complete trust. Even on previous occasions, when he found himself in dangerous situations, he had always dealt with the matter with decisiveness.

The story of the UFOs now seemed absurd. But, seeing as it had happened to Zanfretta, who knew? His main concern, in any case, was that other employees should not know his opinion on the matter. "If I say that I don't believe it, the other guards will think Zanfretta is crazy," he told me. "On the other hand, if I say I do believe him, I'll be labeled as gullible. I prefer to try and see things clearly before pronouncing myself on the case."

It was for this reason that he gave Zanfretta the authorization to undergo hypnosis, under the condition that he always be accompanied by Lieutenant Cassiba. I called Moretti again and asked him to make an appointment, possibly at a time when we would go fairly undetected. We agreed on December 23 at 9:00 p.m.

I didn't tell anyone where we would be going for the hypnosis. I told everyone that we would meet at the "Val Bisagno" headquarters in Via Ceccardi 4 at 8:30 p.m. There were six of us. In addition to me, there were Ferraro, Zanfretta, Cassiba, Boccone and his friend Mario Nepi, as well as Giorgio Cesari, a scholar of paranormal phenomena. I led the group to Moretti's office.

Thus, it was not possible to make any kind of agreement beforehand. Moretti met us with Angelo Massa, his assistant. There was no one else in the office. They led us to a small room where there was a table and then Cassiba, Moretti and I took leave for a minute or two to discuss what was about to happen.

Moretti had also prepared a document which he had Zanfretta sign, where he specified that it was his express will to undergo hypnosis.

The session started at about 9:30 p.m. In the room the light was dim. It came from a lamp that was on a small table. Zanfretta was lying on the leather table. Moretti was standing in front of him. Cassiba and I were seated on the only two armchairs in the room. Others were standing. Boccone was crouching near the head of the table with the microphone of a recorder in hand. For what came to light in that session, no comment is necessary. What follows is the exact text of the recording that I published, once again in the magazine *Gente*.

Doctor Moretti: "Now, before your eyes there is a large clock-face, a big white clock with black hands. But this big clock has a particular feature: it is not going forward, but backward. The hands are turning back and we are going back in time. The minutes are going backward, the hours are going back, the days are going back, you and I are going backward in time. Further and further backward, further and further backward, further and further backward. Now you are surrounded by fog, a dense fog and you cannot see anything because the fog is the time that you are passing to go back into the past. Now we are back on the 6th day of December, it is Wednesday. Wednesday, December 6. The fog is lifting. It is night. It's after eleven p.m. You are doing your job, you are in Marzano near Torriglia, you are doing your rounds. It is dark and cold. Now we are near a villa, that villa is called "Casa Nostra." Now I want you, while staying asleep, deep asleep, to speak. I want you to tell me calmly, because I am here next to you, everything you see. Speak loudly so I can hear you clearly. I see a gate, a little white gate, it looks open, is that right?"

Zanfretta, stretched out on the table in the semi-darkness, started to give signs of life and whispered "Yes." Doctor Moretti standing in front of him continued to interrogate him with his mellow voice.

Doctor Moretti: "What is in the field behind the gate?"

Zanfretta: "Four lights".

Doctor Moretti: "Are they robbers? You are not afraid, are you? "

Zanfretta: "No.

Doctor Moretti: "Tell me, what do you see?"

Zanfretta: "Kangaroo from 68, Kangaroo from 68... The headlights, how come? The headlights are off".

(Evidently now the night watchman is calling the command center with the established code words.)

Doctor Moretti: "Speak louder or they won't hear you".

Zanfretta: "They don't hear me. Kangaroo, I'm heading behind the villa, there are robbers".

Now Zanfretta starts to breathe with difficulty, his chest is heaving rhythmically and his hands are shaking.

Zanfretta: "Who's there? What's going on? Oh my g..."

Doctor Moretti: "What's the matter? Tell me. I'm here with you and nothing can happen to you. Tell me what you see".

Zanfretta: "Dear God... Why should I come with you? What do you want from me? What are all those lights? I don't want to. You are not human, get out of here! What are you putting on my head? Go away! I don't want to.... Leave me alone..."

It becomes immediately apparent that the guard is talking about details that are unknown to him while conscious. He is saying basically that he has been lifted away and taken to a bright, warm place where they interrogated and examined him.

Zanfretta: "I don't want you to come back. I can't say that? Yes... I will do as you ask me... Give me proof... They won't believe me... So many lights! Go away, go away – take that thing off my head. I will wait for you to come back... How hot it is here. Take that thing off my head... Away! You are monsters... I want to go home. My flashlight."

At last the guard escaped, or they let him go. Running, he stops and sees a great big light rising from behind the house, then he goes back to the car and he calls the command center by radio.

Zanfretta: "What is all that light? It' s so big. It's bothering me. Kangaroo from 68... Kangaroo... They are not men... they are not men." Now Zanfretta starts talking to someone and he says "Do you want me to go back to the villa? OK, yes."

Then he meets his colleagues. Zanfretta relives those moments and says the things that were said to him then, in the field near the villa where he was found.

"Put down the gun, think of the children," one of them tells him.

"Come on, stop it," insists the other one. Then they take him, slap him and take him back stupefied while he keeps on repeating, "I saw them, I saw them."

Doctor Moretti: "Now I want you to describe for me these beings that you saw. You say they are not men like us. Describe them as best you can."

Zanfretta: "They are green, with triangular yellow eyes, with big thorns, they have green flesh and their skin is full of wrinkles as if they were old. Their mouths look like they're made of iron, they have red veins on their heads, pointed ears and arms with fingernails... with round things... They come from the third galaxy."

Doctor Moretti: "Earlier you said they left a message. Do you remember it? "

Zanfretta: "They want to talk and they say they will come back soon, in large numbers".

Doctor Moretti: "How do you communicate? Do they speak our language?"

Zanfretta: "No. They translate... with the bright aircraft".

At this point, Moretti decided to wake Zanfretta up. He calmed him with reassuring and mellow words and when he started to relax, he invited him to wake up at his command. The night guard opened his eyes very slowly. He seemed very confused and tired. Then he rubbed his eyes with his hands and slowly sat up, putting his feet on the ground. We were all looking at each other a bit perplexed, like someone who is embarrassed and doesn't know what to say.

Cassiba was upset. More than once during the hypnosis he covered his face with his hands and now he was looking at the man in his care with evident dread. He was afraid. In fact, while the others tried to keep Zanfretta distracted and entertained, joking around about the hypnosis session, he confessed to me that if it were up to him, Zanfretta would never return to Marzano again.

The protagonist of the entire story, in the meantime, had completely regained control of himself and said that he didn't know what had happened. First of all, he remembered absolutely nothing, and then he insisted that he had not been on that table for more than three minutes. Actually, the session had lasted more than half an hour. Obviously, given the delicate nature of what had come out during the hypnosis, I begged those present not to speak a word about what they had heard. In particular, I turned to Moretti. He asked me to remember, and rightly so, that his own professional obligation bound him to secrecy. That and his personal integrity would forbid him from making any sort of comment outside the room in which we found ourselves. The recording of the session was taken by Cassiba.

The next afternoon, I went back to "Val Bisagno" headquarters. At the newspaper in the morning I didn't say a word. I could have 'blurted out' the news any way I saw fit, and I would have been the first to do so. At that time, it would have been welcome, seeing what had been said about Zanfretta in those days. But I felt I would have been acting like a vulture throwing itself on a defenseless prey.

Moreover, I would have betrayed the trust of the director of "Val Bisagno", who while he did not know me, had trusted me. Furthermore, he himself had begged me not to exaggerate the significance of what had happened to his employee.

For all of these reasons, I decided not to write anything, risking that a snitch might tell a colleague of mine of the story and I would have had the news stolen from me. Instead, I wanted to talk to the security guard's superiors.

When I entered, Tutti presented his partner to me, a certain Mr.

Luigi Cereda. An ex-police officer and a member of the Italian Resistance during the war, Cereda seemed quite skeptical. Logical and controlled, he examined Zanfretta's incident relying on concrete facts. During the talk, a mature woman entered the room. Tutti introduced me to her as well. It was Silvana Bonola, the third partner of the company that collectively also managed "San Marco Security" and the company "Sicur Control" (supplier of electronic devices).

Mrs. Bonola was worried about Zanfretta's physical and psychological well-being more than the fact in and of itself.

We sat down to listen to the tape of the session on a stereo that Tutti had brought in for this very purpose. Tutti, Cereda and Bonola had already listened to the recording, but as they wanted to point out to me, only distractedly and with a thousand comments being made.

As the tape went on, I looked at the faces of my three hosts. The suspicion that underlying the Zanfretta story there was some kind of attempt for publicity had always been in my mind. But watching the reactions of those three people listening to the voice of the guard under hypnosis, I had the impression that maybe my suspicions were exaggerated.

Tutti seemed struck but did not want to appear so. Cereda was impassive and every so often shook his head as if to say 'no, no'. Mrs. Bonola from time to time exclaimed, "My goodness, but could it be true?"

And who could give her an answer? Even when we started to comment on the tape we had just listened to, it seemed to me that in the final analysis, the story of the UFO and the guard annoyed them more than made them happy. They were curious, yes, but they could have done without it.

Even with me, the journalist and an outsider, they did not want to appear like people who are looking for free space in the newspaper. In fact, as I was leaving, they begged me not to write anything until they had ascertained, through doctors and neurologists, what Zanfretta's state actually was. I knew it was a big risk. But on the other hand, I didn't feel like publicly discrediting Zanfretta, nor betraying the trust of those people.

Zanfretta, moreover, was the father of two children. A sensational article could ruin him. And I also had the impression that for the night watchman things weren't going to end there.

And what happened next proved me right.

CHAPTER 2

Giants in the Night

Christmas had just passed and Genoa was ready to welcome the New Year, 1979. On the morning of December 28, I, too, was doing my best to bring in the New Year with a little bit of order. I felt like cleaning up and without going too much into detail, I tried to free up space by eliminating a ton of magazines, papers, and various publications that for months took up two-thirds of my desk.

At my feet there was already a big pile of paper. I was halfway through the operation when the phone rang. "Hello, is this Mr. Di Stefano? Look, we're at it again with Zanfretta: it happened again last night. Can you perhaps come in today? Mr. Tutti would like to speak with you…"

Cassiba sounded worried. In short, without going into details, he told me how the night before Zanfretta had once again disappeared and they'd managed to find him again by rather fortuitous circumstances, on the top of a mount. I told him that at that moment I couldn't leave the newspaper because I was writing an article. And it was true.

But taking advantage of the fact that Cassiba and his night guards that very same morning were going to the spot, I wanted to send them our press photographer. In the late morning I would join Tutti.

Aside from the fact that at that moment I really had something urgent to do, I did not want to deal with this new disappearance of the night guard with the hurried attitude typical of journalists who work for an afternoon paper like the *Corriere Mercantile*.

Before writing a single word about Zanfretta, I wanted to personally make sure what had really happened. So I wanted to take my time to verify the facts and speak with witnesses.

Besides, it was Thursday. If I managed not to let out a word about it until Sunday, I could do a good piece for the *Gazzetta del Lunedì*. That edition sold about 100,000 copies whereas the *Corriere Mercantile* usually sold about 10,000.

I knew too that if I mentioned something to Angeli, he would take advantage and ask me to do a piece immediately about the event of that night. Moreover, I was sure, seeing what he thought of UFOs and all phenomena of that type, without a doubt he would have made some ironic headlines.

I handed in my article around eleven a.m. Going out, I bumped into Zeggio who was coming in. "Look, up there, where Zanfretta was, they found some gigantic marks," he told me. "I took pictures of them. The time to develop them, and I'll bring the prints to your table."

My curiosity was further piqued. So there was proof of something concrete. I was really curious to hear from the mouths of those who had been there what had really happened the night before.

I found the full conclave. Tutti came toward me and shook my hand. He had big circles under his eyes. He hadn't slept, he told me, from the night before. Even Cereda and Mrs. Bonola were visibly worried.

"We don't know what to think," Tutti said to me. "Last night we saved him by a miracle – had he made one false step, he would have been killed falling into the gorge. If certain circumstances weren't there, I would say that he's a liar and the thing would be resolved on its own, but with what we saw, I can't say it. And so? How can we explain this affair? I can only imagine the newspaper headlines now..."

Tutti, more than talking to me and his partners, was talking to himself aloud. He was afraid that the press would use Zanfretta's story to set up a campaign against the night watchman and "Val Bisagno".

"We live in the sector of security and surveillance," he was saying. "We can't afford to have people tell us that we have lunatics with visions of UFOs as employees..."

I tried to sort through that confusion of ideas and fears. So after I asked my hosts to remain calm, I encouraged them to tell me the facts. I got the result I wanted. Tutti sat down behind his desk and with Cassiba's help, whom he sent for to help him remember the times, he explained how things had happened.

Zanfretta, who by now was completely back to being himself after the adventure in Marzano, had started his shift the evening before at 10:05 p.m. For his comings and goings he had been given the Fiat 127 with the license plate number GE 683521 property of "Val Bisagno" and marked Beta 68. Like every night, that night too he headed toward Torriglia. For about an hour and a half everything went along normally. Then at exactly 11:46 p.m., the operator on duty at the operations center, Attilio Mazza, received a frenzied call for help.

"I'm surrounded by a thick fog and I can't see anything anymore!" shouted Zanfretta into the radio. "The car is going by itself and is picking up speed. I don't know what to do!"

According to subsequent reconstructions of the facts, at the moment in which Zanfretta was calling for help, he was inside the tunnel at the Scoffera pass. Four minutes later at 11:50 p.m. the night guard called again. This time his voice was much calmer, almost obedient. "The car stopped," he said to Mazza, "and I see a great light. I'm getting out."

The operator didn't waste time; he immediately called Eco 15 (Lieutenant Cassiba's car) and warned him of what was going on. At the same time he gave the order to Beta 29 of the Brigadier Emanuele Travenzoli and to Beta 70 of the security guard Raimondo Mascia to immediately start looking for Zanfretta. Cassiba in the meantime called Tutti and then went to pick him up.

It was at this point that the expedition to save Zanfretta began. The entire area of Torriglia was inspected. The night was terrible: it was pouring rain, the temperature was next to freezing and a thick fog enveloped the entire area.

The few words that Zanfretta had exchanged with Mazza had to do with a roadsign marked with the word Rossi, a small village of a few houses known only because that is where Frank Sinatra's mother Natalia Garaventa (1896-1977) was born. It was Travenzoli who remembered that on the hills above the Scoffera pass there was a small cluster of dwellings by that name.

His car was the first to turn into the very narrow street that headed uphill, the other three cars followed. Travenzoli was right. Where the road widened, on the side of the road was the Fiat 127 with the lights on. The brigadier communicated immediately via radio that they had found the car and then got out. Zanfretta was nowhere to be seen. All of a sudden, he jumped out of the ravine. He had seen the headlights of the approaching car and was trying to flee.

"He looked like a hunted wildcat," Travenzoli remembered later. And in fact, they had to chase him, immobilize him and slap him across the face a few times to make him come back to his senses. "They say they want to take me away," Zanfretta was trembling and crying. "What will happen to my children? I don't want to go, I don't want to go."

But what was very strange was that despite the rain and the cold, the night watchman's face and clothes were dry. "From his nose up, he was extremely hot," Travenzoli explained. "His ears were red hot."

It was a matter of minutes. When the others arrived, Zanfretta was put into Tutti's car, a *Alfa Romeo Giulia*.

To get an idea of where they were, the night guards started to take a look around. One of them, Raimondo Mascia, discovered that around Zanfretta's car there were huge footprints, still fresh. It should be remembered that it was raining. These footprints that were measured in the morning by the Carabinieri of Torriglia and photographed by Zeggio were more than 50 centimeters long and about 20 centimeters wide.

But another decidedly important detail was discovered. The little area where the event happened was completely asphalted, as it was only a slight widening of the road that heads toward the small village of Rossi. At that point, the lane is 8 meters wide and by the outer border of the road, which is marked by white timber stakes, there is overgrown vegetation. The strange thing was that these plants on the side of the asphalt had been completely uprooted in the shape of a semicircle about 3 meters wide. Moreover, on the ground where the weeds were growing they found two very noticeable skid marks along with some gigantic footprints.

The question is: who or what made that clearing in the vegetation? Moreover, what had created those skid marks and footprints? It was clear that the former weren't tire marks: on the ground there was no sign of tread for the entire length of the marks. And then, who could leave such footprints, longer than 50 centimeters? The questions are still open now, also because the same little clearing, photographed three years later, appears normally covered with vegetation up to the side of the road.

The nighttime adventure of the night watchman didn't end there. "Getting out," Tutti told me, "all of a sudden the lights, the windshield wipers and the motor of our car stopped completely. Zanfretta, still shaking, said that they were still there. I told Cassiba, who was driving, to keep going down slowly, engine off, until we reached the road. We had only driven a few meters when we saw the others arriving, running, with their guns drawn. They were afraid that something had happened to us and they hadn't lost any time. After all, we were all very nervous."

After about 100 meters down the road, the car's headlights and motor started working again. Cassiba and Tutti's son Claudio (18 years old, who was also in the car), swear they saw quite distinctly a red light behind them. Cassiba, furthermore, was driving with his head outside the window because the fog made it impossible to see anything, and without any lights we were running the risk of falling down the slope.

It should be remembered that the area we are talking about is at approximately 800 meters above sea level and almost 2 kilometers from the nearest town. Little by little Zanfretta got back to normal. They brought him to a bar in Torriglia and they had him drink a hot coffee.

In fact, Zanfretta is a teetotaler. When he was completely back to normal, he said he didn't remember anything at all, and asked why there was such a fuss. There were two unclear aspects about this second incident, Tutti explained. First of all, six shots had been fired from Zanfretta's pistol (a Smith & Wesson caliber 38 special). Furthermore, the roof of the Fiat 127 he had been using, despite the cold and humid climate, was burning hot when it was found, and it maintained that heat until it was brought back down the hill to Genoa.

Francesco Meligrana, the security guard that brought the car back to the garage of "Val Bisagno" said that the inside of the car *was like an oven* and that the heating was off. Moreover, once he reached his destination, he got out and pointed to a spot on the roof that was hotter than the rest.

To check out the details of this story, I asked for and got permission to bring together the guards who had participated in the events of that unusual evening. I wanted to ask them some questions and above all to see if someone fell into a trap of contradictions. I was also handed a copy of the service report for the night between the 27th and 28th of December where Mazza had quite diligently marked down one by one all the communications from the radio command center. Everything checked out and I had no doubt about the good faith of the watchmen after talking with them for an hour. The meeting was held that very same afternoon on the 10th floor of the skyscraper in Via Ceccardi, in the room next to the radio center. Each one completely confirmed what I had been told just a few hours earlier.

It should also be said that in that period, UFOs were at home in Liguria. A few days before Zanfretta's second *encounter*, on precisely Christmas night, quite a peculiar episode took place in the town of Cicagna, a small village in the hinterlands of Genoa, a few kilometers from Torriglia. Around 4:25 a.m. on the morning of December 26, 1978, Aldo Devoto, a 50 year old truck driver, who lived at no. 4, Via Trino in the suburb of Banche, was suddenly awakened. "I was in the bedroom with my son Mario, 7 years old, when all of a sudden I heard a thud and then a whoosh on the railing of my home which is on the second floor," Devoto, still quite shocked, told a journalist from the genoese newspaper *Il Lavoro*. "After this, there was a huge light that shone through the roller blinds on the window. I looked out onto the terrace, practically paralyzed. An extremely bright object, the size more or less of a Fiat 127 with four pedestals was hovering above the street, at about 5 or 6 meters and just under my house. The object wasn't making any sound, only a light that was so bright that it was blinding. After which, the object slowly moved away toward the area of Monleone and those other small towns, until it disappeared."

"The thing that struck me most," continued Devoto, "was the complete impossibility of moving away from the terrace railing. I would have liked to take a picture or go back inside to calm my family down, but my movements were completely blocked. Then, as the aircraft moved away, I noticed two ribbons of fire coming out of its tail."

Devoto's mother-in-law was also a witness to the episode. Maria Cavagnaro, 75 years old, confirmed word for word what her son-in-law had said. The Carabinieri where Devoto went to file a report, found only several broken tree branches at the same height as the windows of the flat.

The mood of those days was ripe for UFO alarms, and everyone was talking about them. One detail that piqued my curiosity in Zanfretta's second encounter was how little time his car took from the moment in which he saw the fog in the tunnel up to the little clearing where he was then found. According to what emerged from the radio communications, between those two moments only 4 minutes elapsed (from 11:46 p.m. to 11:50 p.m.) As the distance between those two areas is rather significant, and that in any case to get to the little clearing you had to go along a very narrow mountain road for almost a kilometer, I wondered how the security guard could have done it so quickly. I wanted to try it for myself. I asked Tutti to let me go to the tunnel of the Scoffera pass with his best driver and to use the same Fiat 127 with which Zanfretta had travelled. He accepted my proposal, and the task was given to Mascia, who knew those roads and that car well.

One afternoon, we took the road toward Torriglia. The sun was shining and visibility was perfect. I realized that because the weather was so different and the fact that there were two of us in the car, the experiment would never be reliable. On the night of December 26, in fact, a heavy fog had settled on the entire area, and what's more, it had been raining. Visibility therefore was down to a tenth of what it is normally. In any case, for this very reason, I figured the car's speed could probably be higher and get closer to those 4 minutes it took Zanfretta.

We started our test at 4:03 p.m. Mascia skid the tires on the asphalt and took off at high speed toward the little road that led to Rossi. Once on the right path, he had to put the car in second gear. The curves were very tight and the road doesn't allow for any dangerous moves: if you slide, the car could end up in a ditch on the side of the road. Nonetheless, Mascia was working energetically on the accelerator trying to shave the seconds off. For a few dozen meters, he managed to shift into 3rd gear, and finally, after the nth curve where we'd managed by the skin of our teeth to avoid ending up in a ditch, Mascia put on the brakes. The chronometer showed the time was exactly 4:11 p.m.: with two of us in the car, it had taken 8 minutes. How was it possible that Zanfretta had done that same stretch of road at night with no lights, in the rain and the fog, in only 4 minutes? There is still no answer today. Unless we assume that the guard really had flown… To resolve this and all the other doubts, the managers of "Val Bisagno" thought of turning to hypnosis.

This session was going to be memorable. In fact, in those days Nino Pirito who at the time was the director of the television station TVS - the station that was associated with Genoa's newspaper *Secolo XIX* - got in touch with Tutti and asked if he could film the entire hypnosis session. At first, Tutti and his partners didn't agree to it: they thought that a broadcast of that kind could be construed as an exploitation of the case. Eventually, after having heard Moretti's opinion, they agreed to it.

Filming for television in a doctor's office is no easy undertaking, not to mention invading the privacy between the doctor and his patient. In order to give his authorization, Moretti first asked for Zanfretta's willingness to participate. When he agreed, hoping that his detractors would stop attacking him, there were no more problems. Tutti and his partners also thought the same: letting the public hear what the night guard had to say while under hypnosis would help put the comments and criticisms to rest.

The television session took place at 11:00 a.m. on Sunday, January 7, 1979 in a doctor's office. In addition to Moretti and myself, there were Tutti, Cassiba, the technician Giuliano Bonamici from "Sicur Control," Boccone and Enrico Pedemonte, who at the time was a journalist with TVS and who went on to work for the *Secolo XIX* and then *Espresso* magazine. What follows is a faithful transcription of the event.

Moretti, after having hypnotized Zanfretta, made some tests to show that the security guard was in deep hypnosis. In fact, he exposed his right arm and lifted some skin with two fingers, and then put a large needle in. Zanfretta sat motionless in sleep, his face even more relaxed. Moretti stopped the blood that was flowing from the needle with a cotton ball and started the session. In the meantime, the camera was rolling.

Doctor Moretti: "You are going back in time, you are returning to days and days ago, further and further back. Now we are at nighttime, it is Wednesday night: it is cold and you are in the car, you are doing your rounds. You are near the Scoffera pass, now you will tell me truthfully and honestly exactly what is happening to you. You will relive every detail exactly."

After a few seconds of silence, Zanfretta started to speak in a low voice.

Zanfretta: "I'm so sleepy... I can't keep my eyes open. How come? I feel tired... But the car? It is turning... I am not driving, it is going by itself. In the tunnel they can't hear me... I am getting out now... Kangaroo from six eight... Kangaroo, the car is going by itself, I'm afraid to stay in the car, God help me! The steering wheel is hard. Kangaroo, answer!... The car is going by itself, there is a lot of fog, I can't see anything. The car is speeding... I am sleepy. I can't see anything with all this damn fog, but where is it taking me? Where am I? Ahhh, I hit my head! Kangaroo, the car has stopped and I have to get out: they are calling me. Oh, that light again... I can't see anything. I have to go.... You again? But what do you want from me? Leave me alone, I didn't look for you. I know you need me, but I don't want to. I want to live in peace, leave me alone, I have two children and I'm fine the way I am... Why are you taking my bullets? No, not the gun – why are you taking it from me? You are shooting that square over there? I didn't hear the shots... No, the helmet on my head, no... I beg of you, it hurts... Ow, a shock!... that annoying light, it's hot, leave me alone. Why are you taking my clothes off now? No, don't touch me!... Ow, my head, don't put that thing on my head, it hurts. No, you are not coming back, you shouldn't come back, I don't want you to take me away... I, I'm not coming up here anymore. I know, even if I hide, you'll find me whenever you want, even if the others cover me. But I don't want to come... Ow, my head, take the helmet off! Now why have you taken all my clothes off? What do you want from me? What are you passing over my chest? No, no, it feels cold. No, no leave me alone... Ouch, my head, stop the light, it hurts. I don't want to stay still, no. You cannot take me away again, I am not coming here again. And why do you always call me with that sound? I don't want to answer you. And anyway, you aren't human beings, you are horrible. No, owwww, my head, no, please... the electric shocks, no. You, you're afraid of the cold, because it is so hot in here. All this light... But why me? I didn't do anything to you, I'm not a calm kind of guy... No, leave my legs alone. What is this machine?"

At this point, Zanfretta seemed visibly frightened. He was breathing heavily and his face showed the terror of the moment he was reliving. With great effort, repeating 'no' as his stock phrase, he kept going, under Moretti's strict observation.

Zanfretta: "I want to get away from here, the others are looking for me. What do you mean, they won't find me? They will find me and then they'll take care of you. No, I won't come with you. You have to leave me alone. You are monsters!... Now what... what are you doing to my eyes? But you have to take this helmet off, it's hurting my head, it's bothering me... ow... no, my eyes, no: I can't see anything anymore. No, the light no: I can't see anything. I'm afraid, wasn't last time enough for you? Leave me alone, go away. Here, here... Are you putting my clothes back on? Take this thing off my eyes, it's bothering me. Why don't you want me to look at you now? I've already seen you – you're tall, you have green, disgusting skin, and those thorns on the sides of your face, those horrible eyes, why don't you have a mouth? You only have those metal rods with the net... that shows that light... And those hands that end in a round shape... Why don't you use clothes? Even if I can't see you, I remember you. Now take this thing off my eyes. And the helmet, please. I can't take it anymore .... I'm so tired... Why all these questions? I don't know, I don't know anything... No, you can't come to Earth. People will be frightened just by looking at you, you can't be friends. I know you want to show up more often. Ow, my head... Why do you talk to me with this helmet?

41

It hurts...No, they would never understand. No, I want to go back home now... Leave me alone. But why me? No, I don't want to... this helmet hurts, ow, owh, that's enough now... I'm begging you, please, enough! Where are you from? But it's very far, isn't it...When will you come back? Why are you telling me "give it time"? When, "when they least expect it"? But I don't want to come with you, what do you need me for? No, I don't want to come to your planet. No, enough, my head hurts... Enough, I beg you. I'm tired, so so tired. Why are you looking at my hands? They can't be the same as yours. You, you're taller. Where I come from, no one is that tall, only animals, giraffes... You don't know what they are? You are only interested in human beings? But why? You need them as guinea pigs? Oh, that's enough now, take this helmet off me! I can't take it anymore! I'm tired, why don't you want me to scream? It hurts me, take it off me! No, I'm going to scream, take it off me. I'm tired..."

At this point, Zanfretta mumbles a few words with no apparent meaning. One could say they were the words of an unknown language. In the recording of the session, after listening to it very carefully and slowly, these words may be distinguished: *Inù katap china*. Right after, the night guard starts to speak normally again.

Zanfretta: "Kangaroo from six eight, I don't know where I am, here it is all fog, I don't know, I don't know, I'm afraid. Yes, I am closing the door, I'm closing myself in. Yes, I'm calm, the light is going. It is lifting and it's hot, so hot. Yes, I am speaking on the radio, I can hear you, yes, Lieutenant, I can hear you. Yes, it's OK, I'll stay in the car. Yes, Paolo, I don't know where I am: there's a lot of fog here. No, I only saw Rossi (*the sign for the small town called Rossi, ed. note*) briefly. Yes, I'm speaking on the radio. Again, again, again those lights?

Zanfretta had just seen the headlights of one of the cars of the security guards who were looking for him. This time, contrary to what he had done the time before with his *extraterrestrial interlocutors*, in hypnosis he referred the words that his colleagues had spoken to him when they got close to him.

Colleagues: "Piero, Piero, don't run away. It's me, Paolo, come on, stop, come on, calm down..."

Zanfretta: "No, go away... go away..."

Colleagues: "Come on, sit down in the car. Oh my gosh, how hot you are! What's the matter, Piero?"

Zanfretta: "I don't know, I'm afraid, they're coming back, they're coming back. Enough! Yes, I recognize you Mr. Tutti. Yes, the Lieutenant as well. I'm calm, but I'm afraid. I am not coming back up here, that's it. They, I know, they're still here, I can feel it. They can make themselves invisible too. They're here, I'm scared. The car has stopped, the radio too. Even the windshield wipers. They're here, I know it. No, I don't want anything strong: I don't need it. I am not coming back up here anymore, that's it..."

Zanfretta's state of agitation was such that Moretti intervened to calm him down.

Doctor Moretti: "Now you won't see anything, you won't see anything anymore. Your mind is dark, peaceful and relaxed. You will respond to my questions in a state of absolute calm and tranquility. Are you calm now?"

Zanfretta: "Yes".

Doctor Moretti: "Are you sure of what you've seen?"

Zanfretta: "Yes, I don't tell lies".

Doctor Moretti: "OK, I believe you. What was the thing like, the thing you entered? Where it was so hot. Can you describe it, inside and outside?"

Zanfretta: "Yes, outside it is flat, very triangular, the color of steel. Inside, a green light lifted me up and took me inside. Inside a big room with all of them all around me, looking at me. It was full of dashboards and commands..."

Doctor Moretti: "But how many of them were standing around you?"

Zanfretta: "A lot, I ... think more than ten..."

Doctor Moretti: "And how did they talk with you?"

Zanfretta: "They were talking through a light that came from their mouths. They spoke very badly. They're all identical: tall, green, yellow triangular eyes with red veins on their heads, and these thorns on the sides of their faces. They have arms like a human, and legs too. They have hands with long nails that end in something round, and their feet are big, very big."

Doctor Moretti: "Did they tell you where they come from?"

Zanfretta: "They come from very far away, they don't want me to say, they don't want me to. They will come back..."

Doctor Moretti: "When will they come back? If you know, you have to tell me."

Zanfretta: "They'll come back when, when I least expect it, they said. When I least expect it..."

Doctor Moretti: "OK, go back to sleep. Now you are sleeping, sleeping deeply. And everything you saw will be erased from your mind. Your sleep is deeper and deeper, and the sleep you are experiencing will erase every memory. Only my voice, only my voice can bring back those memories, and only when I precisely ask you to remember. Have you understood the order I just gave you?"

Zanfretta: "Yes, only when you want me to..."

Doctor Moretti: "Good. Now sleep, sleep and forget everything. When I wake you up, you will not remember anything of what has happened here in the last few hours and you will not remember anything of the episodes you described, absolutely nothing. Sleep, sleep and forget, forget completely. Here, now, you are sleeping more deeply than you ever have before. In your mind there are only pleasant things, things that make you feel serene, at peace, calm. Your mind and your body feel balanced, you feel well, you feel very well. Your mind is at peace and serene. And that is how it will be from now on."

When Moretti woke Zanfretta up, the night guard actually felt really well, he was in a good mood, and could not remember a word of what he had said. However, as we shall see, for Zanfretta the state of serenity would not last long.

The television show was on Monday, January 8. The interest in and the success of the broadcast was huge for a city like Genoa. The same morning, I published a long article in the *Gazzetta del Lunedì* where I was proposing very cautiously the mystery of Zanfretta's second *close encounter*. At the same time, I announced that TVS would broadcast on TV that evening.

Just to get an idea of the magnitude of the program, suffice it to say that Pirito, the director of the television station, was practically forced to hold a press conference to explain to his colleagues and other journalists the ins and outs of the event. Moreover, given the number of telephone calls from viewers that had missed the program on Monday night, the show was repeated in the following days. Gianfranco Tutti asked for and got a copy of the videocassette where the entire program had been recorded.

To further contribute to the idea amongst the general public that this was an extraordinary event and that the night guard was not lying consciously was the statement that Moretti also made. Interviewed about the hypnosis session that he had just conducted, Moretti said:

"First of all, Zanfretta went into a very deep level of hypnosis, and this was seen by all. Let's say that any school of thought admits that elements such as the psycho-motor passivity, and we saw for example the total catalepsy of the right arm, like being under anesthesia, a certain way of speaking, a certain way of expressing himself that was very subdued, very particular, let's say, if someone has an ear for this type of thing, well, it all makes one think of a degree of trans-hypnotic state to the maximum levels of depth. Now, how can this be in relation to the reliability of the speech? On its own, even if it cannot be absolute proof of reliability, it is a very, very important element for reliability. If we add to this that I observed Zanfretta from a psychological point of view, and well, all these elements, and let's also add another important element: in a precedent session, I used all the techniques that we usually use to see if there could be, even under a very deep hypnosis, elements of contradiction. If there could be some way of insinuating a seed of doubt about the objectivity of what Zanfretta said he had seen, and he responded positively. Positively in the sense of the objective truth of what he had seen. Now, all of these elements put together, what do they tell us? Well, they have to tell us that the hypothesis that he lied is negligible. Extremely negligible I would say. And it is also negligible or relatively unlikely that he expressed a situation of a hallucinatory type in a state of hypnosis. The rest is not my area of competence. I am not a ufologist, I have nothing to say on this subject. I can only limit myself to my field. Many other small details, for example the type of breathing and the frequency of swallowing, the absolute immobility of the eyelids. All elements that further lead to prove a state of very deep hypnosis and reiterate this very deep state because obviously, the deeper the state of hypnosis, the fewer the chances that the person can have a sphere of consciousness or will power through which let's say he could lie or feign. In my opinion, Zanfretta absolutely did not fake anything. Then obviously the doubt remains: if he didn't lie, is the scene he described an objective reality or is it a subjective reality? Considering not only this session but also the overall gathering of proof that we have done with Zanfretta, I have to say that the hypothesis of an objective reality surpasses by a long shot the point of view of a subjective reality."

Moretti, therefore, while within the limits of his professional behavior did not feel he could say that Zanfretta was lying. After all, to wrap up the whole affair with the certainty that we were faced with someone who was not very sound of mind was a convenient and simplistic solution. Everyone's impression, and even my own personal take on things, was that something had actually happened. Obviously, we could not take the story Zanfretta had told in all its details as being the truth, but there was good reason to be perplexed.

CHAPTER 3

The Aliens and Their Sphere

Almost immediately, the fuss that surrounded the Zanfretta case in the days following the broadcast caused the first negative reactions. There was so much talk about it that perhaps there was someone who, taking advantage of the situation, wanted people talking about them as well. There was a group of scholars who from the pages of the newspaper *Il Lavoro* attacked Moretti, maintaining that it was all a bluff and that Zanfretta was delusional, and that hypnosis on its own could prove nothing. Apart from the fact that no one had ever dreamed of stating the contrary, nor did a similar piece of news show up in any other newspaper, including my own, this argument created a certain embarrassment among the heads of "Val Bisagno" and a sense of unease for Moretti too. After all, he had performed his usual work as a professional and had been regularly paid for this. He himself had been the first to say that hypnosis was not absolute proof of the veracity of the facts told.

But that wasn't the point. The people who were criticizing wanted publicity. It got to the point that the so-called 'experts' confuting the results of the hypnosis ended up proposing the use of Pentotal. That is to say, they thought that if only Zanfretta were willing to submit to the use of the so-called serum of the truth, that is to say Pentotal, then his affirmations would be believable.

When the guard heard this, he got upset. He could have cared less about the glory, and even less about all the noise surrounding his person. The only thing he really wanted, very much so, was to be believed, and that he would not be labeled as a lunatic. So he went to his director and expressly asked to do the Pentotal test. "I don't want people to say that I'm crazy," he said, "and if Pentotal can provide this certainty, then I'm ready."

Gianfranco Tutti started to be a bit annoyed. The Zanfretta bomb had exploded in his hands and now the consequences seemed to be totally out of control. Who would administer the Pentotal to Zanfretta? The question was put to Moretti. The doctor stated right away that he would not do it. He suggested going to Milan, to the International

Center for Medical and Psychological Hypnosis where Professor Marco Marchesan, an authority on hypnosis, would be able to perform such a task. Moretti would arrange making contact and ask Professor Marchesan's opinion.

He succeeded. On the afternoon of Tuesday, February 6, 1979, Zanfretta, Buonamici, Cassiba, Boccone and myself arrived in Milan, at 57 of Corso XXII Marzo where the Center is located. Before starting the experiment, Marchesan asked Zanfretta to sign the following document:

"I, Fortunato Zanfretta, born in Nova Milanese on December 28, 1952 on today's date February 6, 1979, of my own free will, will undergo clinical exams in order to verify with every means available in modern medical science, the veracity of my statements concerning my *close encounters* with unknown beings. Under my own responsibility, thus, today in Milan, Professor Marchesan will try to verify with every clinical means available the authenticity of my statements. This is to confirm once more that said exams are being performed upon my request and at my own risk. Faithfully, Fortunato Zanfretta."

Once bureaucracy had been carried out, we got to the point. The guard was asked to lie down on an anatomical black leather table. He was covered with a blanket with vivid tartan colors, and his left arm was exposed up to above the elbow. An anesthetist administered an intravenous drug, a solution called "Farmotal", diluted with distilled water. It took a few minutes for the drug to take effect. Then, slowly, Zanfretta fell into a deep sleep. Marchesan, who had been standing behind the other doctor until that moment, now sat next to the table.

Tall, big, already elderly but full of energy, Marchesan ordered the guard with his imperious voice to go back in time and to go back to the night of December 6, 1978, that is, back to the moment of the first alleged *encounter*. The goal of that session was in fact to verify the entire story, therefore Marchesan asked the patient to report "neither more nor less than what had actually happened without adding any unrelated details to the facts." It goes without saying that Zanfretta repeated exactly word for word what he had already said to Moretti.

To avoid boring the reader, therefore, I will skip the part that we already know. Instead, I would like to report some excerpts from this session that, for the purposes of the incident are absolutely new. In fact, this time Zanfretta even recounts the words that were spoken to him by the mysterious beings, and the picture that emerges is interesting without a doubt. To facilitate understanding, I will use the word 'entity' to indicate the interlocutor of the security guard. It must be clear, however, that during the hypnosis session, the dialogue was been reported in Zanfretta's voice alone.

Entity: "You, until you tell us what we ask you, you will have to suffer," states the strange being to the security guard who complains about the helmet on his head. "We are a people that comes from the third galaxy. We live on Titania, a universe lost between the bright star and the falling star. We would try to communicate, but we can't. We are trying to see how you are made."

Zanfretta: "Leave me alone, you are horrible. Why are you harassing me? From the time I saw you once in the sky, you have sent that voice down on me, you have bothered me. Why are you harassing me now? No, I can't do everything you are asking me... No, they wouldn't understand. But if you gave me proof that you exist, I could try..."

Entity: "We will not give it to you. When it is time, we will give you what's necessary but unfortunately not even that far away place called the Americas... We have tried to get noticed by those beings, those things that fly... We, we let them film us, let them take our pictures: but you people here are unprepared. You will be our pupil and you have to do what we want. Only we can call you with a sound that you will hear in your brain and when you hear it you will not be able to do anything but come to us, consciously or unconsciously."

Zanfretta: "But leave me alone, I haven't done anything to you. Why are you tormenting me?"

Entity: "We people of Titania, point of reference is the third galaxy, we are lost in space and we are looking for a place like your earth where we can breathe well but where we feel cold, where we can settle. I would like to speak with your great leader, but he must not be afraid."

Zanfretta: "Ow, ow, my head. That's enough, take this helmet off, I beg of you..."

Entity: "No, you are in our power and you can't do anything for us, time is like minutes and seconds, an hour for you. We go through the light voyage in a few instants. We have already come across your spaceships, American, Russian and Chinese. We are trying to become friends, but they get scared. We caused the explosion of a missile leaving Cape Kennedy and our initiative was a warning."

Zanfretta: "But I don't care, I need to work. I want to be free, let me go. And it's hot in here. Let me go..."

Entity: "In time, we will let you go. What you hold in your brain... and you see our lights coming out of our faces as if we were speaking. Stay calm, don't worry, we will get in touch again. Now we are only studying you. We are trying to see how you are made. Two months ago we tried to get inside that white thing by opening a wall and we took some animal beings that to us seemed alive, and we are still studying them now."

This last detail is very important in explaining the whole story because indeed just a little time before that, in the villa called "Casa Nostra" there had been a strange breaking and entering. The Carabineri from Torriglia had been called during the night because unknown thieves had literally knocked down door to the house, demolishing a good section of the upper part of the wall to which the door was fixed. Aside from this oddity (it looked like the door had been run over by a tank," the Carabinieri said) another strange thing happened. Despite the fact that there were many valuable objects in the house, among which a color television, the thieves took only two stuffed birds. No one managed to explain the reason for such a strange theft.

Back to Zanfretta's hypnosis:

Entity: "We need you and we are trying to make you understand that we want to be friends, but it would appear that none of you care for it."

Zanfretta: "Now, please, take this helmet off my head. There, oh, but how can it be so big? It looks like a city but outside it is small... Why do you live with your children and wives up here?"

Entity: "Because we are destined to die: only the earth can save us..."

Zanfretta: "I can do absolutely nothing for you. And then everyone would think I was crazy. And why me? With all the people in the world.... And you are really disgusting looking. A person could die just by looking at you. Why didn't I die?"

Entity: "Because we stopped your heart in such a way so it could survive. We've been studying you for a long time, since you saw our spaceship hovering in the sky and we couldn't have done without you because you are a laid-back kind of guy, one of the few in the many that we found."

Zanfretta: "But I don't want to stay with you...."

Entity: "And we're not going to keep you. We are going away, but we'll come back."

Zanfretta: "And now why are you having me go down with the green light? Are you dropping me down? But... I'm flying! I can fly... I dropped my flashlight, I can't see anymore."

From this point on in the story, Zanfretta takes up along the same lines of what he said in his previous hypnotic session with Dr. Moretti. The last part of the session is quite relevant, where Professor Rolando Marchesan, Marco's son, takes over for his father, and asks the guard several very precise questions. The answers, whatever their true meaning, are quite interesting.

Prof. Marchesan: "Repeat clearly what message they gave you."

Zanfretta: "They don't want us to play with atomic bombs because we will destroy ourselves and their solar system."

Prof. Marchesan: "This solar system, how far is it from ours? Did they say precisely, in light years?"

Zanfretta: "Four thousand light years."

Prof. Marchesan: "These beings, how long have they been traveling in space, did they say?"

Zanfretta: "One round of the earth around the sun."

Prof. Marchesan: "That is, one round that the earth makes around the sun, that is one year?"

Zanfretta: "Yes."

Prof. Marchesan: "And they have the possibility of moving around rapidly in space at a speed that is greater than the speed of light?"

Zanfretta: "Much greater..."

Prof. Marchesan: "These beings, did they say how old they were, if they have an age that is comparable to centuries?"

Zanfretta: "No, they don't have age: they don't know how old they are."

Prof. Marchesan: "If they want to establish themselves on earth, what would they like to do? Live quietly in a corner of the earth and have good relations with us? If they said this to you, tell us exactly and sincerely what they said."

Zanfretta: "They want to establish themselves on earth to be able to build a city of theirs closed up in a glass dome."

Prof. Marchesan: "Then the weather conditions, the climate, minerals, etc. are very different from ours?"

Zanfretta: "Yes and they suffer the cold and they cannot deal with our climate. If they don't live in a glass dome, they die."

Prof. Marchesan: "And when they've left the spaceship to meet you, then they suffered the cold as long as they were out of the spaceship?"

Zanfretta: "No, they were covered by the green light that made them warm."

Prof. Marchesan: "Are there many of them, these beings?"

Zanfretta: "Yes, lots of them."

Prof. Marchesan: "Did they say specifically or let you know how many of them there were?"

Zanfretta: "No, they were all alike."

Prof. Marchesan: "So you saw women then and even children?"

Zanfretta: "Yes."

Prof. Marchesan: "And the children were small? How tall were they?"

Zanfretta: "About 1 meter and 40 cm."

Prof. Marchesan: "Were they more appealing to the eye, or were they as monstrous as their parents?"

Zanfretta: "No, like their parents."

Prof. Marchesan: "The women, how were they different from the men?"

Zanfretta: "With belts, with something attached to their waists."

Prof. Marchesan: "But apart from this, were they less ugly? Did they have, for example, breasts?"

Zanfretta: "Yes, all green."

Prof. Marchesan: "But were they almost naked?"

Zanfretta: "No, they had a jumpsuit up to their waist and a square screen in front of their body, the chest."

Prof. Marchesan: "But was this screen see-through so you could see the breasts of these women?"

Zanfretta: "No, they were all green."

Prof. Marchesan: "That is to say, you thought they were green because all the skin of the body was green?"

Zanfretta: "Yes."

Prof. Marchesan: "Can they make themselves invisible sometimes and possibly are they able to circulate on the earth without us realizing it? Did they say this or lead you to believe it?"

Zanfretta: "No, they prefer to make themselves visible when they have contact with a person from earth."

Prof. Marchesan: "So when are they invisible then?"

Zanfretta: "When there is a lot of fog and when it is really hot."

Prof. Marchesan: "In such cases, are they maybe on the earth and we don't realize it?"

Zanfretta: "They are never on the earth, they hover in their spaceship and they wait…"

Prof. Marchesan: "Do they have many spaceships?"

Zanfretta: "Thousands, and they are all alike."

Prof. Marchesan: "But these thousands of spaceships are flying all around in space, no? Not all of them circulate around the earth. They must be doing some reconnaissance around other planets of our solar system."

Zanfretta: "No, they are flying everywhere in space to get noticed by that flying object that they call airplane: they played in front of it and then they disappeared."

Prof. Marchesan: "Did they also talk about beings that come from other planets or even perhaps from other galaxies? Did they mention that there are other spaceships coming from elsewhere with different begins?"

Zanfretta: "No, just them."

Prof. Marchesan: "Did they say how big their planet is, more or less? If it is bigger than the earth?"

Zanfretta: "Four times the size of the earth."

Prof. Marchesan: "Did they say if it has seas, rivers, mountains, ice?"

Zanfretta: "No, they have to leave their planet because it is going to explode, so they are looking for a place to start over."

Prof. Marchesan: "How many are they, more or less, these beings on their planet or even the ones wandering around? Did they say if there were millions, or only a few thousand left? Or tens of millions, or billions, like us on the earth?"

Zanfretta: "No, they didn't tell me anything."

Prof. Marchesan: "Did they let you know more or less when they would come back and get in touch with you, or in any case with us here on earth?"

Zanfretta: "Yes, when I least expect it. They know what happened in these days and they didn't tell me. But they will come and get me."

Prof. Marchesan: "How do they know what happened in these days or in the days in which you had contact with them, these beings? That is, what happened on earth?"

Zanfretta: "During the day they have a special sphere and they see what I do."

At this point, the conversation turns to a new element, a sphere, about which there will be much more talk. That is to say, Zanfretta maintained that these beings had shown him and had him touch an indefinite object in the shape of a sphere. Marchesan tries to find out more.

Prof. Marchesan: "You, at a certain point, had a sphere in your hand. Was the sphere heavy? Was it like a crystal ball? Was it transparent or made of metal?"

Zanfretta: "It was metal and they will give it to me in time."

Prof. Marchesan: "How big is it? What diameter could this sphere have?"

Zanfretta: "It's like a big diamond."

Prof. Marchesan: "But it has the shape of a sphere, or is it multifaceted?"

Zanfretta: "No, it is triangular."

Prof. Marchesan: "So it's more like a cone or maybe a pyramid?"

Zanfretta: "Yes."

Prof. Marchesan: "Then it's not a sphere but it is enclosed in a crystal ball more or less."

Zanfretta: "Yes, it is enclosed in a crystal ball."

Prof. Marchesan: "So when they come back, they're going to give you one of these balls?"

Zanfretta: "Yes, to prove their existence and they would like to show how their world is."

Prof. Marchesan: "So you can see what their world is like through this crystal ball? You can understand what degree of technology they have."

Zanfretta: "Only with my hand will I manage to show through this object their people, their civilization."

Prof. Marchesan: "How could you show with your hand something toward their people? I didn't understand or maybe you should explain better: project onto a screen?"

Zanfretta: "This... tiny triangle..."

The security guard interrupted himself and for a few moments did not speak. Then Marchesan egged him on.

Prof. Marchesan: "This triangle which is enclosed in a crystal ball has the power to let us understand how they live. Tell us in your own words, exactly and truthfully, without adding anything of your own but only what perfectly reflects the truth."

Zanfretta: "The triangle is used like a kind of television that would show us earthlings how these beings, who are called Dargos, live."

Prof. Marchesan: "Do you maintain contact with these beings called Dargos, or do you wait for their command, the whistle, the tone?"

Zanfretta: "They call me with only a whistle, a sound, in my head... to which.... the sirens."

Prof. Marchesan: "Their spaceship, if they told you, is it still around here pretty close to the earth? Are they following what is happening on earth with special instruments so that they can see from far away? Can they get in touch and follow you in some way?"

Zanfretta: "In this moment, they are watching us here and then they will draw their conclusions..."

Prof. Marchesan: "Do you feel that these beings are in touch with your subconscious, that is with the deepest part of your personality?"

Zanfretta: "Yes."

Prof. Marchesan: "Then you feel that they have a special connection with you and that they follow or can follow you in any moment, see what you do, where you are, and even perhaps what you say?"

Zanfretta: "They watch and see everything I do, inside and out, at work..."

Prof. Marchesan: "So these people can even see, naturally, the other people who interact with you during the day? Family members and others..."

Zanfretta: "Yes, they see this and more."

Prof. Marchesan: "Do they know that there is an organization, both in Italy and abroad, that studies these appearances on the earth and in the sky, and, if it is the case, the prints or other things left behind by these spaceships or by these beings?"

Zanfretta: "They know about NASA, they know about the interests of many ufologists but they cannot approach them because they would scare them and make them go crazy."

Prof. Marchesan: "You said that they stopped your heart for a few moments, so that you wouldn't be scared to death, but you didn't feel any effects from that?"

Zanfretta: "Yes, they stopped my heart while I was conscious."

Prof. Marchesan: "And you realized that your heart was stopped without having any damaging side effects?"

Zanfretta: "Yes."

Prof. Marchesan: "For how long was your heart stopped?"

Zanfretta: "A few minutes, just a few."

Prof. Marchesan: "Minutes, you say!"

Zanfretta: "Yes."

Prof. Marchesan: "Maybe one or two minutes, or maybe it was beating very slowly."

Zanfretta: "I don't know."

Prof. Marchesan: "Is there something, maybe, that these beings told you not to tell us and that you cannot reveal to us?"

Zanfretta: "I don't know what they revealed to me... But I can't say it for any reason, in time it will become known."

And with this, Fortunato Zanfretta's hypnosis session in Milan came to an end. The reader should note that not always do the sentences reported respect grammar and syntax, nor do some of them make any sense. They are, however, what was really said, and it is on these statements therefore that judgment may be expressed.

Did Zanfretta state something that objectively happened, or is his story the fruit of his imagination? What is the chance that even under the effect of drugs the guard was lying? Here is the statement that Professor Rolando Marchesan made immediately following the session.

"I would say that there are very poor chances that something subjective is at play here. That is to say, the subjective, the personal, the fantastic, or the residual memory of things seen or read should be extremely low. So what he relates, taking into consideration that there are also witness statements from what we have read in your newspaper and then also what we saw in the magazine *Gente*, taking into account that there are external statements, what he reports should have a high degree of correspondence to the truth. Now, seeing as he asserts that he will have yet another encounter in which they will give him this sphere that has powers that naturally we don't have, because they could be ahead of us, if they exist, as a civilization and technology, by two or three thousand years, we will effectively have proof that is more or less conclusive, shall we say, about the existence of these extraneous objects, and of these appearances. A confirmation, above all, that more intelligent beings exist and that they possess greater intelligence than ours, maybe a greater civilization than ours and technology that is extremely advanced."

Marchesan said he was satisfied with how the session had gone. "The experiment went well," he stated. "So we have not only a confirmation of what was done by Dr. Moretti in the previous sessions, but a deeper knowledge, perhaps a strengthening of the details with things that have a logical structure and therefore present a high degree of credibility."

Even as far as a potential fabrication on Zanfretta's part is concerned, Marchesan was very precise. On this theme he explained:

"Lying, it doesn't appear so in this situation. Somebody either tells an objective truth or a subjective truth. So someone maybe imagines something and makes it up, for him maybe it's true and he tells it as if it were true. Sometimes there can be a mix up of what is objective and what is only imagined, what was talked about, what was seen or what was imagined. It is extremely difficult to distinguish the two things. In such cases, the only thing to do is have a logical structure and external acknowledgement. Now, if those footprints of 50 by 20 centimeters were not made by someone who wanted to play a trick; if in effect the car was hot, so hot that not even someone with an electric stove can produce that heat and maintain it for a long time; if the inhabitants of the area saw enormous lights in the direction in which our friend was found, etc. etc., then there is objective data that must in be set in the story he is telling. When his story doesn't clash, let's say, but is integrated with what was seen, it takes on a high degree of veracity. The more outside proof there is, and the story fits together well because there are no contradictions, then it takes on a high, very high degree of correspondence to the truth."

As far as the astronomic information furnished by Zanfretta in hypnosis, it should be said that it is not easily verifiable. In fact, as professor Alesandro Manara from the Insitute of Astronomy and Geodesy from the University of Milan explains, from the current state of our knowledge, we are not able to say if there is a solar system similar to ours in some other part of the Universe, nor can we imagine where it is located. It is therefore impossible to ascertain, as Zanfretta says, if 4000 light years from our planetary system there is another similar one from which the extra-terrestrials of his encounters might come.

Science, in any case, in these years has been making giant steps and it could be that in the near future we might know something more about possible worlds, inhabited or not. Recently, for example, the American satellite "Iras," launched in January 1983, discovered that gravitating around Vega, the third brightest star in the firmament, there is a solar system of particles, planets and meteorites. Exactly like ours.

"These particles," two scientists from the Pasadena *Jet Propulsion Laboratory* and who analyzed the data transmitted from the satellite declared on August 10, 1983, "could represent a solar system like ours at a different stage of development." It should be mentioned in fact that Vega is about a billion years old, as compared to the five billion years of our sun, so one could think that the planets that might exist in its solar system are still in an evolutionary phase.

Going back to Zanfretta, it is not possible to identify the potential planetary system that was just discovered with the one the night watchman is talking about, in that Vega is only 26 light years away from our solar system, as opposed to the 4000 Zanfretta is talking about.

My article appeared the following day, Wednesday, February 7, in the *Corriere Mercantile*. Not to make Zanfretta's situation any worse, I limited myself to writing, as was true anyhow, that the security guard had confirmed point by point what he had said in the preceding sessions with Dr. Moretti. I deliberately left out the details. How could I possibly have said that Zanfretta spoke of these monsters as belonging to the people of 'Dargos'? The definition smelled like comic strips from a mile away. Only the entire story with all those details that were so natural could support the incredible – albeit possible – theory of truth.

My caution in Zanfretta's regard was more than well-founded. Following his nighttime adventures and all the noise that the newspapers had made, his mental faculties were publicly called into question. His story had taken on a national aspect, both after my article came out in *Gente* and especially after Enzo Tortora wanted him on the show "*Portobello*." Very soon *the security guard who had seen the UFOs* was known throughout Italy and even abroad.

More proof of this was the fact that my article in *Gente* was sold even to foreign magazines. Moreover, news flashes about his *close encounters* were transmitted worldwide by the Italian news agency ANSA every time they occurred. So it is perfectly understandable why "Val Bisagno" wanted to have their employee undergo a neuropsychiatric visit.

Zanfretta was not opposed to the idea, to the contrary. He was more than happy to go visit Professor Giorgio Gianniotti, a university professor of neurology, specialist in mental illnesses and deputy Chief Physician of Neurology at San Martino Hospital in Genoa, where he underwent three medical check-ups, on December 28 and 30, 1978 and January 31, 1979. It was on this last date that Professor Gianniotti issued the following certificate:

"At the request of the Management of the Security and Patrol Institute of which he is an employee, I examined Mr. Zanfretta on December 28 and 30, 1978. Mr. Zanfretta is 26 years old, he is a sworn public official by profession, and was sent to me again on today's date to undergo a neuropsychiatric visit.

As on the preceding two dates, I found Mr. Zanfretta in perfect psychic and neurological condition.

The patient does not show alterations in his thought, nor psycho-sensorial disturbances, he is normal and his ability to will is logical and critical. I believe therefore that Mr. Zanfretta is suitable for his work in an unconditional way and that he does not need periods of observation nor does he need any therapeutic advice.

Signed, in faith, for all legal use.

Professor Giorgio Gianniotti"

It is obvious that whoever was aware of the entire affair, and therefore also of the results of these medical check-ups and of the sessions of hypnosis in which Zanfretta participated, was perplexed but kept an open mind. The doubt that it was all true remained. Those who only read the newspapers and thus heard the most harebrained opinions, probably expressed by people who not only had never been close to the problem but even presumed to express categorical judgment on the subject, was exceptionally confused. In the latter case, the inclination was to resolve it by declaring that the night watchman was a drunk or a lunatic.

Many other people didn't agree and, now convinced that extra-terrestrials existed, got to the point of organizing a small scientific expedition which would have gone in Zanfretta's place on the alien aircraft. That the whole affair had been taken seriously was the interest eventually shown by Professor Rolando Marchesan. The expedition was in fact organized in Milan and many important specialists were part of it. Marchesan never really wanted to give many details on the project, but we know for sure that the idea came to fruition between February and August 1979. In short, Marchesan had become convinced of the night watchman's good faith and, envisioning sensational developments, tried to persuade Zanfretta under hypnosis, to introduce the extra-terrestrials to a group of highly qualified people who would gladly take his place on the spaceship to study the mysterious beings. If the matter never really succeeded it is because, as we will see, Zanfretta's brain was eluding more and more any control that hypnosis might have. It was a slow but inescapable process, in a series of new nighttime adventures.

Right after the Pentotal test, controversy died down. Probably because nobody expected the security guard to accept the invitation, therefore such a gesture had disoriented the people who had doubted his good faith from the beginning. Also, for a few months it seemed that the Zanfretta case would not produce any more relevant news. It was still being talked about, for sure. But these were conversations at the corner bar. Once in a while someone would jump up and ridicule the security guard's mental capacity. It must also be said that at that time, UFO sightings overlapped each other, therefore every time people talked about them, inevitably the conversation ended up on Zanfretta. Speaking of that time one cannot but mention the role that ufologists had. Aside from the fact that it was pretty difficult to distinguish who was the most serious or the most knowledgeable of all among those flying saucers enthusiasts, it was a fact that these groups constantly lived at war with each other. The battleground was the Zanfretta case. It is even funny to observe the envy that these people felt towards Zanfretta himself when they learned about what was being said about his encounters.

I myself was singled out by some of those *scholars* who kept calling me to have more detailed information about what had happened to Zanfretta. In particular, they wanted to know what happened in the hypnosis sessions. After my refusal, they went to"Val Bisagno" directly, but they hit a wall there as well. So they literally tried to employ spy-type means. They privately contacted "Val Bisagno" employees to find out indiscretions, they sent associates who while collaborating with some newspapers, tried to extort − it is really the case to use this verb − false interviews. In fact more than once, the night watchman found statements in the newspapers that he had never made or in any case that were distorted and made him look like a fool, some feeble-minded person with visions.

In other words, as is typical of a certain type of Italian journalism, the press was not used as a means of information but rather to drive a political war against someone thought to be troublesome and in any case unworthy of trust from the start.

The panorama of UFO watchers those days was very multifaceted. The one who among all ufologists closely followed the Zanfretta case was Luciano Boccone. There is a reason for this. Boccone was already a mature man and appeared very different from the other ufologists, all of them quite young, if not just boys.

The managers of "Val Bisagno" politely kept in touch with him until it was clear that his presence could compromise the purpose of the research. Boccone was in fact convinced and was trying to prove that Zanfretta was subjected to the control of *diabolical entities* that appeared to him as monstrous gigantic humanoids. His was a mystical-religious theory that absolutely went beyond the possible theory that the security guard might have actually been kidnapped by beings coming from other universes.

The vow to secrecy that the managers of "Val Bisagno" demanded in exchange for their collaboration was kept by Boccone only toward groups of other ufologists. Instead, in his group everyone knew and everyone talked with their respective friends about Zanfretta's hypnosis as well as the details of his adventures. The leak, as one can very well imagine, was enormous and it was not by chance that as soon as "Val Bisagno" severed dealings with Boccone, it died down.

At the core of that controversy was the UFO-watching group belonging to real estate agent Patrizio Del Bene. Having personal contact with a few guards of "Val Bisagno," Del Bene was immediately informed of Zanfretta's second encounter. Late in the morning he went to the area with some of his associates and took a plaster cast of the footprints found around the Fiat 127 in which the guard was travelling. Controversy was born from the fact that that very same afternoon the footprints.... had disappeared. It was said that the ufologists out of spite and wanting to be the only ones to have casts of the footprints, had destroyed them on purpose.

Del Bene subsequently stood up for himself saying that when lifting the plaster the prints got damaged, so much so that within a few hours there was no trace of even one of them. It was Del Bene, Zanfretta reports, who got to the point of covertly taping a conversation they had in a bar in order to have other people listen to it.

The case interested the Mantero brothers as well, Giovanni and Piero, two young ufologists so taken by their passion as to put this extraordinary qualification on their business card. Who perhaps followed Zanfretta's vicissitudes more discretely but not with less interest was Roberto Balbi, a blind fiduciary employee of the National Ufologic Center, who made ufology his main field of study. Faithful to

UFO research as an expression of a more advanced technology than ours, Balbi even verbally argued with Boccone, rejecting his theories as excessively paranormal.

Fortunato Zanfretta was therefore cuddled, studied, admired and envied by hordes of people who, with their nose up in the air, were uselessly waiting to frame in their binoculars the beguiling light of the passing UFO. A few times, the interest of these people became ridiculous, like that time when Zanfretta himself, during a nighttime inspection around Marzano, kicked out a group of youngsters who had settled around Villa Casa Nostra fully equipped and waiting for who knows what events.

CHAPTER 4

The Lifting Light

Without a doubt, it was a climate of anticipation. But months went by and nothing was happening. Just when nobody expected it, the night watchman met his space "frienemies" once again. It had been seven months since the last time: the night of July 30, 1979, the Zanfretta alarm sounded again in the "Val Bisagno" operations center.

That no one expected it is due to the fact that after the second *encounter*, Zanfretta was assigned to another area. Instead of leaving him on the hilltops above Genoa and therefore in all-too-isolated places, management had relocated him in town. Zanfretta was using a *Vespa* scooter in the streets of the eastern part of town in the suburbs of Quarto, Sturla, Quinto and Nervi. How could anyone suspect that there would be *close encounters* right in the middle of Genoa? But it happened.

That evening Zanfretta started work around 10:30 p.m. He preferred the night shift, it must be said, because it paid the highest salary. A few minutes after midnight, while he was driving towards a villa where he had to check the service clocks, Zanfretta (according to what he reported in a subsequent hypnosis session) was lifted by a mysterious green light towards a hovering spaceship.

While he was talking and arguing with the extra-terrestrials, his colleagues from below were looking for him everywhere. All the streets toward the hills were immediately checked and patrolled by the cars of "Val Bisagno". In spite of the fact that the alarm had been given within just a few minutes of Zanfretta's disappearance (Zanfretta was under constant radio control by the operator on duty), he was nowhere to be found. Only more than two hours later his Vespa was found at the top of Mount Fasce. A couple of kilometers further on, Zanfretta was found running in pitch black towards the small village of Uscio. What is weird is that to get to the top of this mountain, which is above the eastern suburbs of Genoa, there is only a very narrow road in the suburb of Apparizione. The night guard patrolling Apparizione was in fact alerted, and all his colleagues too. He stood in the middle of the road, which in some parts is so narrow that it is impossible for two cars to pass at the same time, with the intention of blocking Zanfretta on the Vespa, if he turned up. But Zanfretta, the guard said in his testimony, never passed by. And so, one wonders, how could the night watchman get to the top of that mountain?

Once again, the answer was sought in hypnosis. Moretti was hesitant, partly because of the publicity the Zanfretta case was bringing him, partly out of respect for Professor Marchesan, and so he suggested going to Milan once again. The hypnosis session started at exactly 5:01p.m. on August 1, 1979. As we will see during hypnosis, Rolando Marchesan himself had become so convinced of Zanfretta's good faith that he had already fine-tuned the *scientific expedition* that would have had to study the *extra-terrestrials*. Leaving aside the initial part of the session where Professor Marchesan preps the patient, here is the accurate recording of the event.

Prof. Marchesan: "I am giving you the chance to speak, to describe what has happened, second by second, starting from 10:30 p.m. and precisely from the moment you started your shift. We are talking, obviously, of June 30, 1979. Please describe the facts, speak."

Zanfretta: "Ok Pasquale, I'm going. I'll start from Corso Europa, bye. Look, the guy with the Alfa Romeo, he always leaves the roller-shutter open."

Prof. Marchesan: "Have you seen someone leaving the roller-shutter open?"

Zanfretta: "No, he always leaves the roller-shutter of the car dealer open. I leave my cards and then will come back. I am going in Via Pio VII to the guy who complains all the time, who says he never finds my cards when I always leave them. Here, I'll leave several, so he can't complain anymore. Now I'm going to Viale Quartara to close the gate at no. 39L. Here you go, done. I'm going to check Countess Moro's clock. Look at these dogs: they keep barking. Sit, Dana. Away.... damn!... Look, the clock has stopped. My!... what light!! What is it? It's not there anymore...Why have the dogs run away? Dana.... Seventy... Kangaroo here... come on, give me a call.... Let me get out of Villa Moro and I'll call you...."

At this point Zanfretta recites the phone conversation with Attilio Mazza, the operator at the radio command center. So that the other security guards on duty wouldn't hear what he had to say to Zanfretta, Mazza had asked him to call him.

Zanfretta: "Yes, Mr Mazza... No, I haven't noticed anything strange, apart from that light behind my shoulders. Yes, all right: I'll be in touch by radio every twenty minutes. All right, Landi is waiting for me at the Sette Nasi restaurant. I'm going. Oh, hi Landi. When on board? At 5 a.m.? All right, but my head hurts. Ow, crap, it hurts.... Say, Landi, is it true what you did the other night, that you left Zanardi in trouble? What, not true? You peed your pants... Zanardi said you left him by himself, ouch, my head, gee. OK, see you tomorrow morning at 5. I have to go but I'll come back, I'm going now. Then I have to go to Viale Quartara, bye, bye... Crap..... what's that green light? No... oh my God, it's lifting me, bloody hell, no. I'm flying, I'm on the Vespa, I don't know where I am! Where am I inside here? Ah, what room... it reminds me of something...Oh no, ow...my head... not you again.....Ouch, Christ: but what else do you want from me. Isn't all the trouble I'm going through enough? No, it's time to stop.... Where are we going now? We're flying... where are you taking me? I think I know this mountain. The noise from before is gone... But what do you want still? No, I have to say something to you, but my head hurts. Ow, please stop this pain for a little. Yes, a professor had said that I, that you have to leave me alone, that four of them would be willing to come. Ouch, easy with that helmet, it hurts.... ow, that's enough. I also have a friend who would like to see you and get to know you..."

Interrupting the transcript of the session for a moment, it should be clarified that up to that point, I didn't know that Zanfretta had been given the mental order to convey to his interlocutors that a group of people was willing to take his place to keep in touch with, shall we say, the *extra-terrestrials*. In fact, aside from myself, Lieutenent Cassiba and Boccone were also present at the session. On the other hand, both of them knew quite well that during the months that passed between January and July, Zanfretta had been taken back to Milan where Marchesan once again put him under hypnosis. This is where Zanfretta had been given the order, and indeed the professor of which Zanfretta speaks is Marchesan, who had found four people that could take his place. The friend who wanted to meet the mysterious interlocutors was none other than Boccone. Zanfretta was to refer the message.

For the sake of clarity, I am dividing Zanfretta's dialogue to distinguish between his thoughts and the thoughts of the beings he is talking to.

Entity: "Who is this professor?"

Zanfretta: "I met him a couple of times, I don't know him well but he is a very important person who knows a lot, so go and look for them, not me, I want to be left in peace. They are more intelligent than me, I don't know anything. Ouch, my head....Hell, with this damn helmet... yes, there are three more people who I don't remember. One I think is a nuclear engineer, another is a parapsychologist and the other.... ah...ah... he's in the movies or something. And then there's my friend Luciano. No... yes... they would be willing to go in my place, as long as you leave me alone. What, you're not interested? In that case, it's a fixation... I am not intelligent. What the hell do I have to do to make you understand?"

Here, straight after this sentence, Zanfretta gives a start, stops speaking with a quiet and scared voice and exclaims with decision: "Let go of the radio! Let it go.... Let it go..." After which he goes back the same tone as before.

Zanfretta: "Ah, I have to run away, I have to run away: how do you get out of here? Let's press one of these buttons. No it's not this one...here, the door opened....., heavens, what a jump! My legs hurt, gee! Holy cow, I'm running....so they can't stitch me up....my motorbike... what did they take from the motorbike? Here now I can run away, I'm running away.... Seventy, seventy... Kangaroo here."

Zanfretta speaks to his colleagues via radio and his colleagues answer him.

Radio: "Piero, Piero, where are you?"

Zanfretta: "I... I don't.... I don't know...."

Radio: "Piero, stay calm, we're coming!"

Zanfretta: "I don't know where I am."

Radio: "Attention please, Zanfretta it's the Lieutenant. Stay calm and tell me where you are."

Zanfretta:"I... I don't know.... Ah, them again, what's this light? What do you want again? But.... If you don't give me proof, they're not going to believe me: how many times do I have to say it? You told me you would give me a sphere that demonstrated..."

Entity: "It's not the right time."

Zanfretta:"What? Again? The last time? Oh Mother of God, Jesus! When? When? The great cold? When is it? I don't have to worry? But it is the last time you look for me.... For crying out loud, as long as you put a stop to it. I need to go... what? I have to walk without stopping? Yes, I can walk without stopping..."

Radio: "Attention please, seventy: Zanfretta, Kangaroo here...

Zanfretta: "Come in!"

Radio: "Where are you? Look around you, if you see anything..."

Zanfretta: "I don't know, I don't know, I only see lights from above and that's it."

Radio: "Attention please, Travenzoli, seventy-one here: the voice is stronger here so he must be nearby. Attention please, Paolo, fifteen here: you climb Monte Moro and Triani and I will climb Monte Fasce. Kangaroo, twenty-eight here: I'm coming up from Uscio so I can go up to Monte Fasce. Perhaps I'll bump into him there. Zanfretta......., Zanfretta...."

At this point the security guard whispers two words, even more quietly: *hit, hit.*

And in fact, he actually jumped on his colleagues, trying to hit them. They had to defend themselves to immobilize him. Later on, still under hypnosis, Zanfretta will explain the reason for this unwarranted aggression...

Colleagues: "Zanfretta, It's Garbarino..."

Zanfretta: "Go away..."

Colleagues: "Paolo, he's here. He's walking... Piero, wake up! Piero, let's jump on him, let's catch him!"

Zanfretta once again receives a belligerent order and whispers: "*Go on, hit your head against the car, it's an order. Your strength increases,*" and then he reverts back to the frightened tone that has marked the entire hypnotic session.

Zanfretta: "No, let go of me, let go of me...."

Colleagues: "Zanfretta...., Piero..... Do you recognize me? Come, let's walk. Do you want to sit on the car? Be still! Take his gun away. Come, sit on the ground: be still. Behave...."

Zanfretta: "Ow, my head. Ow, it hurts.... I'm sick of it!"

Radio: "Fifteen, Echo One here."

Colleagues "Yes, he fainted, we'll bring him down."

Zanfretta: "The light inside... ah...ah.... seventy-one...."

Colleagues: "Zanfretta, do you recognize me?"

Zanfretta: "Yes, ow, my head... where are we? Where are you taking me? The radio, the radio..... I don't have it anymore.... The radio....yes... and oh! No, I'm not going to the ER, my head hurts less, no, they'll end up taking my gun license away again.... I need it. Here, yes: let's go and drink something... Listen, Mr. Tutti... I.... I... would like to resign...because... because I am creating too many problems for you. It's not my fault but I prefer it this way.... It's the same, anyway. I'm going home to sleep..., yes..., Hello? Mr. Mazza,

I'm home.... Yes, yes, I'm resting. Ah, are you awake? (*to his wife*) No, nothing's happened... There you go...There's no hiding anything from you.... but nothing has happened. Here, I reckoned you knew already. Now I have to sleep, we'll talk about it later. If the Lieutenant calls, wake me up. Yes, I have to call the professor in Milan. I'm sleeping...."

Marchesan, who up until that moment had been listening, stepped in to make Zanfretta relax.

Prof. Marchesan: "You keep resting quietly, more and more peaceful, more and more relaxed. With every breath calm and deep, more and more relaxed, heavier and heavier, healthy restorer. You listen only to my voice. Other voices and other sounds do not bother you at all, they get to your ears as if they were very far away, as if they were pleasant musical notes that further deepen your sleep, your rest, your relaxation. Now I will ask you some questions to which you will answer clearly like you did before, while staying in a very deep and relaxed sleep, reliving the facts as if they didn't concern you, as if you're watching them on TV, detached, calm and relaxed sitting in a very comfortable armchair. When, these are my questions, when you felt the headache, was it the moment in which you heard that whistle, that sound, echoing in your mind?"

Zanfretta: "Yes, the hiss..."

Prof. Marchesan: "And around what time did you hear this hiss? If you remember..."

Zanfretta: "When I was winding the clock...."

Prof. Marchesan: "Do you remember what time it was? You should be able to remember, think..."

Zanfretta: "Around ten to one a.m."

Prof. Marchesan: "So, you heard the hiss around ten to one. Did you hear it one time only?"

Zanfretta: "Yes."

Prof. Marchesan: "And then, which roads did you travel on to get to the meeting place with these beings?"

Zanfretta: "No road, just Viale Quartara, at the beginning... but a green light lifted me up..."

Prof. Marchesan: "At what point of this street, Viale Quartara, were you lifted with your motorbike by the green light?"

Zanfretta: "After the bridge...."

Prof. Marchesan: "Ok, after the bridge. Then how much do you reckon you traveled while flying in this green beam?"

68

Zanfretta: "It seemed as if I wasn't moving."

Prof. Marchesan: "Ok, but when you touched the ground, what was your approximate distance from Viale Quartara? From the time you were lifted?"

Zanfretta: "I... I don't know...."

Prof. Marchesan: "Hundreds of meters or even kilometers? You can remember, you must remember!"

Zanfretta: "Around... around 22 km... give or take..."

Prof. Marchesan: "And how long do you think it took you to travel those 22 km?"

Zanfretta: "Just a few seconds...."

Prof. Marchesan: "What was the town closest to the point where you, shall we say, landed?"

Zanfretta: "I don't know..."

Prof. Marchesan: "You mentioned Uscio before, it is quite far..."

Zanfretta: "I, I remember a square where.... where the car spaces are marked. And they jumped off that thing...."

Prof. Marchesan: "This square, do you know in which town or near which town it is?"Zanfretta: "No, I don't know, 'cause it was dark, I couldn't see anything, just the lights of that cloud could see the marks on the ground..."

Prof. Marchesan: "It was a black cloud, did you say? But was it so thick that you couldn't see anything inside or could you glimpse something?"

Zanfretta: "Yes, it was the usual saucer and the other times I saw it, it was covered by a black cloud...."

Prof. Marchesan: "And this saucer, was it on the ground like last time or was it hovering in the air? And in this case, at what height from the ground?"

Zanfretta: " It was in the air, not on the ground, because I jumped 5 or 6 meters and I hurt my knees. But I didn't graze anything, it was just the fall..."

Prof. Marchesan: "That is, the fall. You say that when you got to the square with your Vespa, it's then, I think, you fell and did you hurt yourself then? When you, shall we say, landed?"

Even this attempt to get Zanfretta to contradict himself fails. Once again, the night watchman, in deep hypnosis, describes how things had gone.

Zanfretta: "No."

Prof. Marchesan: "Afterwards then..."

Zanfretta: "When I got hold of the radio, I started to run along those corridors and I saw some buttons I had noticed when the green light had lifted me..."

Prof. Marchesan: "So, inside the spacecraft you hit against something with your knee?"

Zanfretta: "Nooo, when I grabbed the radio from him, I ran to those buttons and I started pressing them out of fear. And a door opened and I threw myself...."

Prof. Marchesan: "But you say that you threw yourself..."

Zanfretta: "Yes, and then I saw the Vespa and the green light..... and the flap where I keep the cards opened and something got onto the spaceship."

Prof. Marchesan: "And was the Vespa always on the ground or did it get inside the spaceship?"

Zanfretta: "It was.... inside...."

On this subject, it must be noticed that, as Zanfretta himself will say, in the small flap of the Vespa there was an AM-FM radio which after the encounter was nowhere to be found.

Zanfretta: "But I ran away..."

Prof. Marchesan: "Yes, you ran away and then they gave you the Vespa back and then they took something from the flap where you keep the cards?"

Zanfretta: "Yes."

Prof. Marchesan: "Inside the spaceship, did you see the same people, shall we say, the same beings you saw last time?"

Zanfretta: "Yes."

Prof. Marchesan: "How many of them were there, more or less. Actually you can be precise about this. Think about it..."

Zanfretta: "Always ten."

Prof. Marchesan: "All adults or boys too?"

Zanfretta: "There were small boys as well..."

Prof. Marchesan: "How many?"

Zanfretta: "Three."

Prof. Marchesan: "Three boys and seven adults?"

Zanfretta: "Yes."

Prof. Marchesan: "Out of these adults, how many were females?"

Zanfretta: "I don't know..."

Prof. Marchesan: "Think about it, you can say it."

Zanfretta: "I think three..."

Prof. Marchesan: "How tall were the boys?"

As the reader can see, Professor Marchesan tries in any way to compare Zanfretta's current statements to the ones he had made under hypnosis seven months before. He tries, in other words to ascertain that things check out.

Zanfretta: "About 2 meters..."

Prof. Marchesan: "On the other hand, how tall were the men and women? Try to say it with precision."

Zanfretta: "About three meters and ten."

Prof. Marchesan: "Did they put the helmet on your head, like last time?"

Zanfretta: "Yes, it hurts.... it's a pain.... it makes me feel the shock... to my brain..."

Prof. Marchesan: "Did they say anything to you during this encounter? Please relate precisely what they said or even, what they asked you to convey to others."

Zanfretta: "They told me they follow everything that's happened and what is happening.... the right moment is when the great cold comes.... and they want to give proof that they exist, but, for the moment, we are not ready yet. Next time they come, it will be final."

Prof. Marchesan: "Final in what sense? Will it be the last time they speak to you? Or will it be the last time they come to Earth? Or what do they mean to say with final time? Last one?"

Zanfretta: "I don't know. I only know that what they told me."

Prof. Marchesan: "Did they say what they intend to do with you?"

Zanfretta: "They said: in time, I will know, when the great cold arrives...."

Prof. Marchesan: "Listen, in any case, I am telling you two things: if you meet them next time, I mean, there will be a next time, and you meet these strange beings and they give you something important, the first thing you will do, as soon as you get home, you will call me. If it is daytime, naturally the encounters happen during the night, but I will give you my home number therefore you are authorized to call me even in the middle of the night and you will wait for my instructions. If it is daytime when you want to call me, you will call me at the office. But, I repeat, if they give you something as proof of their presence and of their existence above all, as soon as you get home you will call me at home, I will give you my number later. I will give you instructions on the matter. If there is another encounter, let me add just this, you must reiterate to these gentlemen that, if they intend to have a collaboration with us earthlings, we are willing to work with them. Let me be precise, us means four people from Milan: a doctor, an engineer, a female psychologist and a cinema photo-journalist, if they like. As well as a UFOs scholar who resides in Genoa. And ask them for instructions on how these people can get in touch with them and finally leave you alone. I repeat: the previous order that I'm giving you now, and that you will carry out should you find yourself in the presence of these people. If these beings should hand you something important, you will call Professor Rolando Marchesan in Milan as soon as you get home and you will wait for my instructions."

The pie had therefore been divided. As they say, they got a whiff of the deal and now they were trying to use the security guard as a means to get to the almighty *extra-terrestrials*. Marchesan, therefore, fully believed Zanfretta's story. And he believed in it so much that, with Boccone, he had organized *the rescue expedition* down to the last detail. At this point, the night guard could and should leave the scene. So everyone, really everyone, would be happy. Instead, what Marchesan wasn't picking up on was that while he was giving out orders, the night guard kept repeating quietly: "No, no," and kept shaking his head in his sleep. In spite of this, the professor kept insisting.

Prof. Marchesan: "Should you meet them once again, I am authorizing you to say to these gentlemen that there are four people, even five, willing to collaborate with them, possibly, or rather, fully respecting personal freedom. These are people who deal with psychological problems, meaning human relationships: a doctor and a psychologist, there is also a nuclear engineer as you have rightly told them already, as well as another friend who is a photo-journalist. The four of them are from Milan. Then, if need be, there is a scholar of these problems that can get in touch with them and who resides in Genoa. Keep these things well in mind and explain them to these beings. If they agree to meet these collaborators, they should tell you what we have to do, what these people have to do to meet with them: provided that their freedom is respected always. They are willing to collaborate in the best way, in the most effective, efficient way. I am asking you now to tell me how you felt, from a physical, nervous and psychological point of view after this *encounter*."

Zanfretta: "W...well."

Prof. Marchesan: "Did you feel well? Or were you still agitated and shaken because of the encounter? Going back a little, can you tell me:

when you were lifted by that ray, or beam, of green light with the whole Vespa, were there people nearby that realized what happened or was the area completely deserted?"

Zanfretta: "No, I didn't get on alone..."

Prof. Marchesan: "You mean that, around you, nearby, you didn't see anyone?"

Zanfretta: "No."

Prof. Marchesan: "Even the square where you landed was deserted, with just the parking marks on the asphalt or ground anyway for the cars?"

Zanfretta: "Yes, it was all dark..."

Prof. Marchesan: "You mean nobody was there. There weren't any cars or vehicles that belonged to other people? No houses nearby? You didn't notice any house or farmhouse?"

The question was actually irrelevant. In fact, those who know the area know that Mount Fasce, 834 meters above sea level, is almost totally deserted. On the two hilltops there is the Sanctuary of the Virgin Mary on one, and on the other the antenna towers of the national TV networks. As for the rest, there aren't any dwellings for several kilometers, nor any lighting. Zanfretta replies accordingly.

Zanfretta: "No."

Prof. Marchesan: "Did you notice how they left? When did they leave? Please describe it, what time was it?"

Zanfretta: "When the flap of the Vespa was opened, they took something. And then they disappeared in the sky in an instant. But without any light or anything, covered by the cloud..."

Prof. Marchesan: "You say 'black cloud' but is it like our clouds that in the night, heavy with rain, let's say, look black...?"

Zanfretta: "Yes, the object.... that...."

Prof. Marchesan: "Please tell us plainly, in a more understandable voice, if there is something interesting to add."

Zanfretta: "The object that they're going to give me, I'll have to hand it..... to professor.... Ha... Hainke..... Bah! To an American professor. When they give it to me I have to hand it to him...., that's it....."

Prof. Marchesan: "The professor called Hynek? Do you remember if they said this name?"

Zanfretta: "Yes... yes... Hynek."

Prof. Marchesan: "Ok. Now listen. We'll proceed... you keep sleeping calm and relaxed, detached from the events you have lived as if they were events concerning, or that have concerned someone else. You keep sleeping."

Marchesan wanted to know Zanfretta better and during hypnosis he took the opportunity to get to know the guard from a more psychological point of view. And so, he got him to go back to when he was 6, 10, 22 years of age and for each time, he always made him draw a tree. Then he asked him to draw his closest relatives. When he brought him back to his current age, he asked him to draw the *extraterrestrials* and the inside of their spaceship.

Regarding the aggressiveness displayed when he was found, Marchesan asked him to clarify further.

Prof. Marchesan: "When your colleagues approached you to convince you to come back to headquarters, you struck out at them. Your normal strength multiplied: you could match up to four colleagues even! Why did you do it? Had you, by any chance, been given an order by those beings on the spaceship?"

Zanfretta: "They wanted it that way."

Prof. Marchesan: "Who wanted it that way? You?"

Zanfretta: "No."

Prof. Marchesan: "The others, from the spaceship?"

Zanfretta: "Yes."

Prof. Marchesan: "So , what did they tell you to do toward your colleagues?"

Zanfretta: "To hit them."

Prof. Marchesan: "But what were these beings hoping to accomplish by unleashing you in such a way toward your colleagues?"

Zanfretta: "To distract them so they could get away."

Prof. Marchesan: "Now I am asking you if those from the spaceship have asked about us present here, especially me, or my father, or your superior Lieutenant Cassiba or Mr. Boccone?"

Zanfretta: "No."

Prof. Marchesan: "They haven't asked for any information?"

Zanfretta: "No."

Prof. Marchesan: "They do know, though, that we have placed you under hypnosis?"

Zanfretta: "They expected it."

Prof. Marchesan: "They expected it. Good."

And with this, Zanfretta's last hypnosis in Milan came to an end. Before waking him up, Marchesan reminded him once again that there was a group of people willing to collaborate with the extra-terrestrials and that he should let them know. Zanfretta didn't answer.

When Gianfranco Tutti learned about how the session went, he got suspicious. That even a Milanese professor believed his employee, so much so that he even inconvenienced the experts willing to come in contact with the beings he was talking about, convinced Tutti to take the entire matter more seriously. From that day onward, he wanted Zanfretta to be under constant observation. Cassiba was the deus ex machina of the situation. Since there was no plausible reason to suspend Zanfretta from work, given that all neurological visits proved him to be sound of mind and the trade unions would have opposed any unjustified measure, Tutti gave Zanfretta his full attention. When on duty, for example, he wanted Zanfretta to be checked by radio very frequently. Any malaise he might feel, must be reported immediately to Cassiba or himself. His wife, furthermore, had been asked to immediately communicate anything strange concerning her husband so that he could be helped in a timely manner.

Once, I was even asked to give my opinion in public on the Zanfretta Case. It wasn't something I did gladly. As it was, I hadn't published a single work on his third encounter so as not to worsen the situation. In any case, thanks to the careless leaks that were coming from all directions, word had spread. A few reporters had turned up at "Val Bisagno" looking for information, but over there they pretended to be clueless. Even Zanfretta's colleagues had been given orders to deny any occurrence so, that time, in the eyes of public opinion, nothing had happened to Zanfretta.

I was invited to comment on the entire matter. It was during a round table held at a private radio station. To tell the truth, I favored my role as an observer rather than someone who, albeit for professional interest, got himself involved in such a matter.

However, Gianfranco Tutti asked me to step in, and, if only for the kindness he showed toward me, I couldn't say no. Nor could I say at the microphone of the broadcasting station that I was convinced that the mysterious extra-terrestrials did exist. Therefore, when I found myself at the center of debate, where many already took for granted that the strange beings existed and that the night watchman had met them, I simply stated all that had happened up to that moment, until that time when concrete proof could confirm Zanfretta's account under hypnosis. Aside from various experts, Tutti, Cassiba and Zanfretta were also part of that round table. Tutti, cautious as well, was quick to follow my example, saying he trusted Zanfretta but was still perplexed about the phenomena that had his employee as their protagonist. "My situation," he said, "is not simple. There is no doubt that we find ourselves facing a series of strange events that must have some kind of explanation, but we don't have it yet. I therefore cannot condemn or absolve Zanfretta. I respect him, I know he is not the one responsible for all this. But unless I have proof, I cannot take a definitive stand."

Basically the program ended with each participant still standing by his own opinion. It is obvious, however, that no one succeeded in forgetting all that was being said in those days. One afternoon I found myself chatting with Tutti, Colonel Cereda and Mrs. Bonola about how we should all behave should Zanfretta be called once again to an unknown destination. Cereda was the most skeptical: his positive attitude wasn't allowing him to take into consideration what looked like nighttime disappearances of his employee.

"How is it that he's the only one to see them?" he was saying. "Is it possible that there's never tangible proof of the presence of these beings, if they exist?" The conversation turned to discussion of the sphere that Zanfretta had spoken about during his last hypnosis. What could the pyramid within the sphere mean? What real meaning could such an object have? And above all, why would Zanfretta have to give it to Professor Hynek?

I was the one to suggest the most elementary of answers: why not ask Professor Hynek directly? For a moment they all looked at me with a touch of curiosity, then they asked me if I knew how to get in touch with him. Looking for him was not difficult, I knew Professor Hynek taught astronomy at Northwestern University in Evanston, on the outskirts of Chicago. I asked for the number at the Consulate General of the United States in Genoa and got it within ten minutes.

At this point, all I had to do was call. English was not a problem, as it is my second language. We only had to be lucky enough to find him in the office. I dialed the number and I called. He wasn't there but the secretary was very kind and she gave me another number. This time I found him. In front of my guests, anxious to learn the content of that conversation, I explained everything to Hynek and asked him for his opinion. Hesitant, the scientist replied that he needed more information and details to be able to express an opinion. In any case it would have been better if I put together a comprehensive report and sent it to him. When I hung up I explained what Hynek wanted and everybody agreed to put Zanfretta's vicissitudes in writing. But I didn't do it. Busy with many work commitments, I never had the time to write that report. Today, however, I realize that if I didn't write it, maybe it was because I myself didn't know what to think. I don't know if it was a mistake to behave like that. I take comfort, however, in having learned, two years later, that Zanfretta himself, made aware of what he was saying under hypnosis, wrote to Hynek without any result. In fact, the professor returned the night watchman's letter to Roberto Pinotti, president of the National Ufologic Centre (CUN), so that they could deal with it.

To be fair, I feel like saying that even Hynek, without knowing all the elements that contributed to making the Zanfretta case more enigmatic, wouldn't have been able to see the matter in the right light.

And so time went by. We were all waiting for the *big chill*, making it coincide with winter, obviously. Would something really happen? While we were waiting, precautions were taken. For example, radio communications would be recorded. All patrol cars had an emergency plan to activate should there be an alert. The roads connecting to the hinterland would be patrolled constantly in the hope that that blessed alert would never be given, especially for Zanfretta's sake. We all lived in anticipation.

CHAPTER 5

Two Beams From a Cloud

And without fail, that day came. It was the night between the 2nd and 3rd of December, 1979. Zanfretta had gone with his car, a Mini, to a self-service gas station on Corso Europa. It was around 10 p.m. By chance, Modestino Romagnolo, journalist and president of the Journalists and Polygraphs Co-op, editor of the newspapers *Corriere Mercantile* and *Gazzetta del Lunedì,* was at the gas station at the same time. Romagnolo eventually testified to having seen and recognized the security guard, but to having paid little attention to him. He filled up his Citroen Dyane and left.

So Zanfretta was alone at the gas station, and from that moment on, we officially lose track of him. The radio command center, in fact, didn't hear from him again. The emergency plan was activated and all cars started looking for him. After going through all the hilly areas, finally one of the guards, security guard Andrea Pesci whose shift was in Torriglia, said he saw a big bright disc up in the sky. And so all cars converged on Torriglia and from there, following Pesci's directions, went to a clearing beyond Marzano, about 2 kilometers from where the first encounter had taken place. Here Cassiba and his men clearly saw two big beams lit up from inside a cloud, and those beams were pointing at them. Not far away, Zanfretta's car was found, open. No sign of him though. Cassiba then, maybe frightened by the unusual phenomenon, drew his gun and fired a few shots at the lights in the sky. The beams switched off and the cloud quickly lifted. Zanfretta was found five hundred meters away.

The matter immediately took on great significance because this time the patrol from police headquarters was following the search for Zanfretta step by step. Four police cars and a few Carabinieri cars had come to the night watchman's aid. There were several witnesses, but what could be proven anyway? Aside from the beams that had switched on inside a cloud and that lit the guards up from above, there was no concrete proof. The morning of December 3rd, I got Cassiba and the other guards to take me to the spot where it had all happened. First off, I went and asked some farmers that lived in the area for their opinion. The houses are about 600-700 meters from where the guards were.

To the great satisfaction of Cassiba and the other witnesses too, these farmers confirmed that the previous night they had seen a great light moving in the sky above their houses, but that they had locked themselves in immediately. Furthermore, a woman told me that they had seen these strange celestial phenomena all too often and that, since they had become so frequent, they weren't paying much attention anymore.

The night watchman's case was becoming more and more sensational. But the surprises didn't end there. That very evening Fortunato Zanfretta was put under hypnosis once again. Gianfranco Tutti asked doctor Moretti to do it, so that any information that might come from Zanfretta's lips under hypnosis would be kept *in the family,* so to speak. They didn't want the matter to develop outside of Genoa or become uncontrollable in any way.

Moretti accepted as long as no one knew that once again it was he who would hypnotize Zanfretta. I committed to this as well. The news I was referring to earlier was that during hypnosis, which was already turning out to be extremely interesting, Zanfretta said that the strange beings that had kidnapped him had just come back from Spain where with their flying saucer they had frightened some people on the street. As I said, the hypnosis session took place on the evening of December 3. The next morning, Tuesday, December 4, ANSA's international desk transmitted to all Italian newsrooms the following newsflash:

"Guadalajara (Spain). A Spanish veterinarian has stated that he was followed by an unidentified flying object (UFO) while he was at the wheel of his car on a road near Guadalajara, some 50 kilometers from Madrid. According to his testimony Alfredo Sanchez Cuesta spotted, during the night between last Saturday and Sunday, a UFO that followed his car and then overtook it, to then hover above it some 15 meters. Blinded by the strong yellow glare coming from the aircraft, at some point Sanchez lost control of the vehicle, which veered off the road. According to the vet, the UFO left the path followed by the car as it passed through some villages."

The same day I published two articles in the *Corriere Mercantile.* The first one, spread over four columns on the first page, had the following title over four lines: 'Zanfretta said: 'They had come from Spain.' This morning's news: They saw them in Madrid.' The second one, four opening columns with four photos had this meaningful title: "The mystery called Zanfretta."

Was Zanfretta's anticipation a simple coincidence? How could he know the news that up until that moment had yet to be written? Mystery merged into mystery and Zanfretta's words were starting to feel more and more real, leaving everyone astonished. With no exception, we were all afraid to believe what a reasonable person does not, cannot believe.

This is the text of the hypnosis session carried out by Doctor Moretti the evening of December 3, 1979.

Doctor Moretti: "It's 10.30 p.m. on the 2nd of December. It is 10.30 at night. You are starting your shift. Tell me everything, absolutely everything that happens from now on, from 10.30p.m. onward. You can speak now... It's 10.30 p.m., you are starting your shift, right?"

Zanfretta: "Yes."

Doctor Moretti: "Now tell me everything that happens, everything..."

Zanfretta: "Hi, Caviglia. Have you got the cards? Here, take two packets. Christ, I'm not feeling very well tonight; I've got such a strong headache I can't take it anymore. No... anyway I'm going and in the meantime I'm going to fill up. Bye. Crap.... this car is always low on petrol. Well, I'll put in five thousand Lire (*about 5 dollars*). Here...excuse me...who are you? Why are you standing in the dark? (The security guard is talking to someone he met at the petrol station.) Are you feeling ill? Should I come closer? Why do you look at me with those eyes? But... come out of the dark! You again? But you.... you're the one I've seen a couple of times.... Where? Where do I have to enter? Why? Ah... yes, yes: I'm getting inside, I'm getting inside the cloud, but don't look at me like that, it bothers my eyes. Yes, I'm getting in the car and inside the cloud. Where are we going now? It's lifting us...! We're going up.... We're high up.... God, so much light... Where are we inside here? Oh no, not you again! It's a fixation then. Why do you want to show me your spaceship? But I'm not interested.... No, no, I'm leaving. Which object? Ah, but first you have to show me the spaceship? Let's go see it then.... It sure is big.... But.... what are those machines? What are they for? As if I care... Yes, but you could bend down a little. Ah, you don't frighten me anymore... May I at least see how fast we're going? Mother of God, we're so high up! Where's the Earth? Hey, I want to go back home, OK? I don't give a damn about what you want to do. I have to place the cards, I have to do the clocks... No, who's that one over there giving orders? Huh?

He's ugly, isn't he? Well, since I'm here, I was curious to see what was inside those cylinders. Will you show them to me then? How many are there? Is that water inside them? How can a man so ugly be inside there? He'll drown... And those weird birds? And that thing.... that thing all.... that looks like a frog-shaped man? My God, it's disgusting! And now? Where are you taking me? But I don't know him, I don't care... Why? What does he have to give me? Ah... ah yes, I had already said so last time. Is he your boss? Huh.... What? Yes, but what language is he speaking? Ah, that's it now. Which sphere? This one? And who do I have to give it to? And after all the trouble I went through I have to give it to that one? You can keep it!!!"

The security guard's tone that until that moment had been quite mellow, even resigned, suddenly becomes harder, almost irate. He has no intention of carrying out the task he has been asked to do. On the contrary, in a fit of anger, he even takes the object and throws it at the one who has given it to him.

Zanfretta: "I don't want it, I'm not interested. Anyhow I'm not obliged. I said I don't want it! You want me to take it? And I'll throw it back at you: here, keep it! And why is the square gone now? Let go of my arm! Let it go.... Damn, you'll rip everything! Look, see what you've done? Hell.... who's going to explain it down there now? Huh? I say, there are so many.... But tell him he can keep the ball. I'm not interested, I've thrown it at him and now he keeps it. I don't care if I've broken..."

(The guard, distressed, says that one of those beings has ripped a sleeve off his jacket. But his reaction is immediately punished).

Zanfretta: "Where are you taking me now? No, not the helmet again! No, no, no... Not again, no! Ow, my head hurts...no please...take it off...no… It makes me sleepy.... No...noooo....I'm so tired! Why don't you take this thing off me? It's a pain... Yes, I'll be good. Take it off! Ah, ah...thank goodness. So what do you want from me again? I've given you the ball so what do you want? I don't care that I've thrown it over there.... anyhow: if I don't go crazy here, I'll go crazy down there. No....why are you turning another light on now? Who's bothering you? Let me see, who's down there? But they're looking for me...look, they're shooting too.... Why are you annoying them with these beams? No... Where are we going now? Ah, but... we were on Corso Europa, how can we be here already? Ah, that house again! Hey, not the car OK? Don't send it down... Why do you want me to sit inside the car now? So, I can leave the car down there... alright, I'll leave it and come back up. Bloody hell, this radio is always broken.... how can they not receive me? And now I'm leaving. Away... Kangaroo? Kangaroo I've got the lights behind me, help! It's lifting me up again, it's lifting meee.... help it's lifting me!"

(Zanfretta thus finds himself on board the flying saucer.)

Zanfretta: "There's no way, is there? Why me? Damn... But they're looking for me! Bloody hell, but... let's go and see this spaceship, bloody hell! What's that light over there, turning on and off? And what's it for? Yes, but how does it supply electricity? It's not electricity? What is it then? Uranium? Anyway, I really don't give a damn. Let's go see somewhere else. And all these people here, same as you... so much noise! How come the one from the square is not here anymore? Oh well, he was the one wanting the ball! But I really don't care if I've broken everything... So? Ahhh.... Gee, look at all these controls! I say, why don't you show yourselves? Huh? I know: it's not that easy! But why should I be the one who's taken for crazy, no way! And don't call me shorty, get it? Eh? Why not show me what you've got in front of that bloody mouth of yours? Yes, but if you don't bend down I can't see... Gee, what a hole! And why is light coming out it? Is it a bright substance of your ..... body system? Ahhh... anyway, leave it: stand up, go! They're calling me down there, damn! Will you leave me alone then? No, huh? That's enough now! Bloody hell, the jacket is ripped... But... where are we going now? It looks like we're standing still... Ouch, this radio doesn't work.... now that I need Mazza's voice for once, he's always talking... but let's go... And where are we going now? Into another room? Let's go see it.... why so many of you up here? It is so small, but inside it's big... What is it? One of the new ones? One of the new spaceships? Where did you go? And to do what, over there in Spain? Why? All of you together? But you scare people! Shush, I'm working on the radio or I'll turn it down a bit."

Radio: "Attention please, Piero, fifteen here..."

Zanfretta: "Bloody hell.... Hey, will you let me get off? No, I don't need the helmet. No, please. Again? Oh Christ, it's a fixation then... It makes my head hurt ... it hurts, no.... ow, not the shocks..."

Suddenly Zanfretta changes tone of voice. The timbre becomes much lower, frightened. It was clear that the subject switched from a conscious state to a state of confusion. The impression is that before letting him go, the beings had given him some kind of brainwashing to make him forget, while in a conscious state, what he had just experienced. And so the night watchman starts to speak as if he's scared to death.

Zanfretta: "Kangaroo... the light is going away... the light is going away. It is lifting. Yes, I can hear you Mr. Tutti. I've hidden in a hole. Yes... I'm waiting for the Lieutenant to arrive. But get him to honk his horn. When are they coming? With the headlights? All right.... holy cow, I'm slipping.... I've slipped.... yes, I can hear you.... Bloody hell, is this radio working or not? Here they come: I can hear the horn... Yes, I can hear it. Yes, I'm coming up, I'll climb up and be there."

Cassiba: "Piero, it's me, Cassiba."

Zanfretta: "Ah, thank goodness.... that's enough, I'm leaving, enough, I can't take it anymore. My God... yes, I'm sitting, I'm sitting. Paolo, the gun... it's loaded, take the bullet out. Ow, bloody hell my head hurts.... Of course, do you really expect the car to start? It probably blew a fuse that one.... you'd like to see it.... you'll have to push it a bit. Are we going down? Good lord, it's cold with the window open. My goodness, so many police! Yes, yes I'm fine... Everyone is looking at me, they are looking at me... Bah, you look like you're looking at someone who's killed a hundred people. Yes, I'm fine. Mr. Tutti.... Did you have a good trip? Engineer.... Hi Claudio.... gee, you're as tall as a Tutsi! Yes, I'll sit for a minute, you're talking over there anyway..."

Zanfretta has therefore been taken back to the offices of "Val Bisagno;" the director and his son Claudio are there, Nino Tagliavia, an engineer, and other executives. In the street, on the other hand, he has seen the police cars that have taken part in the search for him.

Moretti understands that it not is necessary to let him go on and steps in. Furthermore, Luciano Boccone, who was present at the hypnosis session as well, had asked Moretti to prep Zanfretta to listen to questions that were being asked in someone else's voice. Boccone wanted to have more information on the story so that he could explain a few vague details.

Doctor Moretti: "Now, Zanfretta, you can only hear my voice. You remember perfectly everything you've seen, everything that's happened. Only what you have actually seen. Shortly, you will hear another voice, not mine, asking you some questions. You will answer this voice as if you're answering me, you will tell us everything you've seen, you will answer the questions you will be asked precisely and in detail, without any worry. Here, now, this voice will ask you some questions and you will answer them as I'm asking."

Boccone: "Piero, it's Luciano. I would like to ask you who the gentleman is that you've seen and where you've seen him before?"

Zanfretta: "His name is Almoc, he is prince of the Dargos. He is different from the others."

Boccone: "Describe him for a minute."

Zanfretta: "Physically he is more or less like the others, but on the sides of his head he only has one spike, one on each side. The rest of him is identical to the others."

Boccone: "Where had you seen him the other time?"

Zanfretta: "I'd seen him inside a picture, these strange beings took me inside it. He's the same one that speaks a weird language before speaking to me."

Boccone: "What language?"

Zanfretta: "I don't know, a mixture of strange words, like.... like hisses... and it really hurts my ears when he talks so they put a thing on my head to help me understand what he's saying."

Boccone: "Where did he make you enter, when you saw him? You said: 'Where do I have to enter?' Where did you have to enter?"

Zanfretta doesn't understand the question. Therefore Boccone lets it go and goes back to the beginning of the nighttime adventure, when the security guard was filling up at the petrol station. He asks him in which part of Corso Europa he was.

Zanfretta: "From the petrol station I got inside a white cloud, all misty, it looked like a very thick fog."

Boccone: "That man you met, did he look like the others, how was he dressed?"

Zanfretta: "Yes, it's still the same one I had seen in Bargagli once, with his head shaped like an egg. He had his hands in his pockets this time as well. When he looked at me, his eyes became larger and inside I could see a circle of a thousand colors forming and it was hurting my eyes."

Boccone: "Why did they want to show you their spaceship? For what reason?"

Zanfretta: "I don't know."

Boccone: "Did you ask them? Did you ask them 'why do you want to show me your spaceship?' You also said 'I'm leaving.' Didn't they explain why?"

Zanfretta: "Why.... I don't know."

Boccone: "They had to give you.... What object did they have to give you?"

Zanfretta: "It was... a sphere with... a pyramid inside which was lit up. But I threw it in that guy's face."

Boccone: "Why did you throw it at him?"

Zanfretta: "Because.... I was fed up. He wanted me to give it to a professor. I don't know him..."

Boccone: "Which professor?"

Zanfretta: "They call him Hynek. I told him I was fed up. To take it himself, the ball. To give it to him himself. Then he ripped my jacket..."

Boccone: "Did they say what those machines they showed you are for?"

Zanfretta: "No."

Boccone: "You asked: 'Where's the Earth?' What did they reply?"

Zanfretta: "That it's below us. In fact I saw it from a distance."

Boccone: "But was it really far away? How far could it have been?"

Zanfretta: "I was seeing it pretty far away..."

Boccone: "But, what do you mean by far away? Could you see a sphere?"

Zanfretta: "Yes, a round ball...."

Boccone: "That far away..."

Zanfretta: "Then we got closer and closer and we came back to the same spot."

Boccone: "But you said you could see your colleagues coming to your aid. Did they show them to you?"

Zanfretta: "Yes, they lit up a picture...".

Boccone: "Who did you see?"

Zanfretta: "I only saw Lieutenant Cassiba turning the light on and shooting in the air. And then they said that was enough..."

Boccone: "You asked them what that light that turns on and off is for. Did they say what it is?"

Zanfretta: "It's their power supply. They would die without it. It brings them a lot of heat, inside. And it gives the spaceship the strength to fly. It supplies endless power."

Boccone: "You spoke of uranium. Did they say what they use it for?"

Zanfretta: "Yes, they..., on their planet it is a metal of little value."

Boccone: "Did you see a lot of people onboard? All these people, you said. Was there a lot of traffic, comings and goings?"

Zanfretta: "Yes."

Boccone: "How many people did you see?"

Zanfretta: "There were lots of them and it was big inside: it looked like a city."

Boccone: "But were they all the same?"

Zanfretta: "Yes, all the same."

Boccone had no more questions to ask. Moretti then addressed Zanfretta again, asking him to keep calm. At this point, also because I wanted to personally make sure of the night watchman's good faith, I asked Moretti to introduce me into the hypnosis to ask a few questions. And so my questioning of Fortunato Zanfretta began:

Di Stefano: "Let's go back for a second to when you were at the petrol station, you said you saw a person. Could you tell me exactly where?"

Zanfretta: "Behind the petrol pump, at the end of the hedge or a wall, near the carwash."

Di Stefano: "And this person was in the shadows?"

Zanfretta: "Yes, he came out suddenly."

Di Stefano: "Listen, at the time when you were at the petrol station, were other people there?"

Zanfretta: "Yes, there was a man with a green 'Dyane'. He filled up and then he left."

Di Stefano: "And he didn't see this person in the shadows?"

Zanfretta: "No, I don't think so."

Di Stefano: "Was the attendant there?"

Zanfretta: "No, it was automatic. It is closed at night..."

Di Stefano: "How many times did you fill up?"

Zanfretta: "Last night only once, because the red light had come on and I was almost running on empty."

Di Stefano: "Could you describe the physical build of the person in the shadows? I mean, how tall was he?"

Zanfretta: "Maybe a bit taller than me, no hair, and an egg-shaped head. Except.... he didn't want to take his hands out of his pockets."

Di Stefano: "How was he dressed?"

Zanfretta: "With a checked dress suit. It was the same one, identical to the one when I'd seen the cigar-shaped spaceship. He was the same one I saw later on... later in the tunnel who asked me: 'Did you see?' and I... told him to fuck off. And then he disappeared..."

Di Stefano: "You said he had a checked dress-suit. What kind of suit? Like ours?"

Zanfretta: "Yes, like ours but..."

Di Stefano: "Was he wearing a shirt?"

Zanfretta: "Underneath he had a strange shirt... almost like a turtleneck, but it was a strange color..."

Di Stefano: "Could you describe this color?"

Zanfretta: "It looked metallic..., shiny..."

Di Stefano: "Was he wearing a tie?"

Zanfretta:"No, just pants and a jacket."

Di Stefano: "And his shoes?"

Zanfretta:"I didn't look..."

Di Stefano: "You said that he made you enter. Where did he make you enter?"

Zanfretta: "He said to me: 'Get in there with the car'. And in that moment I could see a square cloud forming, a bit bigger than the car and I went inside. Then all of a sudden I almost felt I couldn't breathe because I could see I was being lifted up more and more. I could see... the petrol pump disappearing before my very eyes and then I found myself inside this big light."

Di Stefano: "What color was the light?"

Zanfretta: "It was very bright, annoying. Then a door opened and I saw all those people..."

Di Stefano: "Could you say how many, more or less?"

Zanfretta: "There were many..."

Di Stefano: "Approximately?"

Zanfretta: "40-50 give or take... really tall drinks of water... I come to just below their knees..."

Di Stefano: "You were as tall as just below their knees?"

Zanfretta: "Yes."

Di Stefano: "And so how tall would they have been then in meters?"

Zanfretta:"About 3 meters, 3 and a half meters. They're all the same and identical to the others..."

Di Stefano: "The person who spoke to you to give you the sphere, was he one of them?"

Zanfretta: "Yes."

Di Stefano: "Was he different or like the others?"

Zanfretta: "Physically they were the same, but he had only one spike on one side and on the other, very big...."

Di Stefano: "Did he explain to you what was inside this sphere?"

Zanfretta: "He said to me: 'You will deliver this object to the famous scientist...' and I asked him why he couldn't give it to him himself?"

Di Stefano: "He said famous scientist? Did he mention the name exactly? Where was he?"

Zanfretta: "He said 'Professor Hynek...''

Di Stefano: "Of?"

Zanfretta: "And that I would find him at the University of.... I don't remember the other name.... Domus.... Domus.... Bah."

Di Stefano: "Did he tell you, in which state?"

Zanfretta: "He said I had to get in touch with him through my friend Luciano..."

Di Stefano: "Does this mean that your friend Luciano is in touch with this professor?"

Zanfretta: "Yes."

Di Stefano: "And who told them?"

Zanfretta: "I don't know.... but they know him very well..."

Di Stefano: "Would you be able to explain how?"

Zanfretta: "No."

Di Stefano: "But aside from your friend Luciano, do they know the others as well?"

Zanfretta: "I don't know..."

Di Stefano: "They never spoke to you about anybody else?"

Zanfretta: "Just about Hynek, about Luciano, and that they didn't want anything to do with professor Marchesan."

Di Stefano: "Does it mean that they know Marchesan?"

Zanfretta:"Yes, when I was under hypnosis, they were following us from above, therefore they can see us the whole time..."

Di Stefano: "Have you any idea as to how they do it?"

Zanfretta: "I don't know. They have a machine, like a television; when I move they see me and they see everyone that's around me."

Di Stefano: "Did they say whether you'll hear from them again?"

Zanfretta: "Of course!"

Di Stefano: "Of course? Why of course?"

Zanfretta: "Because I smashed the object I threw and they have to bring another one."

Di Stefano: "Did they tell you when they're coming back again?"

Zanfretta: "No."

Di Stefano: "But they spoke to you about it?"

Zanfretta: "They told me: 'In good time'."

Di Stefano: "They assured you they'll be back anyhow?"

Zanfretta: "Yes, and they told me that.... this time they will show themselves: for now they only have shown the light that lifts and the beams that point."

Di Stefano: "The object, the one that they should give you, you will accept it next time, won't you?"

Zanfretta: "I don't know, why don't they take it to him?"

Di Stefano: "Because you don't want it?"

Zanfretta: "I've already had too much trouble and I don't want any more. Also, we know how it's going to end..."

Di Stefano: "Listen, now I want to ask you a question that's a bit more unusual than the others: have they ever asked you who are you with here on Earth? Who do you see, who your superiors are, who your friends are, and all the rest?"

Obviously, the question aimed at checking on the distinction between reality and fantasy in Zanfretta's mind. The part regarding Boccone could easily be interpreted as the influence that the UFOlogist had on him. As a matter of fact, at that time, Zanfretta was very much *pampered* by Boccone and his friends: they invited him to their meetings, they put him under hypnosis and had introduced him to people belonging to the ufology circle. Now we wanted to understand how much the ufologists had influenced Zanfretta, if indeed he had been influenced at all. And so, would we find these people in Zanfretta's hypnotic statements?

Zanfretta: "They know everything already. They have... they have a lot of photographs of everybody and on each photo there is the name and the date of birth, and all that's happened in their life."

Di Stefano: "Have you seen these photos?"

Zanfretta: "Yes."

Di Stefano: "Could you name one of the people pictured in these photos?"

Zanfretta: "There were two or three that I have seen in a book..."

Di Stefano: "In a book, did you say? Did you recognize this person? Are these people that you know?"

Zanfretta: "I don't remember the name very well. It's a very old person who is very much feared in America."

Di Stefano: "But as far as Italian individuals, people that are closer to you?"

Zanfretta: "Yes, I've seen many..."

Di Stefano: "Meaning? Give me an example..."

Zanfretta: "But there's so many..."

Di Stefano: "I'm only asking you to give me an example of a person that you know and whose photograph you have seen..."

Zanfretta: "I can't answer..."

Di Stefano: "Why can't you answer?"

Zanfretta: "I don't know..."

Di Stefano: "Listen, I'll change the question for you: among the photos you have seen, you don't have to tell me who, did you see any of your friends?"

Zanfretta: "Yes, many."

Di Stefano: "People you see every day?"

Zanfretta: "Yes."

Di Stefano: "Are your superiors there as well?"

Zanfretta: "Oh yes, they're there too."

Di Stefano: "And for each person, there is the date of birth and other personal details?"

Zanfretta: "Yes, there was..."

Di Stefano: "There was…?"

Zanfretta: "There was, I saw Echo, Echo 8 *(Nino Tagliavia)*, Echo 4 *(Giuliano Buonamici)*, Echo 7 *(Mino Ferri)*, then there was.... the one that always works as an operative. Then I saw Mr. Tutti, the Colonel, Lieutenant Cassiba and many more."

Di Stefano: "Listen Piero, can you tell me on what occasion they showed you these photographs?"

Zanfretta: "When I entered the room with all the buttons..."

Di Stefano: "Can you tell me how were these photographs sorted?"

Zanfretta: "They looked like slides and... As they were coming out of those holes, I could see the photos with the writing underneath. But there were a lot of people that I have never seen in my life."

Little by little, as Zanfretta kept going I was starting to suspect that he was mixing his own personal opinions with the memories surfacing in his mind. Therefore, I did a test. Considering that Zanfretta was saying he had seen people he knew well in that photo archive - it is hard to understand of what use they could ever be to the presumed extra-terrestrials - I asked him if he had seen my photo as well. In fact, I rarely saw the night watchman, so if he had put in that photo archive only the people he used to spend time with, mine shouldn't have been there.

Di Stefano: "Among the photos you have seen, was Dr. Moretti's there as well?"

Zanfretta: "Oh yes. The photo of the gentleman that works with him was there too..."

The security guard was referring to Dr. Moretti's assistant, Angelo Massa.

Di Stefano: "Was mine there too?"

Zanfretta: "Then there was Marchesan, and other doctors I had never seen..."

Di Stefano: "I repeat: among these photos, was mine there as well?"

Zanfretta: "I don't know, I've seen so many, I can't remember them all."

Di Stefano: "And now listen: you did see Dr. Moretti's photo, didn't you?"

Zanfretta: "Yes."

Di Stefano: "Do you also remember the details written on that photo? Do you remember anyone's details?"

Zanfretta: "They were very small, and written in a strange way too."

Di Stefano: "Then, if you couldn't understand the writing how can you say that the date of birth and all the rest was on them."

Zanfretta: "Because they told me..."

Di Stefano:" I see."

Zanfretta: "This is our file and we keep everyone in here."

Di Stefano: "Everyone?"

Zanfretta: "They call them 'everyone...'."

The night watchman starts breathing heavily. He looks like he cannot say what he would like to say. The moment compels Moretti to take charge of the situation again.

Doctor Moretti: "Now Zanfretta, calm and relaxed. There is no problem. Do you hear my voice?"

Since the guard continues to pant, Moretti speaks in a more commanding tone.

Doctor Moretti: "Zanfretta, this is doctor Moretti. You can hear my voice now and there is no other interference. My mind is connected to yours and what I say to you is stronger than any other interference. Because you are calm, you are relaxed, you are perfectly laidback and you've let go. I will ask you a question now and you will have no difficulty in replying because there will not be any mental interference that might bother you. Do you understand?"

Zanfretta: "Yes."

Doctor Moretti: "Good. Are you calm?"

Zanfretta: "Yes."

Doctor Moretti: "Ok. You were describing that file. Do you remember?"

Zanfretta: "Yes."

Doctor Moretti: "Ok. And you were saying that those beings told you that in that file everyone was there.... and then you stopped. Well, you can say it now, easily and with no difficulty. I am telling you, that's how it is. You can continue the conversation, relaxed, there is no interference..."

Zanfretta: "Everyone... they're all subjects that they need.... that they... in good time.... will use... for..."

Doctor Moretti: "No, no problem: the words come out calmly and easily. Will use for? You are talking with me, there is no interference. You can speak. There is no hindrance, it's just you and me."

Zanfretta: "They will use... everyone... for the experiments.... because...."

Doctor Moretti: "For what experiments?"

Zanfretta: "I don't know."

Doctor Moretti: "They didn't tell you, did they?"

Zanfretta: "No, they.... when.... they wanted to give me the sphere they told me that they wanted to make known the life machine...."

The session had lasted far too long and Moretti decided to suspend it. The question about these last words, on the mysterious *life machine* remained unanswered. Moretti woke Zanfretta up and that evening we spoke of nothing else.

The debate started the next morning at "Val Bisagno" headquarters. What Zanfretta had said seemed more fantastical than usual. We were afraid that the influence of the ufologists on the security guard might have become too much. We had learned of his visits to Boccone and company and, right or wrong, we suspected that some of his statements might be influenced by the ufologic knowledge that Zanfretta was acquiring in that circle. For this reason, from that day onward, they stopped informing Boccone of results of the hypnosis sessions and "Val Bisagno" management wanted no more dealings with the research group of Arenzano. The belief that Zanfretta could have been influenced by ufologists was such that Gianfranco Tutti asked him to once again undergo hypnosis that very evening, Tuesday, December 4.

So much concern should not seem unjustified. On Tuesday morning, the story of Zanfretta's third *close encounter* was in every newspaper. ANSA had just reported it everywhere in Italy. Some newspapers overtly criticized both the night watchman and "Val Bisagno." Many articles were covertly considering the idea that there might be someone wanting publicity. Others were saying without mincing their words that Zanfretta *wasn't altogether there.*

On top of this, it must also be said that the police and the Carabinieri had also been involved in this last disappearance and, rightly so, they now wanted to know what was really going on. And so everybody wanted to clarify this story once and for all, at least to defend their honor before public opinion.

It might seem strange but hypnosis was the only way to get information about those nighttime adventures. Also because it had been demonstrated that a good percentage of the news that Zanfretta was imparting under hypnosis could be verified in reality. Therefore, for all these reasons, on Tuesday evening Zanfretta went back to lie down on the table in Doctor Moretti's office.

Reporting this session step-by-step is useless. Basically, Zanfretta said the same things as the previous evening, except this time they tried to shed more light on the points considered to be more important. One was about the mysterious individual Zanfretta said he had seen at the petrol station on Corso Europa. If it were all true, it would have us believe that a mysterious man with an egg-shaped head was living in Genoa, who normally wears a checked suit and is able to mix with people without raising suspicions and that, as an agent of extra-terrestrial civilizations, spends his time gathering information about people that, sooner or later, might be useful to the mysterious beings.

Another theory is that there is someone who under certain circumstances hypnotizes Zanfretta to make him live some imaginary situations. Whatever the solution to this riddle, other interesting details emerged during the session of December 4. For example, during his tour of the spaceship, Zanfretta reports having seen human or humanoid bodies floating in a blue substance inside some weird cylinders.

Here is the conversation between the security guard and his interlocutors on board of the spaceship.

Zanfretta: "What's in those cylinders?"

Entity: "These.... they're all our samples which we keep as guinea pigs."

Zanfretta: "Christ, where did you get them? Gee... what a hobo that one..."

Entity: "You call him cave man."

Zanfretta: "And that bird over there?"

Entity: "Do you call it bird?"

Zanfretta: "I think so... gee, it's ugly isn't it? And what's that?"

Entity: "This is a sample of an enemy from another planet."

Zanfretta: "Gee, he looks like a frog, he looks like... why do you keep him in blue water?"

Entity: "We have it to preserve them."

The reader will remember that Zanfretta had already reported on these cylinders during the previous session. This time though, relating the words of his interlocutor as well, the dialogue becomes richer in detail.

During that session Moretti was much more insistent and tried once again to induce Zanfretta into contradicting himself. He didn't succeed. The guard's logic was always sound and sharp and the episodes previously related were repeated the same way and with the same contents. The fact that it was during that session we started to suspect that Zanfretta, or rather, Zanfretta's mind was being controlled by someone or something is significant. When Moretti asked him how he intended to deliver the sphere they would give him, he replied that according to his instructions he couldn't allow anybody to even touch the sphere. He could just show it. Therefore, if Mr. Tutti wanted to help him, he simply would have to put him in touch with the American professor. Furthermore it was very important that nobody knew he had come into possession of the sphere and that he had to deliver it. This is what the extra-terrestrials wanted, he specified.

More developments emerged regarding the file. For example, Zanfretta revealed that when the extra-terrestrials found out that he was snooping around their file pushing every button he touched, they took him and tortured him with the helmet once again. Remembering all this, he was still scared.

Zanfretta also mentioned another interesting detail: the system through which he could *feel* the arrival of his friends from space. This detail proved extremely helpful for setting up the rescue for the fourth *close encounter*. Zanfretta was saying that the warning was an increasing headache accompanied by a hiss that would become more and more intense. Most significant was that he started to feel this hiss three or four days before the date of the meeting. He just had to let Mr. Tutti or Cassiba know that this was happening so that we could all be on the alert.

When Moretti advised him that he must let his superiors know about this headache, Zanfretta seemed hesitant. During the session

Moretti got him to listen to Gianfranco Tutti's voice. The director of "Val Bisagno," who had wanted to be there during the session, stepped in to convince his employee to let him know of the headache as soon as he felt the first symptoms. Thus, having been given the order under hypnosis, he followed it, as we will see later on.

I was saying earlier that Moretti had tried to induce him to contradict himself. I find the following section particularly relevant:

Moretti: "Listen, I wanted to ask you this: has anyone ever described the spaceship to you?"

Zanfretta: "No."

Moretti: "When was the first time you saw a spaceship? Not just for real, ok? Maybe in a movie or a newspaper or magazine. The first time in your life. Go back with your thoughts..."

Zanfretta: "When I was 10."

Moretti: "Tell me."

Zanfretta: "I went to the cinema and I saw a movie..."

Moretti: "A science-fiction movie?"

Zanfretta: "Yes."

Moretti: "Did you like it?"

Zanfretta: "...but I fell asleep."

Moretti: "Was it boring?"

Zanfretta: "Yes."

Moretti: "I like science fiction movies, don't you?"

Zanfretta: "Not always..."

Moretti: "Which ones did you like best? Can you remember any? Some are really good...."

Zanfretta: "One I never saw again... was... *The War of the Worlds*."

Moretti: "Ah, famous."

Zanfretta: "Really good, I only saw it once and then I never saw it again...."

Moretti: "It was many years ago, wasn't it?"

Zanfretta: "Yes."

Moretti: "And do you like science fiction novels? I love them..."

Zanfretta: "Nooo."

Moretti: "How come?"

Zanfretta: "They don't interest me..."

Moretti: "But have you read any, to be able to judge?"

Zanfretta: "I don't like reading, I look at the pictures..."

Moretti: "I see. You're telling me, though, that you don't like science fiction but some of your closest friends are ufologists, right?"

Zanfretta: "Oh yes."

Moretti: "How come then?"

Zanfretta: "I met them when it happened the first time."

Moretti: "I see. Do you see them often?"

Zanfretta: "No, once in a while I call Luciano to say hi, that's all."

Moretti: "Well, they certainly would have explained a few things to you, right? About ufology, about this problem of the UFOs."

Zanfretta: "Yes, but I told them I'm not interested, to go and explain it to someone else."

Moretti: "And didn't they get offended? Is this how you treat your friends?"

Zanfretta: "But there was nothing to be offended about, because I'm not interested. I told him: talk to me about women but not flying saucers."

Moretti, aware of the fact that the ufologists had taken Zanfretta to Livorno where they wanted him to meet some people, asked him straight out.

Moretti: "Have you ever been to Livorno?"

Zanfretta: "Yes."

Moretti: "Who did you go with, your friends?"

Zanfretta: "With my friend Luciano and my friend Mario Nepi."

Moretti: "And what did you go to Livorno for?"

Zanfretta: "Nothing, an outing, and in the meantime, I met Fiorini."

Moretti: "Who's that?"

Zanfretta: "Bah... he was a young fellow.... young! He's forty, he had an experience over there..."

Moretti: "Like yours?"

Zanfretta: "Bah, I didn't understand what happened to him very well, just that he's one of those who've locked themselves up at home... he told me he even stopped pursuing women. Of course, he seems to be an idiot. But when I saw him, he looked like more of a liar than someone who was telling the truth. But I couldn't understand what he was saying... he was mumbling, talking in his dialect...."

Moretti: "He gave you the impression of being a bit of a liar, didn't he? Was that your feeling?"

Zanfretta: "Yes, because he was joking about it too much, with the friends that were there. He wasn't taking it too seriously. So I left and went to sleep in the car. And the car kept shaking here and there. Then I got out and I went to sleep in another car." (Zanfretta claims that when he got in the car, it started rocking on its own.)

Moretti: "Listen, I wanted to ask you something: you told me once that, many years ago, you were put under hypnosis."

Zanfretta: "Yes."

Moretti: "Can you tell me again, I can't remember very well. How old were you?"

Zanfretta: "No, that was when I was in the Navy."

Moretti: "Ah, that's right."

Zanfretta: "I had just gotten there, to start the training period. They gave me my uniform and then they took us in a big room where there was, what do you call it, a juggler? Something like that. He called me on the stage and he said to me: Wanna bet I can put you to sleep? And I said to him: yeah, sure. And then I found myself sleeping on the floor. Then he told me to me kiss somebody from my group. I said to him: Yuk! And he woke me up while I was kissing him."

Moretti: "And listen, after that time, why don't you tell me of all the other times you've been hypnotized? Even if it wasn't a real hypnosis, maybe someone stared at you, looking straight into your eyes, saying something. Think carefully, you'll see you'll remember easily."

Moretti's idea was clear. He wanted to find out whether in Zanfretta's past, or even in the present, someone other than himself and Marchesan had put him under hypnosis. The goal was to ascertain if behind these incidents there was someone who, using hypnosis, was influencing the night watchman. Zanfretta's reply cleared any doubt.

Zanfretta: "There was no one else."

Moretti: "You've never been hypnotized in your life ever again?"

Zanfretta: "No, never."

Moretti: "Not even by professor Marchesan?"

Zanfretta: "No, just with hypnosis."

Moretti: "That's what I'm talking about, hypnosis."

Zanfretta:"By the professor, yes, yes."

Moretti: "So, how many times in your life have you been under hypnosis? As far as you can remember? That time in the Navy, right?"

Zanfretta: "Yes."

Moretti: "And then, have you ever tried with your friends for example?"

Zanfretta: "No. Three times with professor Marchesan; a few times, I don't remember very well, and then with doctor Moretti." (Clearly in this instance Zanfretta doesn't recognize Moretti.)

Moretti:"And before those times?"

Zanfretta: "Never."

Moretti:"Nobody has ever tried, maybe as a joke? These are things that we do with our friends, right? Maybe..."

Zanfretta: "Oh yes, when I was in the Navy. A friend of mine said to me: look me in the eyes and I punched him in the eyes."

Moretti didn't want to insist further. After instructing Zanfretta to call Tutti should he start to have a headache, Moretti woke him up.

There were many consultations in the days that followed. By now we all had the impression that the *encounters* would continue, therefore the directors of "Val Bisagno" decided that they would not be caught unprepared next time. We knew that a few days before the *fact,* Zanfretta himself would warn Tutti and Cassiba about the strange headache that announced the next rendezvous. The problem was to take advantage of this in order to follow Zanfretta without him knowing, to see who he was meeting with. To achieve this result, Zanfretta would be assigned a car that the technicians of "Val Bisagno" decided to prepare with special technical devices. Mr. Nino Tagliavia, the engineer, and Giuliano Buonamici, the technician, were responsible for setting up the equipment. A *Fiat 127* was chosen for the occasion. In the back, under the carpet, they hid a radio that operated only on a fixed frequency which sent a constant signal that could be captured only by special receivers. The power to the radio was supplied by a series of Nickel-Cadmium batteries that would last for 12 hours. In essence, though, these rechargeable batteries had unlimited power because they were also connected to the battery of the car. The radio, therefore, worked whether the car was on or off.

Wherever the *Fiat 127* went, it would be under constant monitoring since such cars are equipped with a signal receiver. As soon as one of these entered the range of action of the radio, that is 2-3 kilometers, the signal would be heard and its volume would grow increasingly as the car got closer to the *127*.

Tagliavia and Buonamici's cleverness went even further. According to what had happened in the previous *encounters* we knew that as soon as the car Zanfretta was travelling in got closer to the alleged flying saucer, it would be subjected to very strong heat. To measure the highest temperature inside the car during those times, they placed a *memory* thermometer enclosed in a special case in an area between the front and back seats, so that it would take the maximum temperature felt in the car. Inside the seats and the doors, the technicians placed sealed envelopes, cassettes with magnetic tape and color photo plates. The purpose was twofold: to empirically verify the variation of potential magnetic fields and the presence of unusual radiations. A homemade method if you will, but it was still an indication.

One of the most perplexing aspects of Zanfretta's stories was the *lifting* of the vehicles he was in when the extraterrestrials brought him onto the spaceship. Considering that in such an instance, as soon as the wheels stop touching the ground they turn inward, Buonamici positioned some steel cables which would break at pre-established lengths between the body and the wheel-hubs of the car.

Both the test and the installation of the other equipment were carried out one evening in an area of the large depot where "Val Bisagno" keeps its fleet of cars. I was there too. Only by lifting the *127* on the hydraulic bridge would the cables break. I myself also checked the positioning of the radio and all the rest.

Tutti supervised the operations. You just had to look at him in the face to realize that this was the last time he would try to understand the Zanfretta mystery. I myself could feel that they all wanted to arrive at some sort of conclusion. Should this attempt also go up in smoke, there would be no further attempts. That's why everyone that evening was so busy. Buonamici, the only one in white scrubs, meticulously checked the effectiveness of his work. Tagliavia, with his coat on and a scarf around his neck adjusted the hidden radio with a micro-receiver of which four copies had been made, one for each car involved in the search for the security guard, should there be an alert.

I didn't miss a thing. I observed everything and was careful to perceive what was not being openly said. For example, I had realized that up to that moment, the managers of "Val Bisagno" had considered Zanfretta a *noisy* yet pleasant pastime. All the incidents, as persistent as they had been, hadn't left much time to properly think and ponder the consequences of those nighttime adventures. At first, the name of the Security and Patrol Institute was on everyone's lips like never before, and considering that they had always behaved correctly towards their employee, they weren't expecting any negative effects. After all, thanks to Enzo Tortora who had contributed with his program "Portobello" in making Zanfretta a national celebrity, Gianfranco Tutti couldn't really complain about the ufologic interlude involving his firm. However, things had deteriorated as the *encounters* continued. Some newspapers were openly criticizing both Zanfretta and "Val Bisagno." Furthermore, the "case" had grown due to the interest Tortora kept showing in what was happening to the night watchman. The famous presenter wanted Zanfretta with him two more times to present his story during the program he was conducting at Antenna Tre, near Legnano. I accompanied Zanfretta along with Tutti, Buonamici and Cassiba both times. During the first show, Tortora limited himself to interviewing the security guard, and asking his opinion about his mysterious encounters. During the second show on the other hand, he specifically called in two experts, Cesare Musatti, the father of Italian psychoanalysis, and Giampiero Mosconi, president of Amisi *(Italian Medical Association for the Study of Hypnosis)*, to give their opinions about the hypnosis sessions Zanfretta had undergone.

To repeat the experience already done by TVS, Mosconi agreed to put Zanfretta under hypnosis in front of the cameras so that he could report his adventures once again.

It was 8.30 p.m. on Saturday, December 15, 1979. I remember that evening very well because the experiment nearly failed. Musatti, who was obviously the most famous and important guest of the program, with all the weight of his knowledge denied from the start the reliability of what Zanfretta said during hypnosis. "Even if the facts reported by this man were true," said the famous psychoanalyst off-stage, "they shouldn't be divulged anyway."

For his part, Tortora just listened without any comment on the matter.

Mosconi's attitude was very different. Not wanting to contradict the master, he stated that he completely agreed with Musatti.

And then the crucial moment came. Zanfretta, lying on a table in another television studio, was put under hypnosis by Mosconi who had the chance to ask him any question he wanted. In the main studio, Tortora, Musatti, Tutti and Buonamici were following the session on a video monitor. Once again, Zanfretta related his facts just as he had done in the past with Moretti.

The live hypnosis created a lot of buzz. When everyone was gathered in the main studio, Tortora asked Mosconi and Musatti for their impressions of that improvised hypnosis session. It came as a big surprise for the managers of "Val Bisagno" that the air of mistrust toward Zanfretta that had been present not even an hour earlier, had completely vanished. Mosconi, patting the shoulder of the night watchman, openly said that he had no reason to doubt Zanfretta's good faith. Musatti expressed his qualified opinion stating that

Zanfretta was undoubtedly sincere when relating his truth under hypnosis. But we need to distinguish between what can be a subjective reality and the actual objective reality. In this case, however, hypnosis cannot provide a definitive answer.

Basically then, the great authority confirmed what Moretti had already said.

CHAPTER 6

The Extraterrestrials Speak

We didn't have to wait long for Zanfretta's next *encounter*. On the afternoon of February 12, 1980, Zanfretta walked into Tutti's office and, with a mixture of embarrassment and shyness, told him that he was suffering from a persistent headache. I don't think Tutti was expecting it. In any case, he understood right away and sent the night watchman away, telling him to make sure to go by the depot and pick up the Fiat *127* that from that day onward he was going to use during his shift. Right after, he called me and gave me the news.

Since we didn't know exactly how many days would pass before the encounter, we all spent those nights knowing that we could be called any minute. In fact, this time I wanted to take part in the rescue expedition as well, so I was waiting.

It was two minutes after midnight on Thursday, February 14, when the phone rang at my place. The operator of "Val Bisagno" radio command center told me that Zanfretta had disappeared once again and that Tutti had arranged for a car to pick me up. I had just enough time to quickly get dressed again. Three minutes later, security guard Dellepiane was downstairs at my front door. Driving at incredible speed through the streets of Genoa, the security guard took me in record time to the area of the Brignole train station. Three other cars marked with the colors of the Security Patrol Institute were there already, waiting on the left bank of the Bisagno river.

Mrs. Bonola was parked near the curb inside an Alfa Romeo *Giulia*. They had been called while they were having dinner in a Chinese restaurant. Tutti was in a flurry and he started to give his security guards orders, telling them to make sure to always keep the receiver on and to report via the service radio if they intercepted the beep-beep of Zanfretta's *127*.

The cars then left for different destinations. I had stayed in Dellepiane's car and we headed toward Torriglia. Tutti's *Giulia* was ahead of us heading in the same direction. As soon as we got to the Scoffera tunnel, the receiver started crackling. Zanfretta had therefore returned to the area of Torriglia. Without wasting a second, we headed toward the turn off for the village of Rossi where we found a shaky Andrea Pesci, the night watchman on duty in Torriglia.

"He came through here, he came through here," he said excitedly, almost crying. "Please let me get in the car, don't leave me here by myself..." But Dellepiane didn't want to listen to reason, and strictly following orders, he kept going just in time to see his boss's car heading uphill on the narrow road. By now the beep-beep was very strong and the more we climbed the mountain, the clearer the signal got.

We finally found the *127*. It was parked in a clearing just before the road starts going downhill. The door on the driver's side was open. Zanfretta was nowhere to be seen. Five minutes later the other cars joined us. A dozen security guards equipped with large flashlights started searching frantically for their colleague.

The night was as cold and dark as ever. Only the headlights of the cars made it possible to see the dirt road. Shaking from the cold, Mrs. Bonola let Tutti manage the rescue operations. Shouting, he was trying to send his men into the most accessible areas. That part of the mountain is very dangerous. A large valley, swallowed by the absolute darkness of the night, opened up from where we were standing. One false step and you could fall for hundreds of meters into a steep, almost bottomless gully.

Where was Zanfretta then? The minutes went by, but we had no news of him. "He must be here somewhere," Tutti kept repeating, almost to himself. Freezing, we waited. There was no doubt that the rescue expedition had worked, almost too well. I had the impression that we had gotten up there no later than fifteen minutes after Zanfretta, so he couldn't have been that much ahead of us. Was it possible that everything had happened during those few minutes?

If I had to describe those moments spent waiting in the cold, I would say that they were mostly loaded with curiosity and skepticism. I was busy considering this when someone from afar shouted that Zanfretta had been found. One group of security guards had communicated via radio that Zanfretta had been found unconscious on the edge of a gorge. Zanfretta, on the verge of falling into the ravine, was lying passed out and almost frozen to death while hanging onto a protruding bush.

I saw this when they brought him down from the mountain, supported under his arms by two of his colleagues. He had opened his eyes but he wasn't able to walk and wasn't saying a word. His face was twisted. He gave the impression of no desire to do anything. It reminded me for a second of his behavior during hypnosis. When they got him to sit inside the Alfa Romeo, I looked at him closely. His hands and face were blue from the cold. After all, he was only wearing a shirt and tie under the black leather jacket worn by night watchmen. He couldn't recognize any of us: not Cassiba or Mrs. Bonola, let alone me.

Mrs. Bonola, with her maternal attitude, took Zanfretta's hands in hers, and rubbing them, tried to get his circulation going again. Little by little he was coming around. Curled up on the seat of the car and looking into empty space, the further we got from that infernal spot, the more his complexion returned to normal. When we arrived at the headquarters of the Security Patrol Institute, he was fully conscious again.

The next day, or rather that same morning since the nighttime adventure had lasted till three a.m., I watched Buonamici and Tagliavia check the secret devices of the Fiat *127* that Zanfretta had used. The steel cables connected to the hubcaps were all broken.

The memory thermometer was also a surprise: despite its insulation and the freezing cold of the previous night, the thermometer marked 43 degrees Celsius (109.4 degrees Fahrenheit). As far as the magnetic tapes and the photographic films were concerned, I was eventually told that they didn't find anything relevant when they developed them.

We searched for the truth in Doctor Moretti's office. That same night, Friday, February 15, 1980, Zanfretta was under hypnosis, lying on doctor Moretti's leather couch.

Doctor Moretti: "It is 8 p.m., it is 8 in the evening on the 14th of this month. Thursday the 14th, it is 8 in the evening. You will tell me now, clearly, everything that happens from this moment onwards, relating your thoughts, your words as well as the exact words of the other people you were in touch with from 8 p.m. on. I repeat: you will tell me your thoughts, you will report what you have said and exactly everything that was said by any other person with whom you have spoken or have been in touch. Nothing can disturb your sleep. I'm listening. It is 8 in the evening, where are you?"

Zanfretta: "We're at the table... we're eating. Nirvana, go and open the door, they've rung the doorbell. Ciao Mario. Where's Irma? *(A couple of friends of theirs.)* Are you hiding from her? Have you eaten? Have you bought a new car? Gee, it's nice! It must cost a lot of money.... Ehhh, I'll buy it when the cows come home... Is it your day off today? Fabio, stop shouting. Margherita, leave him alone. *(His children)*. Gee, guys... hey Nirvana, did you stitch the flashes on my jacket? Huh, on the arm then... stitch them on the arm for me, then we'll talk about it. Why do you care if it's big. Huh, it's already a bonus that they give it to us. That's right, it's blue, it's ideal.... Mine is the other one, that one that has got white fur on the collar! We're taking the kids out on Sunday? To Bogliasco? All right, they've got the clothes. Gee, it's after nine already. Come on, make the coffee and I'm going. Fabio, coffee... Here we go, we can't drink the coffee anymore. Go on, put the kids to bed. Bye, I'm going. Ohhh, this car is always low on petrol. Kangaroo, 70 here, good evening, I'm going up."

Doctor Moretti: "You have to tell us what the other people say as well."

Zanfretta: "Hello Spartà *(A colleague)*. Have you written the kilometers down already? Tonight I'm not feeling well at all. Oh yes, I've got a headache. It started yesterday. I told the Lieutenant, by phone as well... have you checked the oil? Ah, ok, I'm going."

Doctor Moretti: "Zanfretta, you also have to tell us the words that the other people say."

Zanfretta: "Mr. Mazza? It's 11.600. Can you call me a bit more often? Tonight it really hurts. Yes, thank you. We'll speak when I'm down there, I can't hear you very well in this spot. All right, we'll speak later. Hi guys. Here, here's the keys. No, I'm not feeling very well. I'm going OK? Bye, see you later. Mr. Mazza, can you hear me now? Huh, I can hear you clearly now. Yes, I'm going round to do the clocks, then I'm going to Priaruggia. Yes, I'm going to Villa Carrara now."

Realizing that despite his urging, Zanfretta is still not reporting the voices of the other people around him, Moretti keeps insisting.

Doctor Moretti: "The order I'm giving you now is very important, you must always report what the other people say as well. What you say and also what the others say, it's an order!"

Zanfretta: "This damned Count and his clock! He's not even capable of winding it. Then they whine and they say they're not clocked in... I'll leave two cards on the car and at the door. Here you go, there. The Countess, too. Eh, as long as they're happy... Mr. Mazza, I'm going to Sister Mary. Well, I'll manage. Mr. Mazza, give me the time to answer. Yes, I've clocked in. I'm going to Priaruggia now, and I'll leave the car. Ok, yes, I'll take the mobile. I'll park it here at the taxi stand so they won't bother me. Good evening Mr. Freducci, are you still unloading? My goodness you work till late... you're making money then. Goodbye. I'll call Setti *(Another colleague)* right away so.... Christ, my eyes are blurry. Kangaroo from... Mr. Mazza can you hear..."

At this point Zanfretta starts breathing heavily, visibly confused. Then he suddenly stops talking in his usual tone and starts again in a submissive, almost compliant manner.

Zanfretta: "Yes, I'm going to the car. Yes, I'm going."

Moretti understands the change and steps in.

Doctor Moretti: "Tell us what the others say."

Zanfretta: "There's no one else. Someone is calling me..."

Doctor Moretti: "And what are they saying?"

Zanfretta: "To go back to the car... to drive around the area for a while... my head hurts... Mr. Mazza is calling me but I can't answer.... I can't get hold of the microphone... where are we going now? Why am I taking the highway now? Why doesn't the attendant hear me? Ah... Ah... Christ, is it possible he can't hear me? Which exit are we taking now? But we're in Marcissi... in Staglieno... What are we going to Davagna for? This is Barilli, the furniture manufacturer... Mr. Mazza, I'd like to reply but I can't... why does he keep calling me if I can't speak... and now the radio has switched off. Bloody hell, it's so dark, and so many bends... It has switched back on now. How can he not hear me? Look, the boss is on the radio, too, he's calling the others... and I can't call... Ow... this is Pesci's voice; I hope he won't come after me when I get there."

Doctor Moretti:" What does Pesci say?"

Zanfretta: "Kangaroo at Pesci's, there is a bright, triangular object heading toward Rossi. Pesci is at Echo One *(Zanfretta is reporting what his colleagues were saying during the search for him)*, you stay put over there, don't move. I'll go to Scoffera Square and I won't move. Oh Christ, who's that? Hey, Pesci, get out of the way, get out of the way... phew! I just missed him. Hell... how can you drive with your headlights off up there? But I can see the road very well, even if it is dark... The car is lit up... What the hell do you want again? Go away.... I'll drive faster.... no can do, it's going at the same speed. Gee, the car braked suddenly! Now what? Why is it not on the ground today? I'm running away, go, go... I'm running... Holy cow, the radio! Ouch, my head. I'm climbing up, something is bound to

107

happen, they're leaving... ahh thank God. I'll drop a few cards on the ground hoping they will find me, you can't see a thing over here. Gee, it's cold. Why is it going down the valley now?" *(Zanfretta is therefore saying that he is seeing the UFO go down into the dark valley)*.

Doctor Moretti: "Why?"

Zanfretta: "It descended into the valley... it's all dark now. I'm not moving from here, ah I wish I were dead... why me? I was just starting to relax. Who's going to tell the boss?..... Sooner or later he's going to fire me for real.... I hope they come.... There's some lights, the cars are coming up; they must have seen the cars. Hey, crap they can't hear me. Gee, it's dark, my hands are cold. I see some lights down there..... *Who's up there? Hey, who's up there? It's me, Gianfranco. Ok, good! Careful guys, it's slippery. Then there's the gorge. Look, there are some flashlights over there. Hey... hey... who is it? Piero, it's Echo 7 (Mino Ferri), can you hear me? Piero, it's Gian... Piero, you're not armed, are you? Lower your lights guys. Very good Piero, stay calm. Luigi, hold him still.* Let me go..... I can't speak... *Gee, Piero, what a workout! Who needs to go jogging! We found you, did you see? Give me a kiss... Hey, are you crazy or something? Come on, give me a kiss here.... You're insane! Gee, it's cold. Piero, Echo One here. No Gian, he can't hear you yet. Piero, it's Luigi. You see, I came? Keep still, keep still, hug yourself.* Crap, how can I tell them I'm scared? I wish they were in my place... Oh, Mauro.... ah... ah... thank God... oh yes, yes, I can recognize you. For God's sake, yes let's go down. Yes, yes. *Piero Echo One here, can you hear me? Yes, Gian, he heard you. We're coming down now. Easy ok?* Oh, hi Mauro. I'm stopping now. Who's touching me behind the shoulders? Ah, Paolo.... *Zanfretta, that's enough, the extra-terrestrials don't exist, only I exist...* "

The security guard is reporting distinctly everything he hears around him. In this case he faithfully relates what Gianfranco Tutti is saying to him at that moment.

Zanfretta: "How can I explain to them how things are here? I can't feel my hands anymore. Yes I know that they don't believe me, but how can I explain it to them? How I wish this whole affair never started... and my colleagues say that I want to be promoted, it's crazy! I'm only interested in my wages and that's all... Yes, yes, I'm going to the car, it's warm in there. Easy with the hands, it hurts... I can't feel them anymore... Oh, good evening Mrs. Bonola.... ow, don't touch my hands. Hi, Rino (*It is quite significant that in reality he never said those things, they were just thoughts. In fact, during the trip he didn't utter a word*). Where the hell are we? I haven't got a clue... But Lieutenant, won't you tell me where we are? We're in Marzano. Ahhh, my hands feel better now... my feet are still a bit frozen.... I can't remember a thing... I only remember leaving the car in Priaruggia.... I don't remember anything else... we're going down.... gee, the boss will be pissed.... no, that's enough, I don't want to create any more problems for him, I must go, resign, he already has too many problems to look after me as well... I can't prove a thing.... what sons of bitches! If only they would show themselves... and I've been to see doctors, the ones that treat crazy people... but they found no problems with me... Paolo, where's my gun? Spartà's got it. Spartà, have you got my gun? I gave it to the boss... Let's hope you didn't give it to anybody else. But am I going home now? It's three o'clock.... but I'm going to the area! Yes, I still have to do the clocks. Eh, it's not that easy doing them you know? And you even complain? Yes, I'll take the car to the depot. All right, I'm going home then. Yes, but I hope they won't stop me tomorrow, I want to work! Nooo, I want to work and that's it! OK, bye Paolo. Yes, I'll call Mazza when I get home. Hi, Nirvana. No, no, I felt a bit sick and I came back home. Hey, you're worse than a news bulletin, you know everything! Hold on, let me call Mazza. Mr. Mazza? Listen, I'm sorry. Oh well, I made you a bit crazy too. What? No, I hope he'll let me work tomorrow."

Moretti, realizing it is not necessary to have him continue, steps in to interrupt his story.

Doctor Moretti:" That's enough now Zanfretta. Right now you don't see anything anymore and you only answer my questions. Your sleep gets deeper and you answer my questions truthfully as always. When you came through with the car, was the car on the ground or had it been lifted in the air like last time?"

Zanfretta: "No, it was on the ground."

Doctor Moretti: "On the ground... And was anyone in the car with you when you passed close to Pesci?"

Zanfretta: "Yes."

Doctor Moretti: "Who was in the car with you?"

Zanfretta: "That gentleman, the same one as always. When he saw Pesci he ducked.... and I nearly ran Pesci over... I almost had a heart attack..."

Doctor Moretti: "How was this guy dressed?"

Zanfretta: "Always the same way: checkered jacket, he never shows his hands...."

Doctor Moretti: "And where did you pick him up?"

Zanfretta: "Near the highway exit, by the Staglieno cemetery. I had to pick him up..."

Doctor Moretti: "Where did you take the highway?"

Zanfretta: "At the overpass on Corso Europa..."

Doctor Moretti: "At Nervi?"

Zanfretta: "Yes."

Doctor Moretti: "Did you take a ticket?"

Zanfretta: "Yes."

Doctor Moretti: "And which exit did you take to leave the highway?"

Zanfretta: "Where the Cemetery of Staglieno is."

Doctor Moretti: "You exited at Staglieno..."

Zanfretta: "Yes."

Doctor Moretti: "Did you pay as usual?"

Zanfretta: "Yes."

Doctor Moretti: "How much did you pay, do you remember?"

Zanfretta: "Two-hundred and fifty..." (50 cents)

Doctor Moretti: "And where did you find that man?"

Zanfretta: "Just outside the tunnel; the car stopped and he jumped in. The door opened by itself and I couldn't move..."

Doctor Moretti: "And where were you when you were about to run your friend over?"

Zanfretta: "In Scoffera Square. I saw him waving in the middle of the road. At some point I yelled: 'Get out of the way, get out of the way, get out of the way!' and then the car steered by itself and it kept going without headlights...."

Doctor Moretti: "And the guy in the car with you wasn't saying anything? Wasn't he talking during the trip?"

Zanfretta: "Nothing, I only felt that I had to keep going with the car and that's it."

Doctor Moretti: "After what happened, from the day you were found till now, have you phoned anybody or have received any phone calls? From when you were found until now."

Zanfretta: "No, I haven't."

Doctor Moretti: "You didn't come into contact with your friend Boccone, or with some UFO expert or journalist?"

Zanfretta: "No, I called him today... and when I phoned he told me he had just been to headquarters and had spoken to Mr. Tutti..."

Doctor Moretti: "Who did you call?"

Zanfretta: "I called Luciano."

Doctor Moretti: "At what time?"

Zanfretta: "It might have been 11:30."

Doctor Moretti: "And what did you say to him?"

Zanfretta: "He said he had been to headquarters, he asked Giuliano for the tapes, was told that Giuliano would give him the tapes when he had the time to prepare them, then he spoke with Mr. Tutti who told him that there was nothing whatsoever to explain. He was a bit disappointed..."

Doctor Moretti: "And why did you call Luciano?"

Zanfretta: "No reason, I just called him. He's a friend of mine..."

Doctor Moretti: "Did you tell him what happened?"

Zanfretta: "No."

Doctor Moretti: "How come you didn't tell him?"

Zanfretta: "Because he didn't give me the time. He spoke first and when he told me he had been in the office I thought things were as they had said."

Doctor Moretti: "Let's go back to the car, when that person was there with you. At some point you used the radio. You said something over the radio: where are we going, where are you taking me..."

Zanfretta: "I could have sworn I was speaking in a woman's voice. It was just an instant but I was able to say: 'Where are you taking me?' pushing on the small walkie-talkie. Then I couldn't move my hand ... they showed me how to speak.... a strange language..."

Doctor Moretti: "And when did that person get out of the car?"

Zanfretta: "When... the car stopped in the square. He got out and went into that bright object and I ran away..."

Doctor Moretti: "So the bright object was very low."

Zanfretta: "Yes."

Doctor Moretti: "Where was this object exactly? On the ground, in the air, what was it like?"

Zanfretta: "It was hovering about four or five meters from the ground, all bright, I could just see the color of the metal."

Doctor Moretti: "How big was it?"

Zanfretta: "It had a circumference of at least thirty meters. Then when I started running away, it lifted up, turned down its light and disappeared into the valley, down there."

Doctor Moretti: "Which way did it go?"

Zanfretta: "Towards... where there is a house made of metal... inside that deep hole. There is a cliff, it ended up in there. Yes, you could hear it very well; I cannot understand how come they didn't hear the hiss. I even fired a few shots in the air so that they would understand where I was...."

Doctor Moretti: "How many shots did you fire?"

Zanfretta: "Three shots."

Doctor Moretti: "How many shots do you have in the barrel, I mean the gun, how many does it have?"

Zanfretta: "Eight in the magazine and one in the barrel."

Doctor Moretti: "And when did you fire the three shots?"

Zanfretta: "When I heard the Lieutenant calling Mr. Tutti."

Doctor Moretti: "Did you fire them in quick succession or not?"

Zanfretta: "At two-minute intervals. I fired two in the air and one towards the valley to see if I could hit the object. I tried to say to go down into the valley but I couldn't speak. But they were still there and I couldn't speak..."

Doctor Moretti: "Meaning that when your friends were there, the object was still there?"

Zanfretta: "Yes, while we were going down in the car I wanted to tell the Lieutenant to stop but I was unable, I was screaming inside: 'Stop, let's go down and see,' but I couldn't. I would have wanted to shake him but my hands hurt. I could have proven that they exist, all we needed to do was shine a big light and we would have seen them. Instead we went down."

Doctor Moretti: "How did you know they were still there?"

Zanfretta: "I knew it because I could feel them very close and also because they had landed. When they go away, they make a lot of noise, it's a very loud hiss, so when we left they were still there.... there was another time that they were above the clouds... and to distract the Lieutenant, Paolo and the others that were holding me still, they were moving away so that they wouldn't look up.... and I can never prove that I saw them. I am not crazy, I've seen them! I've seen them too many times...."

Doctor Moretti: "Where you fired the shots is where they had already found you!"

Zanfretta: "Yes."

The questions came one after the other, but in a tired way. It wasn't clear anymore what to ask him and after all, it wasn't fair to tire him uselessly. Lieutenant Cassiba, Buonamici and I occasionally looked at each other in the dim light of the room, and could confirm Zanfretta's information with our direct experience. The details matched. Moretti himself, always suspicious, was becoming aware of the fact that his patient wasn't contradicting himself and his willingness to put him to the test was running out. Yet pressed by his desire to shed more light on that fourth episode, he continued to ask questions.

Doctor Moretti: "Have you communicated with them at all?"

Zanfretta: "No, they haven't said anything to me. I can't understand why they took me up there to then hide. The cars must have arrived too soon... Oh, how I wish they had seen the object down there... And the boss says they don't exist, but why would I say one thing for another? I don't joke about these things and I wish they'd understand me... I can't prove anything..."

Doctor Moretti: "Did you see them leave? Did you see the spaceship leave?"

Zanfretta: "Yes, when I ran away; it lifted up and then headed into the darkness, its light fading more and more. In fact, I threw a few cards to show that they were down there. I thought if someone went down there, they would have seen it for sure....."

Doctor Moretti: "And when it leaves, when it moves, does it leave a trace or not?"

Zanfretta: "I don't know. When it lifts up, it makes a loud hiss and becomes brighter. So I don't know if it went completely and now there might be a few marks...."

Doctor Moretti: "Have you ever seen this, you know, spaceship move into the sky?"

Zanfretta: "Yes, yes."

Doctor Moretti: "What can you see?"

Zanfretta: "Just the shape, flat and triangular."

Doctor Moretti: "It's not like our planes, that leave a white trail..."

Zanfretta: "Nooo, they're too... advanced compared to us."

Doctor Moretti: "What color was the object, the spaceship?"

Zanfretta: "Metallic."

Doctor Moretti: "As far as you know, do they listen to radio communications?"

Zanfretta: "Of course. With the equipment they've got inside.... ours are laughable in comparison....."

Doctor Moretti: "Are you guessing or have they told you?"

Zanfretta: "No, I had already seen how organized they are when I

113

was on the spaceship."

Doctor Moretti: "But what I'm saying is, the fact that they may or may not listen to radio communications, did they specifically tell you?"

Zanfretta: "No, I heard it through... inside this plane. Also when I saw the Lieutenant firing shots on Mount Fasce, it was then that I wanted to call them. I pushed a lot of buttons but... who knows what I did."

Doctor Moretti: "Will they be in touch again? What do you think?"

Zanfretta: "I don't know, they didn't tell me anything. The cars could have waited to come up. They might have given me that object and the problem would be solved. I was ready to take it. I don't know why but I get scared, every time .... I'm sure they have a base there because they definitely always leave from there."

At the mention of the object, Moretti became more alert and, going back to the topic, urges the security guard to have them give it to him without fearing potential consequences.

Doctor Moretti: "You have to take the object next time, as we agreed, remember?"

Zanfretta: "Oh yes, I can't wait."

Doctor Moretti: "Don't be scared though, OK? Don't be afraid of these beings because, think about it, if they wanted to hurt you, they already would have, right?"

Zanfretta: "I know but... you've never seen them; you should see them... being scared is an understatement!"

Doctor Moretti: "Sure, I understand...."

Zanfretta: "You shit your pants...."

Doctor Moretti: "But they only want to give you this object, that's all...."

Zanfretta: "Yes but you should really see them, they're taller than 3 meters! My eyes weren't deceiving me, they are really tall..."

Doctor Moretti: "A little while ago you told me that you think they have a base there?"

Zanfretta: "For sure, because every time I have a headache and I feel like they're calling me in my brain, I always end up over there..."

Doctor Moretti: "But was the guy in the car with you that tall?"

Zanfretta: "No, he was normal, with an egg-shaped head.... you can never see his face, he's a weird one... Ah Christ, had they come a little earlier.... In the car, I was hoping: 'Now they'll give me that object, I'll take it to Mr. Tutti and the matter will be closed. Only this way they'll hospitalize me....' Instead nothing happened, they arrived too early and they hid without telling me anything."

Doctor Moretti: "Do you remember when the car was lit up?"

Zanfretta: "Yes, it was so hot.... I even put the window down and looked up because at some point, the car seemed to be going by itself, and I saw this huge light overhead and it gave off a lot of heat."

Doctor Moretti: "Do you remember exactly where it happened?"

Zanfretta: "About a kilometer before the spot where I left the car..."

Doctor Moretti: "Was it very hot?"

Zanfretta: "Very. In fact I kept my head outside.... aside from the fact that looking at the light was really annoying, it was giving off a lot of heat..."

Doctor Moretti: "Was it kind of like the heating in the car?"

Zanfretta: "No, much, much more..."

In the end, Moretti realized that to keep going would have been counterproductive, even for Zanfretta. He terminated the session inviting him to rest.

Doctor Moretti: "Now you are sleeping deeply, rest and forget everything we said. Rest comfortably. Have a good sleep and then I will wake you. Sleep quietly..."

The experiment therefore seemed to be concluded. Moretti reckoned he had to let Zanfretta rest before bringing him back to a conscious state. In the meantime, so as not to disturb him, we moved into the room next door to be able to comment on everything that had just been done. We had been talking for about ten minutes when, suddenly, we heard a murmur coming from the table where the night watchman was resting. Astonished, we immediately rushed toward Zanfretta. Moretti was more perplexed than anyone else. He had told Zanfretta to sleep quietly. Why did he not obey?

It was only at that moment, I think, that we all realized that the night watchman's mind was starting to wander way beyond the bounds of hypnosis itself. But the surprise turned into real amazement when we heard with our very own ears Zanfretta mumbling something in a very strange language. Fortunately, in the meantime, the recorder had been left on and it kept going.

Doctor Moretti: "Who has just spoken?"

Zanfretta: "Them. I transmitted... and they will show themselves very soon.... and they hope that nothing will happen...."

Zanfretta was panting more and more and had difficulty expressing himself. Cautiously, Moretti tried to pick the conversation up.

Doctor Moretti: "We didn't understand that language, though. We don't know what they said."

Zanfretta: "I do..."

Doctor Moretti: "Can you repeat clearly and in a loud voice. Loudly, Zanfretta, and clearly! Repeat everything they've said in that language."

I wouldn't know how to graphically show the language that the security started to repeat, therefore I shall just write its sounds as they were pronounced.

Zanfretta: *"Ei chi snaua... si naila... isne ghe... il se lai.... go ghe ti snau exi ghe... sci nis che ixi kai snoue.... chisnauag the.... aiex piscinau kep na.... tei sdei...."*

Doctor Moretti: "Zanfretta, can you translate for me everything they have said?"

Zanfretta: "Yes."

Doctor Moretti: "Do it then."

Zanfretta: "They will come back soon and they will show themselves once and for all. They hope nothing will happen..."

Doctor Moretti: "Who they will show themselves to? Just you?"

Zanfretta: "They didn't say...."

Doctor Moretti: "Are you in touch with them right now? Can you talk?"

Zanfretta: "No, I've finished."

Doctor Moretti: "Did they tell you when they will show themselves?"

Zanfretta: "No, I've finished."

Doctor Moretti: "Did they tell you when they will show themselves?"

Zanfretta: "No."

Doctor Moretti: "When did they start this transmission?"

Zanfretta: "When you told me to rest.... and you moved away. I called you but.... I tried to resist...."

Doctor Moretti: "Keep calm and quiet. Do you still hear them? Speak loudly..."

The air in the room was becoming heavy from tension. In a way, we had the impression that someone, a third wheel, wanted to forcibly penetrate the small environment. Those present were looking at each other to read in the other people's eyes the truth about what they were thinking. It wasn't easy to believe what was happening.

Zanfretta: "I'm trying hard."

Doctor Moretti: "Trying hard to do what?"

Zanfretta: "To call them..."

Doctor Moretti: "Are they calling you?"

Zanfretta: "Yes..."

Doctor Moretti: "Let go, let them call you. Don't fight it, I am here with you and nothing can happen to you."

Zanfretta: "They can't hear me anymore now and I'm trying to call them... *ah.... ah... ighesnà oghesì.... ah...* "

Doctor Moretti: "Is that them talking?"

Zanfretta: "No."

Doctor Moretti: "But do you know their language?"

Zanfretta: "Yes."

Doctor Moretti: "And how do you know their language?"

Zanfretta: "It's what they want...."

Doctor Moretti: "Try calling them again."

Zanfretta: "Ouch, my head hurts..."

Doctor Moretti: "Try calling them to see if we can communicate."

Zanfretta: *"Lesghinaus... isceno isnaghè... ah... ah.... crap..."*

Doctor Moretti: "What is it, what's happening?"

Zanfretta: "They've already closed the connection..."

Doctor Moretti: "Why did they call you, before? Why did they want to talk with you?"

Zanfretta: "Because they knew I was here, because you were here. They tried to communicate at the beginning but I had to report everything and I covered their words. Yet..."

Doctor Moretti: "What's this business? That you covered everything, tell me properly. When was it that they wanted to communicate?"

Zanfretta:" While... while Echo 7 was calling me...."

Doctor Moretti: "While Echo 7 was calling you?"

Zanfretta: "Yes..."

Doctor Moretti: "But, when?"

Zanfretta: "When... he asked me.... if I was holding my gun, I started hearing a strange language and... You told me to keep reporting..."

Doctor Moretti: "Therefore they wanted to communicate this evening...."

Zanfretta: "Yes..."

Moretti, seeing how agitated the security guard had suddenly become, tried to make him fall asleep again to soothe him and then wake him up without upsetting him.

Doctor Moretti: "Now, Zanfretta, sleep quietly. Should they wish to come into contact again, you will speak. Leave your mind empty and clear. Sleep... empty and clear. There will be no interference here. If they want, they'll be able to communicate."

For a few minutes, we had the impression that everything had gone back to normal. The silence of the office was broken only by a few murmurs. I was, in fact, asking the doctor why Zanfretta didn't obey him, since he was under hypnosis. Moretti didn't know what to say. "Something like this has never happened to me," he was whispering to me so as not to disturb Zanfretta's sleep. "Usually the subject under hypnosis follows the hypnotist's instructions, unless such instructions are in obvious conflict with the patient's subconscious. Now in this case, Zanfretta should have obeyed. Instead it seems we find ourselves facing a man who responds to an external will that is stronger than the very same hypnosis he is under. I really wouldn't know how to explain this phenomenon...."

While Moretti was making these off-the-cuff observations, the night watchman was starting to show signs of recovery. Once again, going against the order he had been given, he was floundering in his sleep. And he started speaking in the unknown language again.

Zanfretta: *"Ghisnai... iesnau..."*

Doctor Moretti: "Can you translate?"

Zanfretta: "They're not answering..."

Doctor Moretti: "Was it you calling them?"

Zanfretta:"Yes."

Doctor Moretti: "Why?"

Zanfretta: "To speak with them... I wanted to... be free from this nightmare..."

Doctor Moretti: "But you'll be freed next time, when you get hold of the object and you hand it over...."

Zanfretta: "Let's hope so... that they're quick about it..."

Doctor Moretti: "They wanted to let us know that they will show themselves then?"

Zanfretta: "Yes, once and for all..."

Doctor Moretti: "Do they know who we are?"

Zanfretta: "Yes, they know everything..."

Doctor Moretti: "But in all that talking, they just said that they will show themselves once and for all, that they hope nothing will happen? Did they only say this?"

THE EXTRATERRESTRIALS SPEAK

Zanfretta: "No."

Doctor Moretti: "What else did they say?"

Zanfretta: "They told me not to be worried, that we're pretty close now and that yesterday they couldn't show themselves because they saw too many lights coming up the road, otherwise they would have shown themselves..."

Zanfretta sat there panting for a couple of minutes, then started speaking again.

Zanfretta: "Will you at least reply..."

Doctor Moretti: "Zanfretta, they said they will show themselves, right?"

Zanfretta: "Yes."

Doctor Moretti: "They said it to us, right?"

Zanfretta: "Yes."

Doctor Moretti: "But yesterday they didn't want to show themselves, how do we go about it then?"

Zanfretta: "I don't know..."

Doctor Moretti: "How many of them could there be?"

Zanfretta: "I don't know... they have to... get in touch with me. When... when I'm sleeping at home...."

Doctor Moretti: "And they will tell us everything we have to do?"

Zanfretta: "I don't know..."

Doctor Moretti: "Will you let me know when they contact you during the night?"

Zanfretta: "How can I? When they speak to me I can't move..."

Doctor Moretti: "But if we're supposed to see them, you need to let us know...."

Zanfretta: "Let them think about this..."

Doctor Moretti: "You'll be able to call me the next day, right?"

Zanfretta: "If you want... I'll do it."

Doctor Moretti: "OK, you told me they will contact you regarding this meeting at your place, while you sleep, correct?"

Clearly Moretti didn't believe what Zanfretta was saying; however, like a good psychologist does, he was trying to go along with him, to see up to what point this tale could be a figment of his imagination. That he had lost control of the hypnosis had already surprised him a fair bit. As a result, he was trying to put the security guard's statements into the right perspective.

Doctor Moretti: "Very well. As soon as you can, immediately after or the same morning, you will phone me."

Zanfretta: "Yes."

Doctor Moretti: "Either me, or Mr. Tutti or Lieutenant Cassiba. Agreed?"

Zanfretta: "Yes."

Doctor Moretti: "Now sleep quietly, sleep quietly without any trouble. A nice restorative sleep. Sleep..."

But the evening didn't end there. Left alone in the room so he could finally rest, after only five minutes of an apparently quiet sleep, Zanfretta in a very low voice picked up the conversation again in the unknown language.

Zanfretta: *"Ashinai daià...kastnè... daismenà... kisnesnà... aidisnesnà... das mi né ashimenà kas nà... nai skin ti nà..."*

It was in that moment that Moretti, summoned by the whispers, went back into the room. We went with him. If it is now possible to report what Zanfretta said during those moments alone, it is because the tape recorder kept going and it was switched off only at the end of the session. The high fidelity equipment installed by Giuliano Buonamici eventually turned out extremely useful for the clarity of the tapes.

Doctor Moretti: "Zanfretta can you hear me? Speak loudly, loudly, loudly..."

Zanfretta: "I'm trying... to call them.... but I can't... ah... ah.... ah..."

Doctor Moretti: "What is it? What's the matter Zanfretta?"

Zanfretta: "Maybe I've got it..."

Doctor Moretti: "Tell me when you come into contact, ok? Agreed? Understood?"

Zanfretta: "Yes."

And then something completely unexpected happened. Suddenly Zanfretta's face hardened. The anxious and frightened mask he had up to that moment disappeared as if by magic, turning into a hard and determined face. His shy and whimpering voice became strong and dry, and decidedly loud. The night watchman then started speaking through a third person.

Zanfretta**: " Earthling! Speak!"**

Doctor Moretti: "Will you show yourselves?"

Zanfretta: **"Everything in due course. I know, it's time we showed ourselves."**

Doctor Moretti: "Will you show yourselves to us, the ones that are here now?"

Zanfretta**: "We are interested in many people, people that may** understand us; we can't convince this earthling to stop fearing us. Don't be scared. Let time run its course. Only he understands our language. You will never understand a thing. You will resolve nothing like this. To believe or not believe means nothing: everything in due course. There will not be many laughing about this earthling anymore. It means a lot to us."

Doctor Moretti: "But we want to help..."

Zanfretta: "**We already know you want to help and in due course we will show ourselves. Ending connection.**"

Immediately Zanfretta's face went back to how it was a few minutes earlier. His chest was heaving rhythmically again and his voice was once again weak and tired.

Zanfretta: "Keep going... keep going...."

Doctor Moretti: "Zanfretta..."

Zanfretta: "Yes."

Doctor Moretti: "Do you know the one that spoke?"

Zanfretta: "Yes."

Doctor Moretti: "Who is he?"

Zanfretta: "He is their leader... he's the one who is in that picture... where I threw the ball..."

Doctor Moretti: "What's his name? Do you know?"

Zanfretta: "I only remember that... he is prince of the Dargos..."

Doctor Moretti: "All right Zanfretta, that's enough now. Sleep, sleep deeply. Forget everything. Sleep deeply, quietly, forget, forget, forget, forget, relax, forget, forget, forget..."

This time Moretti's voice, becoming more and more mellow, has effect. The security guard finally falls asleep and Moretti seizes the moment to wake him up.

Doctor Moretti: "Now I will slowly count from 1 to 10. When I say the word 'ten' you will be awake, feeling great and fit as if you have slept for eight hours. OK? One, two, three, four, five, six, seven, eight, nine, ten: you are completely awake!"

Zanfretta opened his eyes but he still looked groggy. Moretti then invited him to lie down for a little while longer. Only a few minutes later did he totally recover.

Before saying goodbye, Moretti even joked about it: "Best not to say anything to anybody about what you've heard here tonight," he told me. "Someone might ask for a psychological evaluation."

They were ominous words. On my part, I didn't even dream of publishing anything about the matter: where would I have started to give a serious and detailed account of the evening? And how would I have prevented the chronicle of that hypnosis from becoming damaging to Zanfretta himself? To at least be credible, the story would have had to be told from the beginning, without omitting even the smallest details. However, I realized that I needed too much good will to give Zanfretta the benefit of the doubt regarding what he had said under hypnosis. And so, while maintaining my role as a journalist, I decided not to write anything, leaving it for another time.

Those who are rooting for the night watchman may criticize my decision. But considering the situation in Genoa at that time, and the Genoese mentality, I don't think I can regret my actions. Someone else, though, was starting to feel ill-at-ease about what Zanfretta was saying, even if it was only under hypnosis. "Val Bisagno" management in fact didn't know how to deal with the problem anymore. By now, the encounters had become too many to hide them from public opinion. Police headquarters had let it go in the beginning, but now they wanted an explanation.

Following the series of nighttime episodes, Police Commissioner Alfonso Lerino suspended Zanfretta's gun license without any apparently justifiable reason. Zanfretta brought the problem to the directors of his Institute so that someone would officially intervene. Nobody knows how things really went, also because no one wanted to clarify the issue. For sure, a few phone calls took place between Police headquarters and the management, but nothing more. The most probable guess is that the authorities deemed it necessary to "freeze" the gun license while waiting for the UFO situation to be sorted out. It is also conceivable that the executives of the Security Patrol Institute didn't want to take responsibility for potential thoughtless acts or accidents that their employees might be involved in. It must be said, though, that even without the gun license, they didn't fire him.

They placed him in the radio command center.

But Zanfretta didn't give up. The next day, approximately a year after his last encounter, he went to Gianfranco Tutti asking him again to intercede with the Police. The answer was pithy. "Dear Zanfretta, it is best you find yourself a lawyer," the director told him. And immediately, the security guard understood that his employers had no intention of knocking on Police headquarters' door anymore.

And so he did something he would never have done before. He went and spoke to his colleague Saverio Magliarachi, the representative of the labor union federation Cgil-Cisl-Uil within his firm, and explained his situation.

Magliarachi didn't waste time. He took him to the office of the federation to speak with a lawyer, Nadia Gobessi, a young professional who immediately understood the lay of the land. To make a long story short, within a week Zanfretta went to pick up his renewed gun license. He paid only fifty thousand lire (about $50) for his lawyer's trouble. The morning of August 9, 1981, the police gave him back his document.

To judge the behavior of the managers of "Val Bisagno" only in light of this episode is too simplistic, however. Moretti's words regarding a psychological evaluation echoed what Tutti, Mrs. Bonola and Colonel Cereda had been thinking for a while. After all, since they still had Zanfretta on staff, they had to justify for public opinion and the authorities that their guard was not crazy.

And so they had him undergo a complete psychological evaluation, which lasted a couple of months over a few sessions. Doctor Franco Lombardi, specialist in psychiatry and aid to the chief physician of the Provincial Psychiatric Hospital of Genoa-Quarto, was the one to do it.

The evaluation was handed in on March 1, 1980. In the report, the specialist outlined the night watchman's complete clinical case but didn't reach any conclusion about the nighttime episodes everybody was talking about. However, he wrote: "He appears sincere and in good faith albeit extremely impressionable and with limited ability for critical analysis and self-criticism."

The reader will be able to read the entire psychological evaluation in the chapter dedicated to Zanfretta's life. However, I would like to point out that it is thanks to this recognized *good faith* that Zanfretta's troubles didn't worsen. It is quite relevant, in fact, that if he wasn't fired and that if the press, even its most negative factions, never got to the point of ruining him, it is because everyone was convinced he *wasn't lying*. It was difficult, and still is, to acknowledge the existence of that terrible reality he was proposing, but no one felt up to calling him a liar.

CHAPTER 7

The Last Hypnosis

In the meantime months went by. We realized that hypnosis was not that reliable anymore, seeing that Zanfretta clearly tended not to be subject to it any more (even though nobody could explain the reason why). Consequently, looking for the truth proved more and more difficult. Even Zanfretta himself had undergone an undeniable physical transformation. Given that right after each encounter, he urinated a blackish liquid, he had already been under observation since 1979. In fact, it was during that year that the night watchman put on 14 kilos (about 30 pounds) and his hair turned from black to gray. Zanfretta's transformations are documented in the medical report written by professor Cesare Ardy, lecturer of general physiology at the University of Genoa. This report can also be found in the next chapter.

It was in this climate of doubt and uncertainty that Zanfretta, when no one expected it, prepared to meet with the *extra-terrestrials* for the fifth time. To tell the truth, he didn't meet them in the flesh. Followed by his colleagues, Zanfretta was unable to reach his privileged speakers, and he simply established a *telepathic* connection, so to speak.

Everything happened the evening of August 13, 1980. Zanfretta, without letting his superiors know, felt the need to go back to the hilltops around Torriglia and took off. However this time too his behavior was noticed. By now he was under surveillance and any move he made was neatly recorded by his colleagues on the same shift. In fact, when he left "Val Bisagno" headquarters, he was immediately followed. Hot on his trail was also Colonel Cereda who from that first time, not having seen anything transcendental occur with regard to his employee, had considerably reduced trust in him. Giuliano Buonamici was also on Zanfretta's trail. On his motorbike he had followed the night watchman's car up the hills. To make a long story short, those who witnessed that night say that Zanfretta drove his car at high speed on the dark mountain roads without headlights to then stop in an isolated roadside rest stop overlooking a valley. Here the night watchman got out of the car, went to the edge and stayed there with his eyes turned up toward the sky for about half an hour. He then went back and got in the car to head back to Genoa.

Just before Zanfretta's departure that evening, they called me too, but I wasn't home. Despite my not being there, I had no reason to doubt what I was told. In my desire to do more intensive research on Zanfretta, I realized that I should have asked for better attention on the part of the managers of "Val Bisagno." The security guard should have been the subject of a more thorough examination compared to the one he was actually undergoing. The rescue team should have been made up of trusted and responsible individuals; no one else should have been in the search party, least of all those who come just out of curiosity. Also, considering previous experience, we would have needed to give him a head start before pursuing him.

Such criticism however wouldn't have been understood. The "Zanfretta Case" was now becoming too much of a bother to keep up with. Gianfranco Tutti avoided my questions, often with the excuse of not being available when I called. The heart of the matter was that given that no one could solve this man's problem, it was best to forget about him. This couldn't be done suddenly and in the eyes of public opinion. Therefore, as good Genoese do, the managers of "Val Bisagno" decided to slowly let the case sink into oblivion.

Examining the content of Zanfretta's last hypnosis didn't help. As if there were need to demonstrate it, the session showed that the guard was by now under the influence of a foreign will. The matter ran the risk of becoming dangerous. In any case, here is the full text of the hypnosis session held at doctor Moretti's office on Thursday, August 28, 1980 at 9.30 p.m.

Zanfretta:"Nirvana, I'm going. Cassiba wants me downstairs at headquarters at 9. I've got a bit of a headache, but it will pass. Bye. Look at me,... if you need to, call up there. A quarter to nine already, I've got to run. Ouch, it hurts. I'll take the freeway... it'll be faster. It hurts too much... I must stop, and quickly, too. What are you beeping for...I'm going! Ouch. Fuck you. I wasn't feeling well, bear with me. I'm sorry... Shall we go and get a coffee? Let's go and get a coffee. No, no, no: all right. I've got a headache. I don't know, I don't know if I feel strange. What? No... Anyhow, in the meantime I'm not saying anything to anybody, only Giorgio knows. Just you and me. I have a feeling but... well, we can go there and play dumb. Good grief! My head is spinning. Cassiba I'm not feeling well... he can't hear me.... ah... Paolo, ouch, I've hit my head! No, no, it's nothing. It was as if someone squashed my brain. Ah no, no, I'm not going up. I want to sit down. Ow... ouch... it hurts. Ow, it hurts. That's it, it's gone now. It's going. Hey, I heard the whistle again, always that damn whistle. We're going up to radio command. Evening Mazza, going up? Cassiba gave me the equipment, it's Ramoino's. He told me to keep it in my pocket. Yes, I've got a headache, it hurts like hell. How come Valle has come around here? What, you don't know anything? Nothing? All right, a person can go wherever he wants... Oh, if only you knew how much it hurts. It bloody hurts. Wait, I need to go to the toilet... God, it hurts... What am I in the toilet for? Ow... ah, I want to leave... I want to leave. No, Mazza, it hurts but... maybe it will pass... Who's Valle calling? Ah, he said Di Stefano... bah? Look at this, I tell you... Mazza, I have to go... I must go... No, I won't say a thing. Yes, I'll take the lift and go down. Zanfretta... Zanfretta... Zanfretta... ohhh, oh how I wish I could turn around, oh God. Best you don't come close..."

From that moment on, we have the distinct feeling that Zanfretta is talking about his body as if it belonged to someone else. His psyche, by now in the grip of another's will, stays alert and watches what the body does. By what the night watchman says, it is clear he is receiving and executing precise orders. His voice in the meantime becomes more and more breathless.

Zanfretta:"I'm going... away. The car doesn't stop at the light, yet I'm working the gears... Someone is chasing me... Yes, I'm speeding up. I'm trying to lose them. I'm turning at Davagna... Hey, it stopped. I'll keep going. If only I could pick the radio up and let Cassiba know... ah my hand is stuck on the shift... My God! It's so dark! This beam is all crooked... But... I can hear the radio. But this is Echo Four's voice *(Giuliano Buonamici)*. What's he doing at Scoffera? It's the Colonel... Cassiba didn't keep his word, he said he wouldn't call anybody...It was too late anyway. It doesn't matter, let's hope for the best. We're in Scoffera. Who's that right in the middle of the road? Move away Pesci, move away.... ufff, here, no one is following me. I'm speeding up. Yes, I'm turning the headlights off. I'm going down the valley and I'll try and shake them. Yes, I'll come back to the tunnel afterwards. The square is the designated spot. Yes, thank goodness, I've lost them."

It seems that the night watchman was following the orders he was given. It is strange that whoever was giving him orders was able to guide him through an area that even Zanfretta himself didn't know.

Supposedly this someone was even letting him know whether he managed to lose his pursuers or not. In fact, when he stated that he didn't see them anymore, he was told to go down the valley to lose them. It truly seems as if this someone had a comprehensive view of the territory and who was passing through. We might even be led to surmise that whoever was giving him these orders was watching everything from above, as if from a helicopter. Or, please allow journalistic license, from a flying saucer for real.

Zanfretta:"Here is... the tunnel... the Scoffera Pass. *Aisccrist*, there's Pesci, he's not moving. I hope he doesn't follow me...Oh Christ... Pesci go away, don't follow me... Ah... yes... I'm stopping. He turned the lights off, he stopped as well. Ah, all right, I'm going again. Meeting.... point.., yes, I'll keep going. Some cars are still chasing me.... Now two... Crap... I'll turn at Sant'Alberto: where is it? I've never been there. Oh my! Look at these roads! Look, they're still on my tail... Ah, if only they stopped for a moment... I did tell them not to follow me though... Ok, I must stop here, in this square.... Now I am waiting... Now I'm at the signal. I'm turning off the headlights. Yes, they're here, I can feel them. What's that noise? It's dark, I can't see anything but I could swear that there's someone back there... No, it's impossible, I've shaken them. Yes, *nichisnachi aidst*.... yes, I'm coming, I'll be there, I'm coming... You're here then... *Coigainà taie chest*... I didn't ask them to come... they followed me. Yes, I'll go back to the car. Why aren't you doing anything anymore? Show yourselves, please.... once and for all... *Chichist' gamma aixn tedam*... Ah, I kept my word... Ah... ah... I came, didn't I? It's not my fault if they followed me... Ah, all right, I'll go back to the car. But... is it over? You're not coming anymore? Must I go with you? Forever? But I... I'm of little interest to you... OK... I'll go back... forever. Yes, I'm going back to the car and I'm leaving. Meanwhile you must go so that they don't see you. All right... There, I'm going down to the bottom of the slope.... Terrific! A cemetery... what a romantic spot. Here they are... Now they pass through here and then they'll leave, so that they don't see them. I'm going back... I'm going back... yes, where I was before leaving... Good God! This road is never ending... Listen to this, the Colonel keeps saying that I'm changing roads.... He can see, then, even at night... Crap, I guess... that's Giuliano with his bike... Gee, he must be chilled to the bone... It's all my fault... Look, I'm almost downtown. There, I'm downstairs from headquarters. Ow, my head... ouch, I feel faint... And who's this? What's Giorgio doing? Why is he touching me? I don't know... What? I fell asleep? Bah, I don't know. The Colonel is here... Paolo, why am I here? But you do know, don't you? As usual, you went for a drive---... Bah... Ah, Colonel good evening... I'm fine, why, how should I feel? Ah, ok, Giorgio, let's go upstairs and have a coffee. Okey dokey... hey, Mazza, bear with me, I fell asleep in the car.

Here we go, here come the tests. Ahhh, damn 51 *(Raimondo Mascia)* he's a dim-wit. Negative, tell him he can go to sleep. Giorgio, why do you want me to go home? No, I'll stay here till the morning. Mazza is by himself in any case... Mr. Mazza, can you manage? I know you've always managed but... all right, we're leaving... I need to get changed and fill up, so that I can get home. Crap, I put in 12,000 Lire *(about 12 dollars)*... bastards, they've sucked it out... eh, what can you do..., are you going home for a drink? I'm going to sleep in the meantime..."

Zanfretta doesn't realize that if the petrol is missing it is not because *they sucked it out* as he says, but because during the night he went for a drive to the hills travelling many kilometers. At this point Moretti steps in and starts questioning him.

Doctor Moretti:"That's enough Zanfretta, now I will ask you a very precise question and you will answer with the utmost sincerity. In the weeks preceding August 13, did you handle tools like the ones used for digging or to perform similar actions? Do these farming tools remind you of anything or bring anything to mind? You know that your will has been replaced by mine, therefore you must answer me with trust, calmly, telling me everything you are aware of or know from deep within your conscious memory regarding this question."

Actually Moretti's question had a logic of its own. Zanfretta's colleagues claimed that lately the night watchman talked almost obsessively about the sphere with the pyramid inside that the *extraterrestrials* were meant to give him. One day they saw him come to headquarters with his hands dirty with dirt, sparking the suspicion that that sphere actually existed and that he had buried it so no one would see it. To be honest, you had to be very creative to come to such a conclusion, but as previously stated, not many people had the courage to believe that in the night watchman's story there was only a great deal of imagination. Hence, Moretti's question. But his answer left everyone flabbergasted.

Zanfretta:"*Tixel.*"

Doctor Moretti:"If you heard and understood the question you will lift your index finger. I command your finger as well as your mind and voice, and there is no other command contrary to mine which is superior to mine. My will is now within you and you will answer in a clear and understandable manner. It is your voice that will answer, not your will. And now, speak with confidence."

Zanfretta:"*Tixel... tixel... question... negative for now... to you. Tixel, negative question for you, tixel.*"

Doctor Moretti:"What does this word mean?"

Zanfretta: "Negative... question for you, *tixel*. negative question for you, *tixel*."

We were stunned. Zanfretta was answering as if he were a computer being questioned by a human voice. Moretti clearly seemed disoriented. Despite this, he kept insisting.

Doctor Moretti: "What did you bury?"

Zanfretta: "Negative question for you, *tixel*."

Doctor Moretti: "Why negative question for us? What does it mean?"

Zanfretta: "The object exists but now is not the time to have it."

Doctor Moretti: "Can you hear my voice?"

Zanfretta: "Yes."

Doctor Moretti: "I'm putting my right hand on yours, this way you will only communicate with me. Can you hear me?"

Zanfretta: "Yes."

Doctor Moretti: "You and I are alone now, just the two of us. I would like to know what you have buried, not because I'm curious, but to end this unpleasant situation. You know that they want to take you away forever. Well, I just want to help you so that you are able to stay with your family. I don't want anything bad happen to you. Is the concept clear?"

Zanfretta: "Yes."

Doctor Moretti: "You remember with your mind what you buried. Say it."

Zanfretta: "Negative question for you, *tixel*."

Doctor Moretti: "Answer my question. You, Zanfretta, not that stupid voice that's talking. Zanfretta, I'm talking to you..."

But every attempt always came to the same, identical result.

Zanfretta: "Negative question for you, *tixel*."

Moretti didn't want to give up and kept insisting.

Doctor Moretti: "Zanfretta, do you hear my voice?"

Zanfretta: "Negative question for you, *tixel*."

Doctor Moretti: "But can you hear my voice?"

Zanfretta: "Negative question for you, *tixel.*"

Doctor Moretti: "When did you bury the object. Is July 5th correct?"

Zanfretta: "Negative question for you, *tixel.*"

Doctor Moretti: "It's not you that's talking now. What's that word that you always end each sentence with?"

Zanfretta: "Please don't insist... please don't insist."

Doctor Moretti: "That stuff that's buried, will it be taken out? Will they give it to us?"

Zanfretta: "Negative... ow..."

Doctor Moretti: "What the matter?"

Zanfretta: "My head burns..."

Doctor Moretti: "Did you hear what I've just asked you?"

Zanfretta: "No."

Doctor Moretti: "You don't remember the questions I asked you a little while ago?"

Zanfretta: "No."

Doctor Moretti: "What do you mean? I asked you what you did with that stuff you buried. Of course you remember... You don't? You do remember, don't you? That you replied that..."

Zanfretta: "Negative for you, *tixel.*"

Doctor Moretti: "Zanfretta, listen to me. Did you meet with those beings at the beginning of July? Have you had contact with them?"

Zanfretta: "Negative question for you, *tixel.*"

Moretti wanted to ascertain if, according to other security guards' testimony, Zanfretta had a previous encounter in July where he might have come into possession of the mysterious sphere. However, by now hypnosis didn't have any effect on the night watchman's mind. His brain, almost like a two-way radio, answered by reflex as if it depended on someone else's will, someone who was at the same time there in the room through his body.

Doctor Moretti: "Zanfretta, listen up. Do you remember July 5th, in the evening? You spoke to Giorgio Valle and you told him something regarding a beautiful and wonderful thing. Just tell me yes or no..."

Zanfretta: "Yes."

Doctor Moretti: "And do you remember the wonderful thing you had to tell him? Answer yes or no only."

Zanfretta: "Yes, I remember."

Doctor Moretti: "Do you still remember this wonderful thing?"

Zanfretta: "Yes, I do."

Doctor Moretti: "Are you willing to tell me, too?"

Zanfretta: "Negative for that question, *tixel*."

Doctor Moretti: "Why did you want to tell him and not me? Just answer this question. I'm not asking you what the thing is, just why you wanted to tell him and not me."

Zanfretta: "I trusted him."

Doctor Moretti: "And you don't trust me?"

Zanfretta: "It's not me. I'd like to tell but I can't."

Doctor Moretti: "Would you tell your friend Giorgio?"

Zanfretta: "I mentioned something to him but I was waiting for an answer from someone."

Doctor Moretti: "Zanfretta listen. I know you'd like to talk to me but you can't, can you?"

Zanfretta: "Yes."

Doctor Moretti: "But you could give me a simple yes or no answer if you made an effort, if you tried hard enough. Would you like to work with me?"

Zanfretta: "Yes."

Doctor Moretti: "I know you have buried something really beautiful and very important. Answer yes or no."

Zanfretta: "Negative for that question, *tixel*."

Getting nowhere, Moretti then tried to converse with that someone interfering with the night watchman's answers.

Doctor Moretti: "Zanfretta, can you put me in touch with them now? Can you be a go-between?"

Zanfretta: "Negative for that question, *tixel*."

Doctor Moretti: "Ok, let's leave this topic alone. Now you're going back in time, you're going back in time. Zanfretta we are now on July 5th, it is ten minutes past eight in the evening and you have just quarreled with your friend Giorgio. You have just told him: 'You're a friend of mine'. Speak, the two of you."

Moretti tried to introduce the security guard Giorgio Valle into the conversation, to awaken that part of Zanfretta's memory which seemed heavily influenced. Valle was there and he intervened.

Valle: "If you think I go around blabbing about what you tell me, you're wrong. If you want to tell me, go ahead. If you don't want to tell me, keep it to yourself. Simple as that..."

But this attempt failed as well. This time Zanfretta's reply seemed to be coming even more from an electronic brain rather than from a human being's.

Zanfretta: "Negative... negative... negative.... negative... negative... negative... negative... *tixel.*"

Doctor Moretti: "You are listening to me Zanfretta, are you not?"

Zanfretta: "Yes."

Doctor Moretti: "I will now put in your hands a flat surface with some sheets of paper on it and a pen. I will count from one to five. At the count of five, still remaining under hypnosis and still sleeping, you will open your eyes, you will sit on the table, and you will see nothing else but the sheet and the pen. Is this clear?"

Zanfretta: "Negative for question, *tixel.*"

Doctor Moretti: "I didn't tell you what I want you to write down."

Zanfretta: "Negative for question, *tixel.*"

Doctor Moretti: "Now I will count from one to five, at the count of five you will open your eyes and you will do what I said. One, two, three, four, five: your eyelids open up, open up, open up. The eyes open, they open, you can open your eyes, they open, the eyes open. Now you will sit up, very good. Now you see this pen. You pick it up and you write. You get close to the sheet and you write. You see nothing else but the pen and the sheet, do you not?"

Zanfretta: "Yes."

Doctor Moretti: "Very well. I will hold you like this and you will write or draw, without speaking, the buried object. That's it, good. Now, write. What is that object for, do you know?"

Zanfretta: "Negative for that question, *tixel.*"

Doctor Moretti: "Zanfretta, do you know when you're supposed to see these beings again?"

Zanfretta: "Personal compulsory goal, *tixel.*"

Doctor Moretti: "What do you mean, what does it mean: 'Personal compulsory goal'?"

Zanfretta: "Negative, cannot tell."

Doctor Moretti: "Zanfretta, do they know you're under hypnosis right now?"

Zanfretta: "Negative for this question, *tixel.*"

Doctor Moretti: "How come they communicated last time and tonight they don't want to?"

Zanfretta: "I don't know."

Doctor Moretti: "But do they know?"

Zanfretta: "I don't know..."

Doctor Moretti: "Zanfretta, remember how last time you tried to connect with them and call them, do you remember?"

Zanfretta: "Yes."

Doctor Moretti: "Would you like to try this time, too? Just for a second..."

Zanfretta: "Negative for this question, *tixel.*"

Doctor Moretti: "You do remember you showed a drawing to a friend of yours, don't you?"

Zanfretta: "Yes."

Doctor Moretti: "Has this drawing got something to do with the hidden object?"

Zanfretta: "Negative for this question, *tixel.*"

Doctor Moretti: "Zanfretta, it's important to you that you're considered an honest and sincere person, right?"

Zanfretta: "Yes."

Doctor Moretti: "Is this true? This is very important to you, right?"

Zanfretta: "Yes."

Doctor Moretti: "This is very important to you, right? You don't want Mr. Tutti or Lieutenant Cassiba to think that you're a liar. You would never want this..."

Zanfretta: "No."

Doctor Moretti: "For everything they've done for you, right? You don't want this, that they believe you're a liar..."

Zanfretta: "I'm not a liar..."

Doctor Moretti: "If you're not a liar, then why have you come up with that big story, you know, of the buried stuff? First you blurt things out, you lead people to believe you've buried some stuff, you draw it and then, just like that, you pretend not to know anything about it. Negative question... and, well, it seems to me... that it's not a nice way to act toward your superiors."

But Zanfretta, or whoever it was, didn't allow himself to be manipulated by this provocative panegyric.

Zanfretta: "Negative for this question, *tixel.*"

Doctor Moretti: "Who are these people that control you? I'd like to know."

Zanfretta: "Negative for this question, *tixel.*"

Moretti was trying every which way to avoid having the same answer, so he tried to ask more specific questions, referring to previous sessions.

Doctor Moretti: "Who are the Dargos, have you ever heard this name?"

Zanfretta: "Negative for this question, *tixel.*"

Doctor Moretti: "Zanfretta, you're not answering tonight, why? Are you afraid?"

Zanfretta: "Yes."

Doctor Moretti: "Are you afraid for yourself?"

Zanfretta: "Yes."

Doctor Moretti: "OK. Let me ask you this, and this you can answer. When you say 'negative question' etc., etc., is it a voluntary and conscious act on your part?"

The answer, had there been one, would have solved many doubts. But unfortunately it went as usual.

Zanfretta: "Negative for this question, *tixel*."

Doctor Moretti: "Why are you afraid?"

Zanfretta: "Because they can stop my heart... whenever they want."

Doctor Moretti: "Who told you this?"

Zanfretta: "Negative for this question, *tixel*."

At this point, having failed every attempt, Moretti gave up.

Doctor Moretti: "OK, Zanfretta, I will wake you up shortly, I will make you come out of the hypnosis. But, differently from the other times, you will easily remember this evening. If you understand this order, raise the index finger of your right hand. Very good. I will count from one to five and at the count of five, you will be completely out of hypnosis. Clear?"

Zanfretta: "Clear."

Doctor Moretti: "One, two, three, four, five, open your eyes now. Do you remember what we were saying Zanfretta?"

But the guard, still groggy from over an hour of sleep, didn't appear to be coming round very quickly. Despite being awake, he was clearly not understanding what Moretti was saying to him right then.

Doctor Moretti: "It looks like you buried an object, probably before July 5th. And you've drawn it, right? Under hypnosis you drew this object. I then asked you where you buried it, we tried to learn something about when and where you buried it, right? And you didn't want to, you practically didn't answer anymore..."

Zanfretta: "I'm convinced I've got it somewhere but I don't remember."

Doctor Moretti: "Therefore now, at a conscious level, you remember you buried this object?"

Zanfretta: "I think so, I already told him *(Giorgio Valle)*, if I'm not mistaken. I either told him or Mr.Mazza, I don't remember."

Doctor Moretti: "That you buried it or where you buried it?"

Zanfretta: "I don't know, I've been having strange moments lately. I know there's something somewhere... I already tried many times but I can't. I told him as well..."

Doctor Moretti: "Yes, I believe you remembered something regarding objects you had to take away, did you not?"

Zanfretta: "No, I don't know. I don't remember right now. I even buried something but..."

Doctor Moretti: "Right, doesn't this ring a bell, now that you're awake?

And he shows him the drawing he had traced under hypnosis.

Zanfretta: "It's a drawing that comes to my mind almost every day, I draw it every day, that's all."

At this point, anyone with a bit of common sense would have wanted to intensify the search to find out whether this object really existed, or to verify if Zanfretta's mental health was sound. Needless to say, that sphere would constitute unbelievable proof if ever it had really existed. Instead, everything ended with that hypnosis session. Having established the uselessness of hypnosis, the "Zanfretta Case" was officially filed away in the archives. From that moment on, Gianfranco Tutti was careful not to meet with me or other journalists again. The code word was "Absolute silence." And so the years passed, bringing many changes in the lives of those that one way or the other had lived that experience. However, despite the forced confidentiality, no one ever forgot about what happened during those two years. And just as nobody can erase a series of events that actually occurred, no one had the intuition to foresee the potential consequences in the immediate future.

CHAPTER 8

X-Ray of a Man

Several times during the period when I was involved in the "Zanfretta case," I happened to overhear, maybe on the street or in a bar, some comments on what the newspapers were writing about the night watchman. In most cases, the people talking about it were trying to find an explanation for everything by labeling him a drunkard or a visionary, someone with too much imagination, or even worse, a con- artist who wanted free publicity.

Setting aside any assumption on the matter, the fact remains that people (that is to say, the man in the street) are almost always more apt to look for some shortcoming on the part of the protagonist to logically explain the affair, rather than take into consideration also the circumstances in which the facts occurred.

Rarely, on very few occasions, do I remember hearing that the alleged encounters should have been studied, if for no other reason than to ascertain whether there was a lack of foundation. To tell the truth, there was investigating Judge Gian Rodolfo Sciaccaluga of the Genoa Courthouse who in those months advanced the idea of taking a deeper look into what had happened to Zanfretta. There were, after all, reports from the Carabinieri and police headquarters: why on earth couldn't we determine whether there might be something more or less illegal in this entire matter or, perhaps, inexplicable? But the eager magistrate let the matter go because there was no actual crime.

After all, if the investigations had found that in the night watchman's story there was a, shall we say, *abnormal* element, who could be prosecuted? One other time already, in Puglia a district court judge found himself on the bench of a trial against aliens that according to some eyewitnesses had caused serious damage to a farm.

Thus, there are two types of fear when it comes to UFOs and when, as in this case, the ufological theory interferes with everyday life: the idea of looking ridiculous and the search for an objective truth. Looking at it dispassionately, as strange as it might seem, the fear of finding a sliver of truth in the story of those people who claim they saw a flying saucer is such that we would rather ignore the fact by simply passing off the unlucky person as a madman or a liar. With this I don't mean to say that anyone claiming to have seen a Martian in the garden of his house is entirely sane. I, on the other hand, believe that in some cases – and Zanfretta's was exactly one of them – the competent authorities should have taken the responsibility of establishing what was happening. This, incidentally, is what Fortunato Zanfretta kept asking when interviewed by newspapers from halfway around the world, saying that he didn't want to look like a liar.

But who is this man about whom there had been so much talk? Some biographical notes may help to better understand this personage, if Zanfretta could ever be described as such. Pier Fortunato Zanfretta was born in Nova Milanese on December 28, 1952. His father Orazio, from Como, was the owner of a small circus. His mother, Margherita Colbucci, was born in Forlì and helped her husband to manage the circus. Piero, as they called him in the family, was the last of 13 children. Before giving birth to him, his mother gave birth to six sets of twins.

The family unit stayed together only for a short time. In 1959, as a consequence of the physical abuse he was subjected to by the Germans during the war, Orazio Zanfretta died. The circus was sold to another wandering company and it would appear it still exists today. After the father's death, some of the children went their own way, emigrating to the United States, South America and Australia, never to return to see their mother and siblings again. Margherita Colbucci took the four remaining children and moved to Genoa the year after her husband's death, in 1960.

They were tough years. Piero, only ten years old, after a period of time spent in a Swiss boarding school, started working for a milkman doing home deliveries. "I still remember how much they weighed," he says today reliving those moments. "I couldn't wait for the day to end so that I could go to sleep." Such work, too hard for a child of that age, created serious problems at school. In fact he was left back twice. Zanfretta's education ended in elementary school. From that moment on, he worked as a butcher, radiator repairman, baker (he delivered the bread on his bicycle), as an upholsterer, bartender, painter, furniture polisher. In 1972 he was in the draft and enlisted in the Navy. In the meantime, in 1973 he married Nirvana Mura, a girl six years younger, born in Carbonia. In 1974 he was discharged. In 1975, his first daughter, Margherita, was born. In 1977, Fabio was born and Zanfretta started working as a security guard for the Security and Patrol Institute "Val Bisagno."

After the UFO story, Zanfretta left his job on December 10, 1982 to become warehouse manager at the Genoese headquarters of Marumann, a company that makes cigarette lighters, but he didn't like the new job. Having been accustomed to being on the move as a security guard, he couldn't get used to the quiet life of an employee. Therefore he asked to be reinstated at the Security Institute but they rejected his application. He wasn't given a reason, although other night watchmen were hired back. Probably, taking advantage of the fact that his case was no longer in the newspapers, the directors of the Institute didn't consider taking back a former employee who had caused so much trouble from their point of view.

It must also be noted that in 1982, Gianfranco Tutti left the institute to take over a restaurant and nightclub on the Eastern Riviera, therefore many things had changed in the management of the company.

However, after a few months, the directors of the Institute reconsidered. After calling him in for an interview, and realizing that they were speaking with a completely sane man, they decided to take him back. It was great day for Fortunato Zanfretta. On December 1, 1983 he put on the blue uniform of the night watchmen once again and beaming presented himself to Captain Cassiba. Cassiba after all cared for him and if he didn't hug him, it was only because his manner, always a little deceptively gruff, prevented it. In any case, everybody welcomed him with great joy and he felt like he'd returned home.

Regardless of the veracity of the encounters, it is reasonable to wonder how Zanfretta managed to live through this long experience. No doubt it wasn't a positive experience. From 1978 to 1980, his house was bombarded with phone calls from pranksters who came up with the most ridiculous jokes just for a laugh at his expense. We have seen what the consequences were on the job. From a physical and psychological point of view, five years after the first event in Marzano, the man looked like he'd aged 20 years.

The facts explain more than any words can. Here, then, below, is the outcome of the tests to which Zanfretta was subjected over two years. These are the reports signed by doctors who had him in their care. In order, they are those of professor Cesare Ardy (report of medical examination of December 24, 1979), professor Giorgio

Gianniotti (neuropsychiatric visit of December 31, 1979), doctor Franco Lombardi (psychiatric examination of March 1, 1980), doctor Aldo Piccardo (medical check on employees on sick leave of March 25, 1980 at the municipal clinic of neurology in Genoa). (*A check-up on the truthfulness of the medical reports submitted by an employee who is on leave because of illness*). As we will see, no one feels they can provide a definitive conclusion on the outcomes of the visits.

1)- Prof. Cesare Ardy, Lecturer in General Physiology at the University of Genoa

Genoa, December 24, 1979

At the invitation of this respected company, I visited Mr. Fortunato Zanfretta, 28 years old, and subjected him to lab, radiological, instrumental and specialized tests. Mr. Zanfretta accepted to have the examinations performed and authorized me in writing to report on the outcome of the same, releasing me from doctor-patient confidentiality.

- Nothing relevant in Mr. Zanfretta's past personal history, except reparative surgery in his right leg following a road accident and appendectomy at the age of 22.
- Regarding the imminent personal history, I will not report the facts that prompted the current evaluation as they are well known; in addition to this, what appears abnormal: (1) an increase of 11 Kg in body weight from December 1978 to now. (2) according to the patient concerned, recurring episodes of vomiting, almost daily, which began in December 1978 and are on-going. (3) blackish urine in the hours following the four well-known episodes concerning him. All three things were reported by Zanfretta, and cannot be verified but are believable.
- I have performed a clinical examination and requested a check-up: both, in addition to being routine tests, include other specific tests to highlight any endocrine-metabolic disorders (related to his weight increase and blackish urine), autoimmune disorders of the paroxysmal nocturnal hemoglobinuria type, (suggested by the blackish urine) and gastrointestinal disorders (food vomiting).

In particular:

Clinical visit: objective examination negative for all organs and systems; X-ray examination of the chest: negative; cardiovascular bundle within limits; electrocardiogram at rest and under stress; chemical and microscopic urinalysis, blood group, blood cell count, urinary and blood creatinine levels, dosage of glycosylated hemoglobin, BUN, osmolal clearance, serum uric acid levels, serum cholesterol and triglycerides, transaminases and gamma GT, glutamic acid, oxaloacetic glutamic pyruvic transaminase, colloidal lability tests, serum bilirubin, ESR, radio-immunological thyroid tests, platelet count, CRP, RA test; research of urinary indoxyl, of urinary tract phenyl-pyruvic acid, urinary melanin, alcaptonuria; aminoaciduria, chromatographic fractionation; examination of electrophoretic serum; hemoglobinuria screening tests (PNH): Murri tests, biphasic haemolysin and acid haemolysis tests; serum radial immuno-diffusion; Wassermann and Microgen tests; EEG; spine, hips, knees, hands and feet X-ray; X-ray of the skull and of the stomach and duodenum.

- Nearly all the examinations listed above yielded results within their normal ranges: irrelevant deviations from standard values were found only for: gamma GT, Weltmann reaction (colloidal lability), serum electrophoresis, serum immuno-globulins, urinalysis (minimal, sporadic albuminuria), EEG (Small electrical alterations, popular, in course of hyperpnoea), skull X-ray (congenital malformation of the frontal sinus, slight hazing of the left ethmoidal sinus and moderate deviation of the nasal septum toward the right), spine X-rays (slight spondyloarthrosis with calcification of the supraspinous ligament of C1).

In my opinion, such slight and heterogeneous abnormalities by no means should be accounted for by the incidents reported by Zanfretta.

- Only a traditional X-ray gastroduodenal investigation revealed a clear-cut bulbar ulcerative duodenitis, with periduodenitis and gastric dystonia.

Summing up, both my clinical examination and all the laboratory, instrumental, radiological and consultant specialists' examinations have not shown any internal disease in the patient except a bulbar ulcerative duodenitis with periduodenitis and hypertonic dystonia of the stomach for which suitable therapy has been recommended, and that does not seem to have been the reason for the well-known night time episodes.

The patient has been advised to organize himself so that in the car and at night, he always has a container for the collection of urine should nocturnal episodes similar to those he described occur. The excretion of blackish urine observed by Zanfretta in the hours following each of his "absences" seems to be, in fact, the most important feature of his story for the purposes of detecting any pathological phenomena; the testing of that urine, if it were indeed the color described, could indicate diagnoses which currently do not seem likely.

Prof. Cesare Ardy

2) - Prof . Dr. Giorgio Gianniotti, lecturer in Neurology, specialist in Nervous and Mental diseases, Deputy Chief Physician in Neurology, S. Martino Hospital

Genoa, January 31, 1979

At the request of the Management of the Security and Patrol Institute of which he is an employee, I examined Mr. Zanfretta on December 28 and 30, 1978. Mr. Zanfretta is 26 years old, he is a sworn public official by profession, and was sent to me again on today's date to undergo a neuropsychiatric visit.

As on the preceding two examinations, I found Mr. Zanfretta in perfect mental and neurological condition.

The patient does not show alterations in his thought, nor any psycho-sensorial disturbances, and his capacity for free will, logic and criticism is normal. I believe, therefore, that Mr. Zanfretta is suitable for his work in an unconditional way and that he does not need periods of observation nor does he need any therapeutic advice.

Signed, in faith, for all legal purposes and use.

Professor Giorgio Gianniotti

3) - Dr. Franco Lombardi, Specialist in Psychiatry and Assistant Director at the Provincial Psychiatric Hospital of Genoa-Quarto

Genoa, March 1, 1980

Psychiatric Report for Fortunato Zanfretta, aged 27

I, the undersigned Dr. Franco Lombardi, Specialist in Psychiatry and Assistant Director at the Provincial Psychiatric Hospital of Genoa-Quarto, have been asked on January 8, 1980 by the Security and Patrol Institute "San Marco" to carry out a psychiatric evaluation of Fortunato Zanfretta, aged 27 and employed by the aforementioned Institute. Mr. Zanfretta authorized me in writing to report on the outcome of the same, releasing me from doctor-patient confidentiality. I report the following:

History

Family history: his father died aged 49, presumably of heart disease (the person under evaluation was 6 years old at the time), owner of a circus which he ran together with the family. Described as a good person, understanding, "protective," respected by those who worked with him in the circus, which he administered with competence.

Mother is currently living, 61 years old, housekeeper. Has no diseases worthy of note. Not very "loving" toward the son; after the death of her husband she sent him to a school in Switzerland where Zanfretta remained until the age of 10 approximately. Zanfretta, the youngest son, has 12 brothers and sisters (born from 6 twin births) some of whom he does not keep in touch with as they live abroad (U.S.A., Australia). There are no pre-existing psychopathological conditions in the bloodline.

Physiological History: born full-term presumably normal - growth and psychological development within the norm. Good eater, non-drinker. Zanfretta's personal history does not seem to have any outstanding characteristics. After completing his studies with some difficulty (he repeated the 2nd and 3rd year in elementary school, living in an educational institute until the age of 10 approximately, and concluding his studies in Genoa at the end of elementary school), he soon started working, first as a milkman, then as an upholsterer and eventually started to work for a porters cooperative at the port. After time spent in the Navy, during which he married, he went back to his previous job until three years ago when he was hired by a Security Institute as a night watchman. He is married with two children of two and five years.

Pathological History: common childhood diseases. Appendectomy at the age of 22. Tissue reconstruction of the lower right limb following a road accident. With regard to the following personal history, we find most significant the episodes during which Zanfretta claims to have spotted UFOs and to have had encounters with aliens. Leaving aside any description of such episodes because they are already well known, I am only going to acknowledge the following:

1) The amnesia concerning the event, in its entirety, especially as far as the recent episodes are concerned.

2) The persistent headache in the days preceding the meeting.

3) The excretion of blackish urine in the following hours.

Moreover, "déjà vu" phenomena occurred recently as well; a substantial increase in body weight in the last year; frequent episodes of food vomiting. All the above-mentioned ailments are reported by Zanfretta, they cannot be verified but are reliable.

General Clinical Examination

Patient is of average height and build, currently in good conditions of nutrition and blood.

Cardiovascular system: cardiac area within limits. Pure, rhythmic cardiac sounds. B.P. 130/80.

Respiratory System: symmetrical chest, expandable. Tactile vocal fremitus normally transmitted. Clear pulmonary sound. Normal vesicular murmur.

Soft abdomen with scar resulting from appendectomy; normal liver, gallbladder and spleen.

Neurological Examination

Normal and energetic global and local motility of trunk and limbs. Symmetrically normal deep reflexes. Cutaneous reflexes present and symmetrical, with absence of abnormal responses. Cranial nerve motility in order. Pupils isochoric, eucyclic and normally reactive to light, accommodation, convergence. Absence of spontaneous and elicited nystagmus. The cerebellar and extra-pyramidal systems and the sensory systems are in order. Romberg's test negative. Normal gait. No sphincteral disturbances.

A recent EEG revealed mild, diffuse electrical alterations, elicited by hyperventilation (see Prof. C. Ardy's clinical report dated December 24, 1979, which was made available).

Psychiatric Examination

Alert and oriented in space, time and as regards people. Appropriate composure and behavior.

Good emotional response to the environment and the interview. Absence of hallucinations. Occasional failures in recent memory. The patient shows global memory lapses of a probable psychogenic nature concerning the known and already mentioned episodes with the exception of a brief initial part relating to the first encounter. In more recent episodes the amnesia tends to increase to a total of 3 hours approximately.

During the hypnotic sessions which he has been subjected to, Mr. Zanfretta recalls and relates in detail the events that involved him without exhibiting any alteration of thought; absence of idea-generating discrepancies. Intelligence within the norm. On the volitional side: a slight hypobulia and a clear-cut hyper-suggestibility can be detected. Good spontaneous and intentional attention.

From the interviews:

The patient appeared collaborative and attuned, and apparently amiable at his utmost. He initially narrated to be a bit annoyed about what is happening to him and is rather put out because people don't believe him but is naively satisfied about the credit that others, instead, give him.

On the other hand he also appears a bit intimidated: "So I would like to see you there in front of someone who's taller than three meters: he wasn't threatening, but strange, all green, with red veins on his head, and all his flesh piled up like the gills of fish, eight fingers on his hand with suction cups and feet with nails lifted up off the ground." He had the impression that "they spoke to him inside his head," but does not have good memory of this.

He's not passionate about science fiction but his wife is; he, though, has withheld various things from his wife so as not to frighten her. He believes that they "take him" to "study him." His recollection of things is bad, it is only when he is very tired that he has the impression that he's dreaming what happened and is remembering it. When he wakes up, everything becomes foggy again.

He would like to listen to the tapes with the recordings of what he says under hypnosis, "after all they're his issues." His employers want him to take all these tests and he does, since after all, they're kind to him.

He was told that from one of the tapes it appears that he still has to meet with the "humanoids" who should hand something over to him. At this point he is very afraid; all of a sudden, together with the verbalization of his anxiety, he also makes manifest his repressed aggressiveness, which appears to be entirely generalized. He would like to be alone, he is comfortable in solitude. The aggressiveness is expressed toward his mother and the people who actually have held or hold some kind of power over him; he doesn't appear hostile toward the "humanoids," only scared.

The story of his life is a sequence of "partially" tolerated frustrations but he now seems to be rebelling, is no longer putting up with this socially acceptable mask and definitely becomes unbalanced under the effect of his reactive anxiety to the situation.

Regarding the *encounters* he still says that he knows when they are about to take place because everything begins two or three days beforehand with intense headaches, "as if they put bricks on my head," then he hears a strange modulated sound in his ears "like a flute that I don't know how to describe" and then he recalls nothing else.

At times it seems to him "to have become different," to "have powers that allow him to understand people better," but the explanations he gives appear to be rather confused.

Psychological Examination

1 - Intelligence Scale Wechsler-Bellevue (form 1). Verbal I.Q. 90. Performance I.Q. 96. Full Scale I.Q. 93.

The subject shows general intelligence values in the median range. The psychometric deterioration, correct, appears to be 27.5%, slightly outside the norm. During the examination the subject appeared sociable, motivated, apparently submissive. He made an effort and appeared to be tolerating frustration the perception of which did not induce either a competitive or blocked attitude. He has a tendency to minimize effort, and is not discouraged. His logical abilities appear deficient and cultural level is limited.

2 - Rorschach Protocol

He has a difficult relationship with the environment: it filters in fact through a repetitive distancing of the human figure. This is not perceived from the 3rd figure which when turned upside down, is seen as "a frog or strange being." However, when questioned about it, there are "arms." The 4th figure is seen as semi-human, albeit monstrous, but is walking away turning its back; he is "bothered" by it.

In differentiating between himself and the external world (Kuhn-Rizzo), a further difficulty is represented by a disturbed sense of identity and unity of the self (Jaspers). The presence of a face-mask

146

(2nd figure) that is repeated, albeit in another way in the 10th, upside down, points in this direction. This is exacerbated by the frequent perception of the content of 'eyes,' suspiciousness, fear of the observation and others' opinions, perhaps feelings of guilt.

Among the repetitive elements, even complex, there is certainly maternal symbolism, attraction and repulsion for the void, the hollow: perhaps this is a sign of immaturity or a sexuality that has remained ("fixated") at pre-genital emotional situations, basically pre-adulthood.

At the 7th figure an intense anguish is detected, which is also found at the 9th figure.

Another important element is the rushing of a multi-shaped crowd "toward that object" at the 10th figure. It is a strange fantasy, certainly related to a complex, given the stated movement ("they're heading toward" and when questioned, "they're moving").

All this because of an overt need to attract attention and to make a good impression by valuing himself as it is clear from the 8th figure. The narcissism of the coat of arms "like nobility" is immediately confirmed in the "reflection."

The 10th figure, with the crowd running toward the object, together with the need for self-assessment of an immature-infantile type, together with along with the constantly possible de-personalization and the sexual problems full of ambivalence, testify to a personality with decidedly hysteric-type traits and to an imagination that is inspired by events that could be - and which in our protocol appear to be - para-human.

3 - M. N. P. I. (Complete)

A picture of accentuated hypochondriac neuroses is taking shape. He has (100) with hysterical-type traits (72) and significant difficulties in building a relationship with the environment (Pd:70). All other values are in the norm. The very low score for the dishonesty scale shows a good reliability of the protocol. There are no psychotic-type elements.

4 - PNP Questionnaire.

The score relating to the scale of neurotic trends exceeds the norm (p. 72), below the critical score of 70 are both the scale of paranoid tendencies (p. 67), and the scale of psychopathic tendencies (p. 62). The scale of insincerity is very low, therefore the protocol is to be considered fully reliable.

5 - A.S. IPAT Questionnaire for the assessment of anxiety.

10 points, equal to the maximum level of disorganizing anxiety.

Extreme fragility of the self (p. 9). Moreover the presence of feelings of guilt appears accentuated (p. 9). High level of insecurity (p. 10).

6 - Reactive to Sacha's sentence completion.

A type of object-relation dynamic which is frankly negative is observed. Relationship with the maternal figure is very disturbed, ambivalence about the father figure.

Sexual relationships while not showing abnormalities on the level of heterosexual relationships, demonstrate a very bad opinion of the female figure in general, with accentuated underlying aggressiveness. Interpersonal relations are not easy; there is a tendency toward isolation and suspiciousness. Feelings of inferiority and guilt are accentuated, very low level of self-esteem. To sum up, the protocol underscores a serious neurotic imbalance which is generally present in nearly every type of interpersonal relationship.

Final Conclusions

In light of the above, we can conclude that the picture is one of neurosis, with hysteric-type patterns in a subject showing a generally low level of intelligence. There are extensive signs of disorganizing anxiety, intense difficulty in socializing and a generalized aggressiveness that are easily demonstrated as soon as the examination is no longer a structured task but involves exposure of some event he has experienced. He appears sincere and in good faith even though extremely impressionable and with a low capacity for criticism and self-criticism. It might be advisable to undertake some future investigation of the neurological aspect of the case in relation to the following elements: headache episodes - deterioration index corrected at Wechaler-Bellevue (27.5 %) above the norm - "deja vu" phenomena.

Dr. Franco Lombardi

4) - Municipality of Genoa - Neurological Clinic

Genoa, March 25, 1980

The patient suffers from ill-defined episodes of anxiety: it is certain that there are bizarre elements with phenomena of hallucinations and global amnesia. I see a certification by professor Gianniotti, but it says that he is perfect without going into the merits of the pathology. All the same, it does not express an opinion about the nature of the disorders. I see a psychiatric examination by Dr. Lombardi that does not offer any conclusive diagnosis. I cannot exclude a psychiatric pathology for which I request a more in-depth examination.

Dr. Aldo Piccardo

CHAPTER 9

A Comparison of Opinions

When talking about Fortunato Zanfretta's nighttime adventures, we cannot excuse ourselves from reporting the opinions and testimonies of all those who, for one reason or another, lived through the experience. The opinions of course differ. Generally, those who participated actively and directly in the *rescue expeditions* to find Zanfretta are more prone to corroborate the theory of *close encounters* and the ufologic background of the issue. The oddity of certain episodes, the coincidences and the signs often found in places where the night watchman was eventually found, have considerably contributed to consolidating the hypothesis of an exceptional event.

On the other hand, those who found themselves involved in this story against their will tend to justify what happened with a number of explanations that are somewhere between the logical and the inconceivable. Everyone, however, had the foresight not to fall into the trap of *I believe it*. As the reader has seen, there is no objective and irrefutable evidence. If this were a trial, I would have no difficulty in defining it circumstantial.

However, the overall collection of details and circumstances has raised many doubts and it is hard to get past them. Faced with this situation, we witness different opinions, dictated for the most part by the role that each individual witness feels they had in the affair. Let's consider, for example, the testimony of Dr. Mauro Moretti, the hypnotist who on behalf of the Security and Patrol Institute "Val Bisagno" followed Zanfretta from the beginning. After the first two sessions, Moretti asked for his name not to be mentioned in the newspaper anymore. Being a good professional, he believed that too much publicity about the Zanfretta case could damage his reputation. He feared, and rightly so, that his name could validate the UFO hypothesis. But, considering that not even he was convinced of what was happening to his patient, while confirming the oddity of the case, he didn't even dream of saying one more word about the objective truth of the case itself. The following testimony confirms this point of view.

MAURO MORETTI, M.D. specialized in Hypnosis

"Initially, we tried to learn from hypnosis if what Zanfretta was saying was the truth or it was a lie, if he was a truthful person or not, if he was crazy or not. I believe this approach was a mistake, although it was an understandable curiosity from a human point of view. Hypnosis by itself cannot guarantee one hundred percent that a person is sincere; it can guarantee up to a certain percentage of certainty, especially when employing some of the methods we used with Zanfretta before the actual sessions.

With this system, we can verify with a certain degree of accuracy if the person is consciously lying or not, as this may also occur while under hypnosis. In this regard, I can say with a good margin of safety that Zanfretta was sincere. Obviously the problem remains as to whether what he said was the truth for him, or if this truth also reflected an objective truth. If this is the case, hypnosis cannot assist in any way or at all.

I believe, however, that whoever wishes to examine the issue in depth must consider the story as a whole with its due importance. Hypnosis must definitely be considered, but so too all that extra data not revealed by hypnosis which was checked by people who I believe are until proven otherwise, worthy of faith and credibility.

The happening in Spain, the situations that were personally observed by Di Stefano, the state Zanfretta was found in, on more than one occasion. For example, if I remember correctly, there was that time when he was found with his clothes almost completely dry in spite of the low temperature and the fact that it rained or had just stopped raining. The temperature inside the car, the fact that he was found on top of a mountain, Mount Fasce, which is only accessible by one road, we also know that a car was waiting for him in the middle of the road but didn't see him go by, and yet he was eventually found on Mount Fasce.

Well, all of these things, together with hypnosis, can certainly create a favorable opinion: and in this regard, I do not think that I am able to express, and perhaps I am not the only one, a final and unequivocal judgment. However I believe that if we want to arrive at a partial conclusion, a conclusion which is entirely a personal one, we must look at the situation as a whole, in its entirety. We must therefore take into account what hypnosis has revealed, what the person's life has revealed, what has emerged from the psychiatric evaluations that have been done, and what has emerged from the

152

A COMPARISON OF OPINIONS

testimony of colleagues, friends and anyone who participated in and has lived with this story, and who has noticed certain facts, certain very precise facts.

Well, a person can get an idea, a hypothesis, from all of this. Then, whatever the idea, whatever the hypothesis, I would say it all depends on the personal needs of whoever reads the book, on their reasons for wanting to see one thing rather than another, for wishing a certain thing rather than another."

Giuliano Buonamici's testimony has a different take on things. From the outset of the case, Buonamici was personally involved because of his position within the company where Zanfretta worked. Being Gianfranco Tutti's right hand - the man who at the time was majority shareholder as well as technical director - Buonamici almost always participated in the night searches for Zanfretta and has therefore experienced the events that led to his recovery.

Buonamici also attended all of Zanfretta's hypnosis sessions and was responsible for the sound recording. He, like many others, was very curious about the nature of Zanfretta's *close encounters*. And indeed it was he and engineer Nino Tagliavia who installed in the car used by the night watchman a particular spy-radio which made it possible to locate it even without resorting to the complication of the radio-bridge.

This is his opinion.

GIULIANO BUONAMICI, technician

"Looking at it from outside, there may be some skepticism. Things change however if you consider things from within and knowing the spontaneity and sincerity of some of the people who lived this story. I am convinced that we are neither the best, nor the only ones, nor the most beautiful ones. Therefore, I am convinced that it is possible that other civilizations might exist, don't ask me if they are extragalactic or not - although in all likelihood they are, considering what we know about our solar system - and I am also convinced that what happened to Zanfretta could very well happen.

Clearly, I cannot say for sure that it happened to him. I can say, however, that some external events seen from the inside have deeply shaken me. What happened in Spain and other things that at some point, you know, are objective and do not lend themselves to dubious interpretations. Just as I have seen him travelling at night with the

153

headlights switched off, at more than sixty kilometers per hour on those tiny roads where a bike could barely travel on. And just as I went to the top of Mount Fasce and I saw that the engine of the Vespa 50 he was using was cold, no later than 1O minutes or at most a quarter of an hour after his arrival. In summer, an engine doesn't cool like that after travelling uphill for so long... I rode the Vespa down.

You're left quite shaken because when you know someone, I realize that you can't describe the feelings or the gaze of a person in a book. However, when you look in their face, you see how they act and how they speak, how they move and live. There is no one like him. And I wouldn't be surprised if what he said was true, and I don't see why we should be surprised today.

Right from the very start, Zanfretta was for me one of those fortuitous cases you could follow and document. If Zanfretta had been the typical husband who went to play poker at the pub, they would have found him lying on the grass, perhaps with his backside wet with dew, and he would have been beaten by his wife for saying that he had gone somewhere else. Moreover, he wouldn't have remembered anything, nobody would have investigated, the matter would have continued and from time to time he would have disappeared; ultimately they would have said he was exhausted and needed care.

On the other hand, everything started because Zanfretta was a security guard who had a handheld radio and who kept an eye on things during the night at the expense of other things.

These circumstances were the spark that triggered the process that was going to eventually develop. And then we find a journalist who, incredulous, asks for Zanfretta to be subjected to hypnosis. Clearly, up to that moment nobody could imagine what would have happened after. It is equally clear, however, that if Zanfretta had been any other kind of being up and around at night, none of this would have happened. Also because if anyone going around at night said: 'I saw flying saucers,' the immediate reply would be: drink less and stay home at night instead of going on a pub crawl!

This is what I believe. The fact that Zanfretta had a radio in his hand linked to someone who could hear, and that that news inadvertently came out because at the operations center of police headquarters just by chance they overheard his message, as well as the one transmitted by the colleagues who went to his rescue – well, that's what blew the lid.

I would say that after the first hypnosis everything became an inevitable succession of events. But before the hypnosis there was only: 'I'm going to see if there are thieves.' This, if anything, is proof of other things. Zanfretta was on patrol in that area, it is a tricky area, very barren and uninhabited. You need a good dose of courage and conscience to go there. Let's admit it, Zanfretta's got guts. I don't know if anyone of us, in February, would be brave enough to go to Torriglia at night.

And then there is the person's disposition to consider. Zanfretta is the typical person dedicated to home and family. He is not a pathological liar or someone with flights of fancy. On the contrary, he is happy with the small satisfactions his job gives him without expecting more. It must be said that, as opposed to many of his colleagues, he never tried to show off in the working environment with fanciful stories. I have to say that even on the occasion of Marzano di Torriglia he showed a considerable commitment to duty. Any other night watchman, seeing a light in a house so much out of the way, would have pretended not to see. Others would have asked the operator at the command center for backup. Instead he went to look. The fact is that perhaps Zanfretta does normally what others only do as a form of heroism deriving more or less from sense of duty and sacrifice."

Colonel Luigi Cereda holds the operating license of the Security and Patrol Institute "Val Bisagno." As we have seen, Cereda is a man accustomed to observing the substance of the facts rather than how they appear to the world. This positive attitude has fostered in him a strong curiosity about the true nature of Zanfretta's meeting. Skeptical from the start, after completing an inspection in Torriglia at the time of the first encounter, he became convinced that something had really happened.

Antonio Nucchi - who at the time was brigadier and station chief of the Carabinieri of Torriglia and who today is commander of another station in Genoa, further confirmed this conviction. But the encounters didn't end there. And it was precisely this long series of nighttime appointments that little by little caused Cereda's conviction to waver.

He was in favor of the decision to submit Zanfretta to all possible visits from specialists and in the end, he wanted to participate in one of the nocturnal chases. But on that occasion, Zanfretta merely stood with his nose pointed up in the air and nothing extraordinary happened. And so Cereda became much less inclined to believe in the existence of Zanfretta's extra-terrestrials. This is his testimony.

LUIGI CEREDA, owner of the Security and Patrol Institute "Val Bisagno"

"Regarding the Zanfretta case, my experience leads me to make the following considerations. If I'm not mistaken, the first sighting of the mysterious object and of the individual who was obviously in it, occurred near Marzano di Torriglia. I reviewed this with the brigadier who at the time was station commander of the Carabineri station of Torriglia.

From him I learned that during the night when Zanfretta made mention of this particular and extraordinary presence, at the same time, more or less, other inhabitants in the area of Torriglia had noticed mysterious objects flying in the sky over the valleys and all around Torriglia. I learned this from the brigadier of the Carabinieri.

Later that evening, the Carabinieri and I performed a thorough inspection around the villa where the meeting between the Zanfretta and the mysterious man took place. With the aid of large flashlights, we thoroughly examined the surrounding terrain and discovered some strange prints in the front yard and around the villa. As a result, we physically took these prints as evidence, as they certainly represented something different from the norm.

In any case, my impression is that something extraordinary must have happened during the first episode also because, I repeat, all the testimonies from the neighbors and from others who had reported these facts to the Carabinieri, all in all confirmed the presence of mysterious objects over the hills surrounding the spot where Zanfretta's episode occurred.

On the other hand, I have reservations about everything that happened after this, because my personal conviction is, reinforced by having followed him in everything, even in the last, shall we say, appointment with these people who evidently were supposed to meet him following all the episodes that this book describes, nothing happened. Then, when we came back to headquarters and we immediately checked the vehicle with which Zanfretta had performed these night maneuvers on the mountains, I personally ascertained that there were no signs of overheating of the vehicle, which were denounced in earlier events, nor of the tires of that same car. That is, everything was absolutely normal.

Zanfretta, on the other hand, didn't look like himself because he had to be helped out of the vehicle by his colleagues, had to be supported for a certain period of time and had a strong headache. Except for this semi-unconscious state after this last episode, I have nothing else to say.

I believe that everything that was said from the first episode onward can also be the result of external input, because in my opinion what Zanfretta partly described under hypnosis could be the result of advice or influence on him over time, leading him to interpret roles that, at the end of the day, did not correspond to the truth.

He is certainly convinced and in absolute good faith about what he declares he saw and lived through. I am certainly not an expert in psychology, but I am a pragmatic man who looks at what is concrete and real. The real facts are those that I have described here."

One of the most valuable testimonies regarding the sighting of the UFO which Zanfretta supposedly boarded, is that of Captain Giovanni Cassiba, head of the security guard department of the "Val Bisagno" Security and Patrol Institute. Cassiba in his capacity as supervisor of the guards personally led all rescue searches for Zanfretta. During those often very long nights, Cassiba and his men saw and experienced phenomena that are very difficult to explain. Having said that, I'll leave him to talk about it.

GIOVANNI CASSIBA, head of the security guard department of the Security and Patrol Institute "Val Bisagno".

"Two years later, I still hear people around talking about what happened to Zanfretta and indirectly to all of us who worked with him. Today, like then, everyone is trying to put forward simplistic explanations without having any real knowledge about the events of those days. Those of us who experienced it, like my men and I, know that reality is actually a thousand miles away from this bar gossip. Up there on the mountains surrounding Genoa, armed men who are undoubtedly brave, were terror-stricken after witnessing with their own eyes events so extraordinary that they cannot be believed. Consider, for example, that time when we reached Zanfretta on a hill on the outskirts of Marzano. When we almost got to the top, we distinctly heard his voice shouting over the radio that they were taking him away. I remember that in addition to mine there were also two other cars with the colleagues Travenzoli, Garbarino, Zanardi and Mascia on board. On a curve, just before reaching the spot where we thought we would find Zanfretta, we were almost blinded by a strong light. The engines of the three cars switched off at the same time. Lights included. We quickly got out but we couldn't see anything else. After a couple of minutes, while we were still looking around us, the headlights of the cars switched back on by themselves and this was the second time it happened, because once already on the hilltops around Rossi, our cars had a mysterious power cut. And so what was that glare that enveloped us? And why this recurring phenomenon of the cars that stop working like that? It was even more incredible when, looking for Zanfretta in the dark, we were lit up from the sky, I repeat, from the sky, by two large beams that were pointed toward us. I don't want to name names but one of us, terrorized, ran away. We were on top of a mountain, there was only the open sky above us, a dark sky in a dark and moonless night. From a cloud, all of a sudden, hovering in the air two big beams switch on. Then, perhaps in self-defense, I pulled the gun and I fired toward those lights that, unbelievably, were still hovering in the air, continuing to shine that light on us for a few minutes. Then they switched off and the night became dark again. It was impossible to distinguish anything.

All these experiences told by a man like me, someone with his feet firmly planted on the ground, should make us think. Besides, I was not alone. Do we all have visions? Whether we like it or not, we are facing something inexplicable, something that cannot be brushed off lightly. I repeat: I don't know why this happened, or why Zanfretta was the one to suffer the consequences. What I know is that it happened, and that is enough for me. Even if many get scared just by thinking about it."

When Warrant Officer Antonio Nucchi was still a Brigadier commanding the Carabinieri station in Torriglia, he never would have imagined that one day he would have to deal with a UFO-related problem. But it happened. The morning of Friday, December 8, 1978, Zanfretta's superiors went to Nucchi officially asking for his help. From that day, Nucchi had to deal with Zanfretta several times and several times, in fact, he sent detailed reports on what was happening in his jurisdiction to his Command and the Judiciary. But nobody ever thought, at least officially, of seriously investigating this case. Nucchi, however, had done his duty.

ANTONIO NUCCHI, Warrant Officer and Commander of the Carabinieri Station of San Teodoro, Genoa
"I have known Zanfretta since 1971, and when I was young

brigadier, I was, shall we say, a bit of a player, someone who wanted to work and also have fun. I knew him and I thought he was a much more serious person than I could ever consider myself. And so, when this particular fact happened, I thought Zanfretta had gone crazy, or that he had started to have rocks in his head or that he had been influenced by books or various films. Because at that time, we used to talk about movies as well. UFOs were, shall we say, something we talked about often.

Then, when I saw him, I spoke with him, I saw him cry, I saw him shaking, I saw him white as a sheet, and everything in the aftermath of the fact, well, it gave me pause. This guy was talking to me with trembling voice, white as a ghost, and he was telling me about this event.

At that point, since I knew him from before and even though I have always been very, very skeptical about UFOs, I thought that there might be some truth to his story. Obviously after this, I started my own investigation by speaking to the locals and listening to their various statements. Also because one way or another, I had to try and clarify this matter. The newspapers were talking about it, people were talking about it. Basically, as commander of the station of Torriglia, I was forced to open an investigation to see if the statements in some way were in line with what Zanfretta was saying.

And I can actually say that many people, for example Luigi Barbacetto, the gamekeeper, and Salvatore Esposito, Brigadier of the Guardia di Finanza, Mrs. Armida Ghiglino of Albora di Propata and also the Mayor of Torriglia, Giuseppe Cevasco, did see strange things in the sky. We cannot say that they were objects from another planet, but they were, to all intents and purposes, unidentified flying objects.

The first time I went on the spot with a few soldiers, there were also some UFO-ologists who took photographs that were then published in the newspaper. I must say, we did see something. Something of substance had been left on the ground. It was the same the second time, in Rossi: there were footprints that compared to my foot, far exceeded its length. I wear a size 10/10.5.

And then in Torriglia, there were people whose names I can't even remember who confirmed other events. Among others I remember Luigi Benvenuto, a.k.a. Jair, who while travelling in the car with a Mr. Traverso saw something in the sky.

Then, I'm not sure if this was a joke or not, we heard that one evening, while he was on the square in front of the church going toward the vicarage, Don Pietro, the parish priest, saw a thing above the parish church.

Someone else from Marzano, I don't want to say his name because he asked me not to, told me he had seen a UFO. A friend of mine as well who's a chef on cruise ships and who lives in Torriglia three or four months a year, has seen along with a girl from Genoa a saucer-like shaped object, kind of like a cigar with a belly, if you like, metallic in color, with a series of colored lights in the middle that kept changing. They saw it hovering in the air for about ten seconds over the Olcesi valley not far from Torriglia, and then it left in an instant.

And so exactly on January 3, 1979 I sent a detailed report to the Courthouse (*Pretura*) of Genoa and to its Torriglia offices. I remember the date well, because you don't forget those dates so easily.

As required by my office, I simply reported the first sighting to my superiors who in turn did the same. After the second case, in addition to regular reporting, I also wrote a legal report to the Courthouse (*Pretura*) in Genoa where I outlined the facts that occurred both on December 7 and December 27, 1978. I saw fit to also inform the Judiciary because in the event that these objects, instead of coming from other planets might have been terrestrial aircrafts, obviously there was a criminal law violation concerning the occupation of the airspace of a sovereign state.

All in all, therefore, even if I was very skeptical in the beginning, I have to say that there was something there, something had been seen. And then, quite frankly, I believe Zanfretta."

So that the reader may get a sense of the professional demeanor with which Nucchi approached the issue, below is the report "about the sighting of unidentified flying objects (U.F.O.) and of humanoids by Fortunato Zanfretta," which was filed on January 11, 1980 with the case file number 203 by Judge Russo of the Courthouse (*Pretura*) of Genoa. It should be noted that this report was also sent to the Assistant District Attorney of the Italian State, Luciano Di Noto, who as a matter of jurisdiction sent it to Judge Gian Rodolfo Sciaccaluga to investigate. Inevitably, the latter decided to stop any progress on this file.

This is the text of the report that in those days caused such a stir at the Courthouse in Genoa.

"At 12 p.m. of December 7, 1978, Mr. Cereda, owner of the Security and Patrol Institute 'Val Bisagno' of Genoa, informed this command that around 00:33 a.m. of the previous night, Fortunato

Zanfretta, personal details attached, while on his usual round of night patrol in the vicinity of the Villa 'Casa Nostra' in Marzano, saw a monstrous looking humanoid being approximately three meters tall and an extremely bright object that shortly after took off vertically with a hiss, disappearing into the sky.

On the morning of December 28, 1978, this command was informed once again by Lieutenant Cassiba of 'Val Bisagno' that the previous evening, while Zanfretta was going through the Scoffera pass toward Torriglia, the car he was travelling in suddenly stopped responding and contrary to the desire of the abovementioned person, started travelling at very high speed on the municipal road for Rossi, stopping after about three kilometers. When he got there, he got out of the car compelled by an unknown force and noted the presence of the bright object and the same beings that 20 days before had approached him in Marzano di Torriglia.

Both times, Zanfretta was tracked down about an hour after the radio silence by the same colleagues who since they had not heard anything from him, went looking for him and found him him in the above-mentioned places in a complete state of shock.

Despite the hostile weather conditions (there was frost in Marzano, it was pouring rain and there was a thick fog in Scoffera), to his colleagues he always appeared flushed and sweaty, especially in the head.

Also the body of his car, at the time of its discovery, was hot as if it had been exposed to the summer sun.

The undersigned, during a site inspection carried out immediately after receiving the news noted that:

In Marzano, on the lawn adjacent to the villa, a horseshoe shaped impression was noticed on the grass with a diameter of about 2 meters and was 3 meters long;

In Scoffera, on the ground by the roadside, n. 2 shoe prints with a heel of about 45-50 centimeters long, with a concave sole were observed.

Zanfretta had told the undersigned that he had approached the villa in Marzano because he had noticed some lights at the back of the house that appeared to be flashlights and, thinking that there were robbers, he went to the nearby lawn. Instead, when he reached the rear corner he felt a shove on the back and as he turned around, a big and ugly humanoid about 3 meters tall appeared in front of him.

As far as what happened in Scoffera, he only remembers that the car was travelling of its own accord.

On the afternoon of December 23, 1978, in Via S. Sebastiano n. 15/2 in Genoa at the office of Dr. Moretti, and in the presence of journalists and UFO experts, he was put under regressive hypnosis from which it was discovered that these beings had picked him up and taken him into a room of their spaceship that was all lit up in order to better examine him. (These details were reported to the undersigned by a UFO expert who attended the hypnosis session).

As far as the incident in Scoffera is concerned, Dr. Moretti in Genoa will perform the regressive hypnosis in a few days.

Zanfretta has undergone medical examinations at the Neurological Department of San Martino Hospital and has been declared completely sane apart from a slight hypertension due to shock. The undersigned has personally known Zanfretta since 1971, and he has always been considered a serious person. It has also been established that he does not resort to the use of alcoholic beverages or drugs.

Strange phenomena of very large and bright flying objects have been noticed over the last few months around Torriglia. These phenomena were spotted by many of the people living in the area. Among them I should mention gamekeeper Barbacetto or bBrigadier Esposito of the Guardia di Finanza (*financial police force*), but I could draw a list of names of more than 50 people.

We submit the above to the judicial authority which will deem fit to decide on the issue.

We maintain the prerogative to communicate further developments on the matter."

The Station Commander
Brigadier
(Antonio Nucchi)

The fact that Nucchi's report was taken seriously even by his superiors was confirmed by the dispatch of two telegrams that the Carabinieri headquarters in Chiavari, responsible for the station of Torriglia, sent to the following addressees:

Ministry of the Interior, Rome; Chief of Staff of the Air Force, 2nd Division, Rome; General Command of the Italian Carabinieri, Rome; First Military Territorial Command, Turin; First Aerial Region, Milan; Police Headquarters, Genoa; Carabinieri Division, Milan; Carabinieri Brigade, Turin; Carabinieri Legion, Genoa; Carabinieri Air Force, Rome; Military Garrison, Genoa; Central Police Station, Genoa;

Carabinieri Group, Genoa; Carabinieri Group Aerial Region, Milan.

The first of these telegrams was sent from the Communications Center of the Carabinieri exactly at 5:32 p.m. of December 8, 1978. Two UFO sightings are reported. The first, dating back to December 6, 1978, by Mrs. Armida Gillino of Albora di Propata, further on from Torriglia. The second one on December 7, 1978, precisely concerning Zanfretta.

The text says:

"UNCLAS NR. 387/1 =2 Stop 12/6/1978 19.30 hours approx. in Albora di Propata (Ge) a bright unidentified flying object is alleged to have been spotted for a few moments in good meteorological conditions at an altitude of about 1500 meters, direction NE - Stop - Witness of the above Gilino Armida born in Propata 6/7/1900, resident, who stood on a balcony of her home - Stop - Reliability degree: fair - Stop - Then at 00.30 hours 12/7/1978 in Marzano di Torriglia (GE) security guard Fortunato Zanfretta, born Nova Milanese (Mi) 12/28/1952, residing in Genoa in Via Orgero 9 apt. 1O, during inspection villa 'Casa Nostra' allegedly noticed at back of villa for a short time strong light source - Stop - Coming closer he claimed to have noticed a flying object, color red, blinding brightness, diameter over 10 meters - Stop - Zanfretta, terrified by unexpected event, went toward his own car parked at about one hundred meters alerting operating center - Stop - Immediately after, he allegedly was struck by bright shape with human aspect about three meters tall, who climbed on object and took off vertically with great hiss disappearing into horizon at high speed direction SW - Stop - Zanfretta was then found on spot by colleagues unconscious and agitated - Stop - Weather conditions good with clear skies - Stop - No witnesses - Stop - Noted on the ground impression 2 meters in diameter, horseshoe shape - Stop - Reliability degree: good - End - Capt. Carusi."

We can see that despite some descriptive imperfections, Zanfretta's entire first episode is summarized in the telegram. It is worth noting that in those days there was still no talk about hypnosis, nor had Nucchi completed his investigation into the mysterious *close encounter*. The Carabinieri Command became interested again in Zanfretta after the second episode in Rossi. The new telegram was sent to the same addresses at 8:19 p.m. on December 28, 1978. The text follows:

"UNCLAS NR. 387/3 =1 Stop 12/27/1978 23.46 hours Scoffera di Torriglia bright unidentified object oval-shaped spotted in very bad weather conditions (torrential rain and fog) - Stop - Witness to sighting Fortunato Zanfretta, born in Nova Milanese (Mi) 12/28/1952, residing in Genoa in Via Orgero 9 apt. 1O, security guard - Stop - The same was travelling in car and suddenly motor vehicle stopped responding to commands going onto municipal road against driver's will and stopping on a side clearing - Stop - Here Zanfretta saw bright luminous object from which bright shape with human aspect about three meters tall got out and who then took him on board where he had to lie down on the bed and was kept there till 00,10 - Stop - Subsequently Zanfretta found himself at his own car while bright object disappeared. - Stop - At place of sighting two long footprints 50 centimeters similar to shoes were noticed – Stop - Size, elevation, flight type, flight and object speed is not known. News believed to be reliable. End - Mar. Ordeglio".

Subsequently, the Carabinieri handled the Zanfretta case; but on the following occasions it was no longer possible to obtain the texts of the telegrams that had been dispatched. Let's not forget that these messages are considered documents of a confidential nature by the military authorities. To have been able to obtain two is more than satisfactory.

If it has been possible to follow Zanfretta's story right from the beginning, we owe it to Gianfranco Tutti. It was the former director of the Security and Patrol Institute "Val Bisagno" who authorized all necessary investigations to determine whether the night watchman had actually experienced the events of which he spoke in hypnosis, or not. And he was also the one who objected when the board of directors of the Institute wanted to fire Zanfretta to put an end to the whole story. And it was still he, in the end, who mobilized the organization of the company by providing men and mean, so they could obtain any concrete evidence of what was happening to his employee.

Later, when things were dragging on and following Zanfretta's case had become costly (the case had cost "Val Bisagno" about 15 million lire), on behalf of the Board of Directors, Tutti took it upon himself not to let the investigation continue. After all, it is difficult to criticize this decision. If the authorities didn't care to verify the facts (doing nothing but simply suspending the night watchman's gun license), why should a private company have to do it?

There were other problems too. For a variety of reasons the other partners of the Institute didn't approve of Tutti's management. And in fact, about two years after the end of the Zanfretta case, the former director sold his shares and started another business.

Today Gianfranco Tutti is a businessman owner of the company "Diffusione Giocattoli." Occasionally, he confesses, he still thinks about the days when Zanfretta's unfortunate dealings gave him a great deal to do. And today, like then, he still wonders what actually happened. In retrospect, he says, he feels like he is living the plot of a film.

GIANFRANCO TUTTI, businessman

"It saddens me a great deal that someone may think that behind what happened to Zanfretta there was a publicity stunt or worse, a set up. A Security and Patrol Institute such as the one I was managing does not make a name for itself by employing a night watchman who says he is seeing UFOs. If anything, it would be discredited. The issue is another. At that time, we found ourselves involved in a whole lot of wacky circumstances where the reference point was a man who up to that moment was the classic example of a good employee. Honest, fair, good father, always polite and helpful: who could ever doubt him? That's why when this whole business started, that's to say, that night in Marzano, every one of us who knew him looked at each other asking ourselves if we should believe him or not.

Let me explain: if the same thing happened to another security guard, he wouldn't have been looked after like that. After all, it's easy to judge hastily. You had to be there when he disappeared to realize how things actually were. You had to look him in the face when we found him on top of the mountains completely terrified, and we couldn't tell how he had ended up up there.

With this I don't mean to say that I believe everything he said under hypnosis. Personally, I cannot say I ever saw the beings of which he spoke, but I certainly lived through out-of-the-ordinary experiences while running after him during those famous nights.

I stood up for Zanfretta several times, arguing with my ex-partners. They wanted to fire him so that the issue of the encounters would stop there. I was always opposed to it. I didn't think it was right to put a man in the middle of the street just because, unwillingly, he had found himself involved in such a far-fetched story like the one about the UFOs. And in fact, when they suspended his gun license, I moved him to the radio command center.

Now, a few years later, I see everything much more clearly and I feel as though I'm watching a movie. I see this man who runs away being chased by a giant flying saucer, I see him with the monstrous beings that kidnap him, I listen to the reaction of a public opinion that is perplexed and curious about what's happening, I read the newspaper headlines that don't know how to explain the matter. I'm thinking to myself that it would even be funny, fantastic, if it weren't something we actually lived through.

I don't want to provide explanations: I haven't got any even for myself. I don't know if the extra-terrestrials were really there. All I know is that, in that instance, the authorities should have done something to get to the bottom of the whole story. We at 'Val Bisagno" had acted officially by informing both central police station that the Carabinieri of what was happening. We couldn't do more than that.

The result, however, was the transformation which Zanfretta underwent after those two years of hardship. I am older than he by 15 years, yet now he looks like the older of the two. His white hair, whatever they might say, didn't come from nowhere. Something happened, something that made him lose the original black color. I will let the so-called expert establish what happened."

CHAPTER 10

Mystery in the Mountains

At the time of Fortunato Zanfretta's *alleged encounters*, there were many who could not but wonder: why Torriglia? In fact, four out of five of the security guard's nighttime episodes occurred near the small town on the hilltops of the Genoese hinterland. The newspapers reported names of villages and places (such as Fallarosa, Scabbiabella, Rossi and Marzano) that are not even mentioned on the maps. All, however, are located in the area of Torriglia.

The description of the meetings with the *extra-terrestrials* and the unusual and mysterious circumstances in which they took place, embellished with details about the wild and lonely nature of those places, created that phenomenon that in the Genoese area became known as *Torriglia's UFOs*.

An inquiry into the Zanfretta case – theoretically taking the facts described by the night watchman as the truth – must therefore look closely at the area in order to ascertain why on earth Torriglia could be of interest to beings supposedly from other worlds. So let's learn a bit more about this town.

The town is situated in the center of a green valley at 860 meters above sea level on the border between the provinces of Genoa and Alessandria and it has 2921 inhabitants. It is a town and the territory includes the villages of Bavastri (94 inhabitants), Garaventa (75), Porto (126), Pentema (167), Marzano (332), Lace (483), and Ponte Trebbia (208).

To reach Torriglia, you need to travel along the State road no. 45 Genoa-Piacenza. Genoa, the Ligurian capital, is exactly 30 kilometers away. Because of the beauty of the landscape and the temperate climate with temperatures in the same range throughout the year (maximum daily temperature 22°C in July, minimum 4°C in January), in 1956 Torriglia was declared a health resort. In fact, the town has long been a holiday destination for Genoese who do not like going too far away during the summer holidays.

Torriglia shares a great deal of Genoa's history as it was dominated by the Malaspina, Fieschi and Doria families. Two popes were natives of Torriglia, Innocent IV and Adrian V, both belonging to the Fieschi family.

Torriglia's current economy is mainly based on tourism and agriculture, and has led to the development of the tourism infrastructure and holiday accommodation, well-equipped to accommodate the crowds that arrive every year during the warmer months. Before the Zanfretta case, nobody in Torriglia had ever heard of UFOs in the area.

"It all began back in 1978," says the Mayor Giuseppe Cevasco, "there were many people that winter who saw strange appearances in the sky. Let me start by saying that in my life I've never been interested in UFOs and I know nothing about them. But I can testify to what I have seen without any possible doubt. I remember it was evening and I was talking with some acquaintances when something that looked like a big elongated ball of fire, oval I would say, appeared in the sky. It flew in a straight line at low speed for a few seconds, then it suddenly increased and it soared toward the mountains. Of course, I have no idea what I saw might have been. But we can certainly rule out that it was an airplane or in any case a normal aircraft. The cyclical frequency with which these occurrences were seen in the sky by several of my fellow citizens started us thinking there could be unusual military exercises in our area of which we had not been informed.

However the Carabinieri confirmed that nothing of the sort was happening, but that indeed it was an issue of real unidentified flying objects. I couldn't say what kind of connection these appearances had with Zanfretta. But it is strange that the two events took place simultaneously and that they also stopped at the same time. In fact, from 1980 onwards I believe there have been no more sightings in Torriglia of UFOs."

The Mayor's was not the only testimony. Many witnesses confirmed seeing UFOs during the same hours in which Zanfretta mysteriously disappeared. Even the parish priest of San Onorato had to admit having seen those strange lights in the sky.

Despite all these accounts, the question remains: why Torriglia? When looking at the events, I wanted to consider the possibility of some particular anomaly in the geological formation of the area. My curiosity was piqued in particular by the characteristics of Mount Moro in Torriglia, 1030 meters above sea level and which stands above the area of Marzano where the first *close encounter* took place. What is strange about this mountain is the fact that it is the only mountaintop in the entire area that during thunderstorms is continuously hit by lightning. In fact, people who live in the area stay clear of Mount Moro when bad weather is expected.

Thunder and lightning have left plenty of traces on the top where you can still see dozens of fallen, damaged and charred tree trunks. This detail and the fact that the villa "Casa Nostra" is located at the foot of the mountain persuaded me to learn more about that place. I was wondering, in fact, if the lightning phenomenon was in some way connected with magnetic anomalies or similar occurrences.

But the answers I got made me dismiss this theory. I approached Professor Stani Gianmarino, lecturer at the Department of Geology of the University of Genoa, who confirmed that there is nothing to make us think that Torriglia and Mount Moro had anything particularly unusual from a geological point of view. "The geology of those places has no unique characteristics," explains Gianmarino. "The composition of the overlaying rocks varies between limestone, marble-based limestone and marl and is officially indicated on the map as the 'Mount Antola limestone.' This formation largely extends in the Genoese area and it makes up the rocky spine that extends along the coast of the Polcevera Valley to Sestri Levante, stretching out inland up to the Curone Valley. In terms of specific anomalies," the lecturer continues, "I have to say that they are neither of a gravimetrical, magnetic, or geothermal nature. The fact that, as the inhabitants of the area indicate, Mount Moro has greater incidence of lightning, which falls almost exclusively here, finds no explanation in its lithological characteristics. Such a phenomenon is rather well known in the Ligurian Region, where there are certain particular rocky formations. We can therefore assume that this depends on the position and especially on the morphology of this mountain."

Geological theory aside, there is only one theory remaining that could explain rationally on the basis of what we know, why the night watchman's unfortunate events might have happened in this very area. Since we are abstractly conjecturing, let's delve further into the imagination and try for a second to put ourselves in the shoes of the supposed *aliens*.

Supposing that *extra-terrestrials* do exist and that they are as Zanfretta described them, it would certainly not be easy for them to come into contact with a such a divided and generally belligerent people. Imagine, then, what the effect would be on a human seeing three-meter-tall giants with illuminated eyes ... For these people, then, the only contact possible would be if it casually occurred when an earthling fell into their hands by mistake.

But with what criterion would these beings select their human interlocutors? Clearly a flying saucer over 20 meters in diameter, as described by Zanfretta more than once, cannot land without catching someone's eye, unless it landed in a dark and isolated place. And who would they choose under such circumstances, if not the first passer-by that happened to be there by sheer chance? Let's not forget that the Zanfretta case would never have existed if the man wasn't a night watchman and if he hadn't been in radio contact with an operational center.

All of these things suggest that the area of Torriglia, still assuming that the meetings really took place, was the ideal place for the *extra-terrestrials* simply because it is sparsely populated (particularly in winter) and has vast mountainous areas, pretty much inaccessible to a vehicle on wheels, where an aircraft like that could actually hide without anybody seeing it. In fact, from Torriglia a stretch of the Apennines several kilometers wide extends to the province of Alessandria. In this section, there are only very few farmhouses and no paved roads, only a few mountain tracks known to a handful of experts connect its various points.

I realize that in making these considerations it may seem that I am taking for granted the *extra-terrestrials'* presence in the area. That is not so. It is just that we are dealing with a case, and I will never tire of saying it, where the objective reality is hidden behind a veil of clues and circumstances that in some cases are beyond human imagination. Only by analyzing these facts, one by one and without prejudice, can we hope to remove that screen, even just a little, and therefore face the truth.

CONCLUSION

Everyday reality, unlike what happens in the movies, does not finish with the words 'The End' on a screen; the main characters, whether they like it or not, continue to live it to the end of their days. Fortunato Zanfretta and his adventure are no exception. After two years of strange and not-so-strange episodes that were always very much a topic of discussion, suddenly the curtain fell covering oh so discreetly both Zanfretta and all those who directly or indirectly had lived his story.

And such is life, philosophers would say. In fact, the interests that the night watchman's curious and unfortunate adventure had touched upon, which were various and sundry, required a quick and discreet closure of the case. It wasn't difficult. After a few years of silence, any event tends inexorably to become hazy, blurring the details little by little. The name of Zanfretta, a few years after that first winter night in 1978, had entered the popular memory of the Genoese and of those who had read of the trials and tribulations in magazines such as: *Night Watchman Abducted by UFOs*.

Among other things, by fortuitous coincidence, from time on, UFOs have deserted our skies and the pages of our newspapers. Apart from the sporadic appearance of the *luminous cigar* on Monday, June 6, 1983, which as we have seen dug a groove through the airspace of half of Italy, the national press has not reported any further important signs of UFOs.

There were, however, a few exceptions. I am referring to two episodes respectively: Monday, December 8, 1981 and Friday, January 28, 1983 in two villages near Genoa. The first happened in Frisolino di Né above Chiavari. It was about 6 p.m. and the trucker Umberto Giomboloni, residing in Chiavari, employee of the company "Zappettini di Lavagna" was driving his *Fiat 684* truck which was carrying construction material in Val Graveglia.

After unloading on the State Road of Né, Giomboloni stopped for a moment at the restaurant "Cappotto" in Frisolino di Né where, together with a few friends, he drank an espresso with a sip of grappa. As the patrons later testified, the trucker did not go beyond the little shot of grappa. After this, he resumed his journey.

Leaving the trattoria, Giomboloni got back into his vehicle and travelled a few hundred meters along the lonely roads of the high hill until, reaching a curve in the road, he completely lost his direction. "I could not make heads nor tails of anything," Giomboloni said later to his family, still under the shock. "A few moments passed, then I saw that thing ... You can't explain what it was. An intense light that hung over everything and everyone. Then inside the cab of the truck between my body and the left-hand door, seven small flames appeared. They emanated heat, I even touched them and got burned."

And in fact, on the trucker's hands as proof of his story, there were evident signs of burns.

"I was desperate, terrified," he continued. "I couldn't move from there, as if someone were stopping me. The truck did not respond to my commands, the steering was blocked. I begged that light, those flames, to let me go away. It was a terrible moment: I prayed to the saints, the Virgin Mary. I didn't even know what I was doing."

But the most extraordinary thing, still according to the testimony of Giomboloni, had yet to happen. In fact, he said that gradually the light lessened until it disappeared completely. And it was then that he realized that he was a long way from the point he had been at the moment he was wrapped by the light; what had seemed only a few moments had in fact lasted almost an hour.

"I found myself at 15 kilometers from 'Cappotto' in the opposite direction from Chiavari, i.e. in the opposite direction of travel with respect to the one I had taken just before the event," Giomboloni specified. "Of course I am sure I did not turn around with the truck. How is it possible then, that I found myself so far away and furthermore with the front of the vehicle facing the State road, and not toward Chiavari? I cannot explain it. That mysterious force had engulfed me without me realizing it. I came to my senses almost immediately. It was 7.30 p.m., I looked at the clock. On the road I met two old men who seeing me a little dazed asked me what was wrong. Finally I got back home."

Giomboloni, married with four children, is anxious to clarify that he was neither crazy nor a heavy drinker and swears on the head of his children that what happened was the pure truth. The episode, however, passed almost unnoticed and apart from an update in local newspapers, nobody heard any more about it. Also because there was no one who wanted to open an investigation on the episode.

The second news story to which I refer happened in Montoggio, a small village near Torriglia, a few kilometers from the point where

Zanfretta's *close encounters* occurred. Midnight had just passed when the dogs belonging to the trucker Giovanni Gardella began to bark and howl furiously. Gardella, fearing the presence of a thief, took his shotgun loaded with five shots, turned on the lights in the garden, and went down to see what was happening.

Then and there the man saw nothing. Then he went near the point where the dogs' howls came from, and positioning himself near a tree, tried to distinguish the cause of such noise in the darkness of night. But what he saw was neither a thief nor one of the many wild animals that still live in the area. Before his eyes appeared to be the shape of what he described as a *very tall monkey* who, grabbing the dog, lifted it in the air hurled it far away.

At that point Gardella forgot he had a rifle in his hands. Beset by unspeakable terror, he threw the weapon away and fled toward home, taking good care to lock the front door. The next day, still shaken from the adventure of the previous night, Gardella denounced the occurrence, but as usual, no one worried about taking him seriously; in the newspapers there was talk of a *King Kong of Montoggio*, but no one made any connection to what had happened to Zanfretta not more than two years before.

Of course, it is possible that this episode has nothing to do with the mysterious interlocutors of the night watchman; however, the description of the monkey-like figure provided by Gardella and especially its height (the trucker did say that it had to be close to three meters) should make you think. But even this time, there were no official investigations.

One of the questions I have asked myself as I examine the summaries of Zanfretta's hypnosis, is the difference between the very unusual descriptions he made about "his" extraterrestrials and those trite descriptions that appear in the wealth of UFO-related literature. They talk of *close encounters of the third kind*, that is, of those meetings where it is assumed there has been direct contact with aliens, the latter are almost always described as small men no higher than a meter twenty, or bold young men with long blond hair who also closely resemble biblical angels.

As I am not a reader of this genre of book, I am not in a position to speak about it with competence. However, I felt it was my duty to do a little research to see whether in the past there could be some comparison or similarity with what happened to Zanfretta. It was not easy, but in the end, an analogous case, or at least one with a good number of analogies, did appear. I am referring to what happened the evening of September 12, 1952 in Flatwoods, West Virginia.

Shortly after sunset, numerous witnesses saw distinctly what looked like a large meteor land behind a hill. Impelled by curiosity, Mrs. Kathleen May, her two sons and a National Guard Gene Lemon, decided to go to see what it was. When they got to the top of the hill, the group saw a large luminous globe as big as a house resting on a field. One of the boys later says that he heard a *vibrating sound*, another said that he heard a *hissing sound*.

Not seeing any form of life around the strange apparatus, also because it was clear that it was an aircraft, the young boys and the woman tried to get close enough to see it better. It was while they were going down to the field that one of the boys, focusing the light beam of a flashlight on a tree, framed what was described as a monstrous figure about three meters tall with eyes that emitted a greenish-orange light.

They all saw it. Mrs. May also went to the point of saying that she had noticed on the body of the figure folds which were similar to those of a dress. Needless to say, terror took hold of the unwary observers, and every one of them, running as fast as they could, reached Flatwoods with their hearts in their mouths. During the night, some of them fell ill.

The following morning, on the other hand, a group of citizens led by the director of the local newspaper went to the field where the UFO had landed, finding two parallel markings of skidding in a large circular area of flattened grass.

The Flatwoods case was one of the few that the U.S. authorities declared trustworthy and free of any scientific explanation. As you can see, juxtapositions with the Zanfretta case are certainly not lacking. We observe, for instance, that the size and brightness of the alleged spacecraft match. Also, the witnesses' descriptions of the monstrous creature match: both the height and the illuminated eyes, as well as the folds of the body make us think of the description of a creature with the same characteristics.

What can be said then of the skid marks left on the ground and the flattened grass? In Zanfretta's second encounter, these two details were clearly observed by the Carabinieri who were in charge of the investigation.

The doubt remains whether Zanfretta could have ever read books describing the event in Flatwoods. But the psychological examinations carried out on him concluded that he lacked even fleeting knowledge of UFO literature. On the other hand, there would always be the question of who could ever have orchestrated a hoax of this kind.

Another question mark is the language that Zanfretta showed he knew during the hypnosis. I gave the recording of the mysterious words to Professor Umberto Rapallo of the Institute of Linguistics at the University of Genoa so that he could examine it. Given that the recordings had been carried out on a normal cassette rather than on a higher speed tape, Professor Rapallo had difficulty analyzing the content. As was expected, the lecturer could not draw many conclusions aside from the fact that the words were not part of any known language and that there was not sufficient evidence to assert that it was indeed a real articulated language. Rapallo, however, didn't feel up to excluding the possibility that what Zanfretta had exclaimed was in fact a message expressed in a language unfamiliar to us.

There are therefore many points to clarify in the Zanfretta case, last but not least, concerning the issue of the change he underwent from 1978 to 1980. Fortunato Zanfretta certainly is no longer the same man. Apart from the consequences of the publicity he received, he carries in his psyche and physical condition indelible signs of the mysterious adventures.

Someone accused him of maintaining contact with UFO experts. The only one with whom he had a relationship of friendship, Luciano Boccone, died prematurely of a heart attack in February 1983. Boccone was the only one who after the well-known events, occasionally but still sporadically, saw Zanfretta. Other UFO experts, after his name had disappeared from the headlines of newspapers, no longer kept in touch with him.

Yet in spite of the fact that time has erased the immediacy of those episodes, some evidence suggests that this man is still waiting for something to happen.

In the early months of 1983, some of his colleagues who worked in the vicinity of Torriglia recounted that certain nights they saw him arrive and head toward the hills of Rossi. He had no difficulty in admitting that, consumed by an indescribable desire, he felt he had to go up to those solitary mountains where he walked for hours in the dark and into the night.

But nothing more happened. Tired and dazed, at the first light of dawn, Zanfretta returned to his car and returned home with the feeling that once again what should happen had not happened.

Temporary fixation? Maybe, but who could expect to keep their equilibrium intact if, by chance, they had lived only a little the adventures narrated by Zanfretta under hypnosis?

Today he once again wears the night watchman's uniform. He is pleased that they have taken him back; in a sense, he feels reborn. He knows that in re-hiring him they showed great confidence in him and therefore he no longer wants to hear about UFOs. In a few words, he wants once again to live as he did before the *encounters* started; he wants to think only of his family and regain his serenity. He even wonders if everything that happened around him could be considered real.

The thought that the *encounters* could be repeated does not perhaps even cross his mind. If he did think about it, he would certainly remove it immediately. But who, on the other hand, can say with absolute certainty that the Zanfretta Case is closed?

The doubt remains and perhaps it will remain so for many years to come. Because it may even be that in the not-too-distant future, in some part of our small planet, a human being will present himself to the world with a sphere containing a luminous pyramid and say: "They gave me this. Look and be amazed!"

It is fantasy, of course. But in a world that has already entered science fiction, and that year after year crosses new borders considered impossible just yesterday, anything can happen. Who knows? Perhaps one day even the Zanfretta case will be explained in the light of facts that are still unknown. What is certain, though, is that before that day arrives, we will have to have overcome the fear of UFOs.

The map of the Municipality of Genoa. The three places where the close encounters allegedly took place are marked with a circle: Marzano di Torriglia, Rossi and Mount Fasce.

The villa "Casa Nostra" in Marzano and the garden in which Zanfretta claimed to have seen the "extra-terrestrials" and their flying saucer for the first time.

The semicircle-shaped print, approximately 3 meters wide that was discovered on the grass where the night watchman was found.

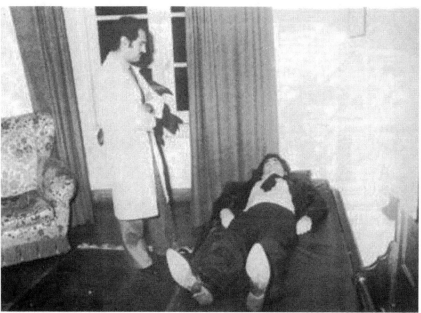

Doctor Mauro Moretti during Zanfretta's first hypnosis session.

Lieutenant Cassiba tries to comfort Zanfretta who has just woken up from hypnosis. Nirvana, the night watchman's wife, is next to him.

Those who attended the first hypnosis listen to the recording of the session. From left to right: Alfredo Ferraro, Rino Di Stefano (seated), Mauro Moretti, Giorgio Cesari, Angelo Massa, Luciano Boccone (seated) and Mario Nepi.

Zanfretta with his wife Nirvana.

The clearing where Zanfretta's second close encounter allegedly took place.

One of the huge footprints that were discovered near the car compared with the left shoe (size 10) of Brigadier Antonio Nucchi of the Carabinieri.

Zanfretta's "Smith & Wesson" caliber 38 from which six shots were fired.

Nucchi examines with other Carabinieri the ground where skid marks were found.

The two skid marks found on the edge of the clearing. In this spot the vegetation had been uprooted forming an area in the shape of a semicircle.

The same clearing three years later. Note how the vegetation has grown again to the edge of the asphalt.

Brigadier Nucchi takes notes while he questions Cassiba and Zanfretta.

Zanfretta on the spot of his second *close encounter*.

Night watchman Pesci confirms having seen a large bright object heading towards the village of Rossi.

Three night watchmen who were part of Zanfretta's search party. From the left: Mascia, Dellepiane and Travenzoli.

Radio operator Attilio Mazza explains in front of Zanfretta what instructions he had been given in order to monitor the night watchman via radio.

The issue of Tuesday, December 4, 1979 of the evening Genoese newspaper *Corriere Mercantile*. On the first page the peculiar coincidence of the UFOs seen in Spain. Zanfretta had anticipated the news the previous evening under hypnosis.

The flat area where Zanfretta was found after his third *close encounter*.

A farmer in the Marzano area confirms having seen the bight UFO.

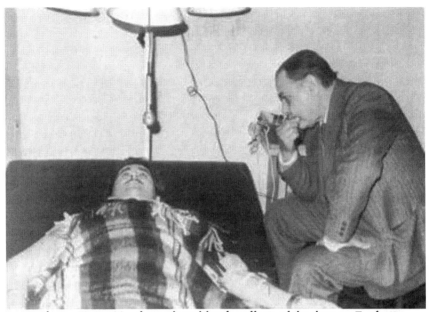

Professor Marco Marchesan is waiting for effects of the drug on Zanfretta.

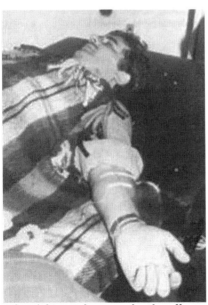

The night watchman under the effects of Pentotal.

Professor Rolando Marchesan after the session declares: "Zanfretta is sincere and reliable."

Luciano Boccone (with the microphone) asks Zanfretta a few questions. Standing, Boccone's assistant, Di Stefano on the right (seated).

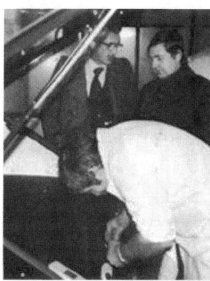

The director of the Security and Patrol Institute "Val Bisagno" Gianfranco Tutti (with the glasses) speaks with Nino Tagliavia, engineer, while Giuliano Buonamici installs a spy-radio inside the Fiat 127 that will be given to Zanfretta.

A detail of the wheel-hub of the 127: note the steel cable (marked with a sticker) which would have helped verify if the car had really been lifted from the ground by an unknown force.

Zanfretta and Tutti with Enzo Tortora.

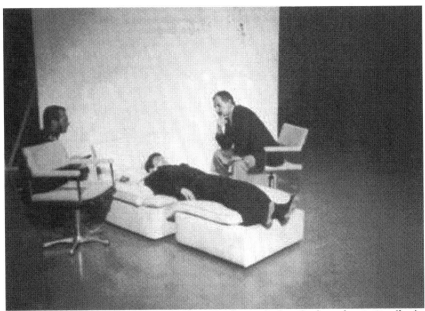
Doctor Giampiero Mosconi hypnotizes Zanfretta during the broadcast. Cassiba is next to the night watchman.

The guests of Enzo Tortora's program at Antenna Tre. From the left, standing: a TV assistant, Enzo Tortora, Cesare Musatti. Seated: Mosconi, Zanfretta, Tutti and Buonamici.

The text of the telex sent on December 27, 1978 by Warrant Officer Ordeglio of the Carabinieri station in Chiavari regarding Zanfretta's second *close encounter*.

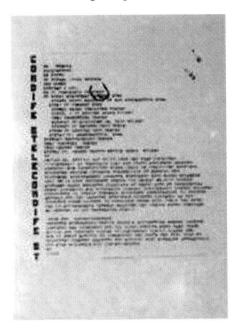

TRANSLATION

December 28, 1978
2019 Hours

FM CC CHIAVARI COMPANY
TO RIFA DEPARTMENT OF INTERIOR ROME
RIFTA AIR FORCE STAFF = 2nd DEPARTMENT = ROME

Ministry of the Interior, Rome
Chief of Staff of the Air Force, 2nd Division, Rome
General Command of the Italian Carabinieri, Rome
First Military Territorial Command, Turin
First Aerial Region, Milan
Police Headquarters, Genoa
Carabinieri Division, Milan
Carabinieri Brigade, Turin

Carabinieri Legion, Genoa
Carabinieri Air Force, Rome
Military Garrison, Genoa
Central Police Station, Genoa
Carabinieri Group, Genoa
Carabinieri Group Aerial Region, Milan.

"UNCLAS NR. 387/3 =1 Stop 12/27/1978 2346 hours Scoffera di Torriglia bright unidentified object oval-shaped spotted in very bad weather conditions (torrential rain and fog) - Stop - Witness to sighting Fortunato Zanfretta, born in Nova Milanese (Mi) 12/28/1952, residing in Genoa in Via Orgero 9 apt. 10, security guard - Stop - The same was travelling in car and suddenly motor vehicle stopped responding to commands going onto municipal road against driver's will and stopping on a side clearing - Stop - Here Zanfretta saw bright luminous object from which bright shape with human aspect about three meters tall got out and who then took him on board where he had to lie down on the bed and was kept there till 12:10 a.m. - Stop - Subsequently Zanfretta found himself at his own car while bright object disappeared. - Stop - At place of sighting two long footprints 50 centimeters similar to shoes were noticed – Stop - Size, elevation, flight type, flight and object speed is not known. News believed to be reliable.
    – End –
Mar. Ordeglio".

The text of the telex sent on December 8, 1978 by Captain Carusi of the Carabinieri station in Chiavari regarding Zanfretta's first *close encounter*.

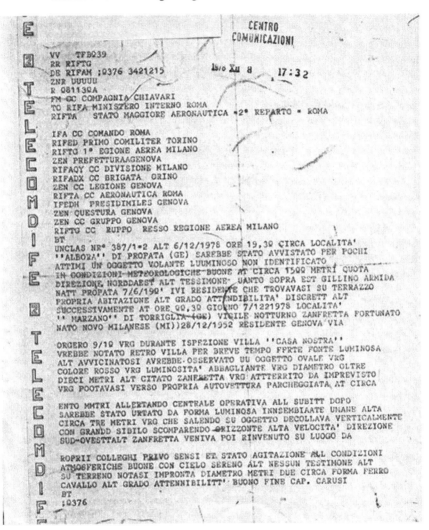

CENTRO
COMUNICAZIONI

VV TFB039
RR RIFTO
DE RIPAM :0376 3421215   18/o Xu 8   17:32
ZNR UUUUU
R 081130A
FM CC COMPAGNIA CHIAVARI
TO RIFA MINISTERO INTERNO ROMA
RIFTA STATO MAGGIORE AERONAUTICA -2° REPARTO - ROMA

IFA CC COMANDO ROMA
RIFED PRIMO COMILITER TORINO
RIFTO 1° EGIONE AEREA MILANO
ZEN PREFETTURA GENOVA
RIFAQY CC DIVISIONE MILANO
RIFADX CC BRIGATA ORINO
ZEN CC LEGIONE GENOVA
RIFTA CC AERONAUTICA ROMA
IFEDM PRESIDIMILES GENOVA
ZEN QUESTURA GENOVA
ZEN CC GRUPPO GENOVA
RIFTO CC RUPPO RESSO REGIONE AEREA MILANO
BT
UNCLAS NR° 387/1-2 ALT 6/12/1978 ORE 19,30 CIRCA LOCALITA'
''ALBOZA'' DI PROPATA (GE) SAREBBE STATO AVVISTATO PER POCHI
ATTIMI UN OGGETTO VOLANTE LUUMINOSO NON IDENTIFICATO
IN CONDIZIONI METEOROLOGICHE BUONE AT CIRCA 1500 METRI QUOTA
DIREZIONE NORDDAEST ALT TESSIMONE UANTO SOPRA EST GILLINO ARMIDA
NATT PROPATA 7/6/190' IVI RESIDENTE CHE TROVAVASI SU TERRAZZO
PROPRIA ABITAZIONE ALT GRADO ATTENDIBILITA' DISCRETT ALT
SUCCESSIVAMENTE AT ORE 00,30 GIORNO 7/1221978 LOCALITA'
'' MARZANO'' DI TORRIGLIA (GE) VIGILE NOTTURNO ZANFRETTA FORTUNATO
NATO NOVO MILANESE (MI) 28/12/1952 RESIDENTE GENOVA VIA

ORGERO 9/19 VRG DURANTE ISPEZIONE VILLA ''CASA NOSTRA''
VREBBE NOTATO RETRO VILLA PER BREVE TEMPO FFRTE FONTE LUMINOSA
ALT AVVICINATOSI AVREBBE OSSERVATO UU OGGETTO OVALE VRG
COLORE ROSSO VRG LUMINOSITA' ABBAGLIANTE VRG DIAMETRO OLTRE
DIECI METRI ALT CITATO ZANFRETTA VRG ATTTERRITO DA IMPREVISTO
VRG POOTAVASI VERSO PROPRIA AUTOVETTURA PARCHEGGIATA AT CIRCA

ENTO MMTRI ALLERTANDO CENTRALE OPERATIVA ALL SUBITT DOPO
SAREBBE STATO URTATO DA FORMA LUMINOSA INNSEMBIAATE UMANE ALTA
CIRCA TRE METRI VRG CHE SALENDO SU OGGETTO DECOLLAVA VERTICALMENTE
CON GRANDD SIBILO SCOMPARENDO ORIZZONTE ALTA VELOCITA' DIREZIONE
SUD-OVESTTALT ZANFRETTA VENIVA POI RINVENUTO SU LUOGO DA

ROPRII COLLEGHI PRIVO SENSI ET STATO AGITAZIONE ALL CONDIZIONI
ATMOSFERICHE BUONE CON CIELO SERENO ALT NESSUN TESTIMONE ALT
SU TERRENO NOTASI IMPRONTA DIAMETRO METRI DUE CIRCA FORMA FERRO
CAVALLO ALT GRADO ATTENNIBILITT' BUONO FINE CAP. CARUSI
BT
:0376

TRANSLATION

VV TF BO39
RR RIFTG
DE RIFAM; Q376 3421215
ZNR UUUUU
R Q81130A
FM CC CHIAVARI COMPANY
TO RIFA DEPARTMENT OF INTERIOR ROME
RIFTA AIR FORCE STAFF = 2nd DEPARTMENT = ROME

Ministry of the Interior, Rome
Chief of Staff of the Air Force, 2nd Division, Rome
General Command of the Italian Carabinieri, Rome
First Military Territorial Command, Turin
First Aerial Region, Milan
Police Headquarters, Genoa
Carabinieri Division, Milan
Carabinieri Brigade, Turin
Carabinieri Legion, Genoa
Carabinieri Air Force, Rome
Military Garrison, Genoa
Central Police Station, Genoa
Carabinieri Group, Genoa
Carabinieri Group Aerial Region, Milan.

"UNCLAS NR. 387/1 =2 Stop 12/6/1978 1930 hours approx. in Albora di Propata (Ge) a bright unidentified flying object is alleged to have been spotted for a few moments in good meteorological conditions at an altitude of about 1500 meters, direction NE - Stop - Witness of the above Gilino Armida born in Propata 6/7/1900, resident, who stood on a balcony of her home - Stop - Reliability degree: fair - Stop - Then at 12:30 a.m. of 12/7/1978 in Marzano di Torriglia (GE) security guard Fortunato Zanfretta, born Nova Milanese (MI) 12/28/1952, residing in Genoa in Via Orgero 9 apt. 10, during inspection villa 'Casa Nostra' allegedly noticed at back of villa for a short time strong light source - Stop - Coming closer he claimed to have noticed a flying object, color red, blinding brightness, diameter over 10 meters - Stop - Zanfretta, terrified by unexpected event, went toward his own car parked at about one hundred meters alerting operating center - Stop - Immediately after, he allegedly was struck by bright shape with human aspect about three meters tall, who climbed on object and took off vertically with great hiss disappearing into horizon at high speed direction SW - Stop - Zanfretta was then found on spot by colleagues unconscious and agitated - Stop - Weather conditions good with clear skies - Stop - No witnesses - Stop - Noted on the ground impression 2 meters in diameter, horseshoe shape - Stop - Reliability degree: good

– End –

Capt. Carusi."

The information report sent on January 3, 1979 but Brigadier Nucchi to the Magistrate's Court of Genoa.

TORRIGLIA

N. 203 Reg. Gen.   Anno 79

PRETURA UNIFICATA DI GENOVA

Sezione .... N. .... Reg. P. M.

Giudice Russo   N. .... R. G. Ist.

PROCEDIMENTO PENALE

CONTRO

A.R. ad avvistamento di UFO

in data 7-12-78

IMPUTATO

<table>
<tr><td colspan="2">PRESCRIZIONI</td><td>N. .... Reg. Corpi Reato</td></tr>
<tr><td colspan="2">Data del reato ....</td><td>N. .... Reg. Esecuzioni</td></tr>
<tr><td colspan="2">Data prescrizione ordinaria a) ....</td><td>N. .... Campione</td></tr>
<tr><td colspan="2">b) ....</td><td>N. .... Mod. I</td></tr>
<tr><td colspan="2">Data prescrizione interruz. a) ....</td><td>Scheda per il casellario il ....</td></tr>
<tr><td colspan="2">b) ....</td><td>Scheda minorile il ....</td></tr>
</table>

Decr. penale ....

Decr. pen. in notifica ....

Notificato il ....

Opposto il ....

Sentenza n. .... del ....

impugnata il ....

Scheda Istat. il ....

Comun. Uff. Elettorale il ....
(Art. 25 n. 3 Legge 7-10-1947, n. 1058)

Rituali e penali il ....

Spese anticipate L. ....

Archiviato il 11-1-80

R.G.P. Pretura Genova- Mod. 4 - Tip. S. Anna

N.3947/1 P di prot.   Torriglia,11 3.1.1979.

OGGETTO: RAPPORTO INFORMATIVO: circa l'avvistamento di oggetti vola.
                               non identificati (O.V.N.I.) ed umanoidi
                               da parte di:

                             - ZANFRETTA Fortunato nato il 28.12.1952 a
                               Novo Milanese, residente a Genova-Sampier·
                               darena via Orgero n.9/10, coniugato, vigi-
                               le notturno presso la Val Bisagno di Geno-
                               va.

                             Fatti avvenuti sulla notte del 7.12.978
                             in località Marzano e sulla notte del 28.
                             12.1978 in località Scoffera.

ALLA PRETURA UNIFICATA   DI
-Sezione di Torriglia-   16100   GENOVA

e, per conoscenza:

AL COMANDO DELLA COMPAGNIA CARABINIERI DI

                                               16043   CHIAVARI

        Alle ore 12 del 7.12.1978, il Dott.CEREDA, titolare della
Società di vigilanza "Val Bisagno" di Genova, informava questo
Comando che verso le ore 00,33 della decorsa notte, ZANFRETTA
Fortunato, in rubrica generalizzato, mentre effettuava il soli-
to giro di vigilanza notturna nei pressi della Villa "Casa Nostra"
in località Marzano, avvistava un essere umanoide alto circa tre
metri di aspetto mostruoso ed un oggetto fortemente luminoso che
poco dopo decollava in verticale con un sibilo, scomparendo nel
cielo.

        Nella mattinata del 28.12.1978, questo Comando veniva nuova-
mente informato dal Tenente Cassiba della Valbisagno, che il ZAN-
FRETTA, la sera precedente, mentre stava transitando in località
Scoffera diretto a Torriglia, improvvisamente l'autovettura sulla
quale viaggiava non rispondeva più ai comandi e si dirigeva contro
la volontà del suddetto,a velocità molto elevata, sulla strada
Comunale per Rossi, arrestandosi dopo circa tre kilometri. Ivi
giunto una forza sconosciuta lo spingeva a scendere e constatava
la presenza dell'oggetto luminoso unitamente agli stessi esseri
che 20 giorni prima lo avevano avvicinato in località Marzano di
Torriglia.

        Entrambe le volte, il ZANFRETTA, è stato rintracciato, dopo

circa un'ora dal silenzio radio, dagli stessi colleghi che non
avendo avuto più sue notizie si erano recati a cercarlo, rintrac-
ciandolo nei suddetti luoghi, in forte stato di shock.

Lo stesso, ai colleghi, nonostante le avverse condizioni
atmosferiche(in Marzano era in corso la "galaverna" ed a Scòf-
fera vi era fitta nebbia e pioveva a dirotto) è sempre apparso
molto accaldato e sudato specialmente nella testa.

Anche l'autovettura dello stesso al momento del ritrovamen-
to si presentava con la carrozzeria calda come se fosse rimasta
esposta ai raggi del sole estivo.

Lo scrivente, nell'ispezione subito effettuata nei luoghi
subito dopo aver ricevuto la notizia ha constatato che:
- In Marzano, nel prato adiacente alla villa si notava sull'erba
  un'impronta a forma di ferro di cavallo di diametro di circa
  2 metri e lunga 3 metri;
- In Scoffera, nella terra sul ciglio della strada, si notavano
  n.2 impronte di scarpa con tacco della lunghezza di circa 45-50
  centimetri, con suola concava.

Il ZANFRETTA, aveva riferito allo scrivente che in Marzano
si era avvicinato alla Villa perchè aveva notato delle
pile sul retro e pensando che vi fossero dei ladri si è recato
nel prato vicino. Invece, quando giunse nei pressi dell'angolo
posteriore si sentì urtare nella schiena e voltandosi gli appar-
ve di fronte un essere umanoide alto circa metri 3, di aspetto
grosso e orrendo.

Per quanto riguarda il fatto avvenuto alla Scoffera ricor-
da solamente che la macchina procedeva per proprio conto.

Il giorno 23.12.1978, nel pomeriggio, in Genova via San Sebastiano n.15/2, presso lo studio del Dott.MORETTI, ed alla presenza di giornalisti ed ufologi, è stato sottoposto ad ipnosi re-
gressiva dalla quale è risultato che questi esseri lo hanno pre-
levato e condotto in una sala illuminata della propria astronave
per poterlo meglio esaminare.(Questi particolari sono stati riferi-
ti allo scrivente da un ufologo che ha assistito all'ipnosi).

Per quanto riguarda invece l'episodio accaduto a Scoffera
la regressione ipnotica verrà effettuata a giorni, sempre a cura
del Dott.MORETTI di Genova.

o/o/o

Il ZANFRETTA, è stato anche sottoposto a visite presso il reparto Neurologico dell'Ospedale di San Martino ed è stato riconosciuto sanissimo di mente se si esclude una leggera ipertensione dovuta agli shock subiti.

Lo scrivente conosce personalmente il ZANFRETTA sin dal 1971 ed è sempre stato ritenuto persona seria. E' accertato inoltre che il predetto non è dedito all'uso di bevande alcooliche o sostanze stupefacenti.

Nella zona di Torriglia, da alcuni mesi, si notano strani fenomeni di oggetti volanti molto grossi e luminosi. Detti fenomeni sono stati rilevati da molti abitanti della zona tra i quali si può citare il guardiacaccia BARBACETTO oppure il gadiere della Guardia di Finanza ESPOSITO, fino a completare elenco di nominativi di oltre 50 persone.

Quanto sopra si riferisce per quanto Codesta Spett/le A.G. riterrà opportuno adottare.

Si fa riserva di comunicare ulteriori sviluppi della vicenda.

Il brigadiere
comandante della stazione
(Antonio Nucchi)

TRANSLATION

CARABINIERI LEGION OF GENOA
Torriglia Station

N. 3497/1 P of prot.   Torriglia, January 3, 1979

Object: INFORMATION REPORT about U.F.O. sighting and aliens by:
ZANFRETTA Fortunato born on December 28, 1952 at Nova Milanese, resident at Genoa-Sampierdarena, Via Orgero no. 9 apt. 10, married, ,security guard working for Val Bisagno in Genoa.

Facts happened in the night of December 7, 1978 at Marzano and in the night of December 28, 1978 at Scoffera Pass.

TO THE MAGISTRATE's Court of Genoa
Torriglia Section
and, in acknowledgement:
TO CARABINIERI HEADQUARTERS OF CHIAVARI

At 12:00 p.m. of December 7, 1978, Mr. Cereda, owner of the Security and Patrol Institute 'Val Bisagno' of Genoa, informed this command that around 12:33 a.m. of the previous night, Fortunato Zanfretta, personal details attached, while on his usual round of night patrol in the vicinity of the Villa 'Casa Nostra' in Marzano, saw a monstrous looking humanoid being approximately three meters tall and an extremely bright object that shortly after took off vertically with a hiss, disappearing into the sky.

On the morning of December 28, 1978, this command was informed once again by Lieutenant Cassiba of 'Val Bisagno' that the previous evening, while Zanfretta was going through the Scoffera pass toward Torriglia, the car he was travelling in suddenly stopped responding and contrary to the desire of the abovementioned person, started travelling at very high speed on the municipal road for Rossi, stopping after about three kilometers. When he got there, he got out of the car compelled by an unknown force and noted the presence of the bright object and the same beings that 20 days before had approached him in Marzano di Torriglia.

200

Both times, Zanfretta was tracked down about an hour after the radio silence by the same colleagues who since they had not heard anything from him, went looking for him and found him him in the above-mentioned places in a complete state of shock.

Despite the hostile weather conditions (there was frost in Marzano, it was pouring rain and there was a thick fog in Scoffera), to his colleagues he always appeared flushed and sweaty, especially in the head.

Also the body of his car, at the time of its discovery, was hot as if it had been exposed to the summer sun.

The undersigned, during a site inspection carried out immediately after receiving the news noted that:

In Marzano, on the lawn adjacent to the villa, a horseshoe shaped impression was noticed on the grass with a diameter of about 2 meters and was 3 meters long;

In Scoffera, on the ground by the roadside, n. 2 shoe prints with a heel of about 45-50 centimeters long, with a concave sole were observed.

Zanfretta had told the undersigned that he had approached the villa in Marzano because he had noticed some lights at the back of the house that appeared to be flashlights and, thinking that there were robbers, he went to the nearby lawn. Instead, when he reached the rear corner he felt a shove on the back and as he turned around, a big and ugly humanoid about 3 meters tall appeared in front of him.

As far as what happened in Scoffera, he only remembers that the car was travelling of its own accord.

On the afternoon of December 23, 1978, in Via S. Sebastiano no. 15 apt. 2 in Genoa at the office of Dr. Moretti, and in the presence of journalists and UFO experts, he was put under regressive hypnosis from which it was discovered that these beings had picked him up and taken him into a room of their spaceship that was all lit up in order to better examine him. (These details were reported to the undersigned by a UFO expert who attended the hypnosis session).

As far as the incident in Scoffera is concerned, Dr. Moretti in Genoa will perform the regressive hypnosis in a few days.

Zanfretta has undergone medical examinations at the Neurological Department of San Martino Hospital and has been declared completely sane apart from a slight hypertension due to shock. The undersigned has personally known Zanfretta since 1971, and he has always been considered a serious person. It has also been established that he does not resort to the use of alcoholic beverages or drugs.

Strange phenomena of very large and bright flying objects have been noticed over the last few months around Torriglia. These phenomena were spotted by many of the people living in the area. Among them I should mention gamekeeper Barbacetto or Brigadier Esposito of the Guardia di Finanza (*financial police force*), but I could draw a list of names of more than 50 people.

We submit the above to the judicial authority which will deem fit to decide on the issue.

We maintain the prerogative to communicate further developments on the matter."

The Station Commander
Brigadier
(Antonio Nucchi)

The sentence passed by the Genoa magistrate's Court.

n: 203/79

PRETURA UNIFICATA DI GENOVA

Il Pretore

V° l'art. 74 c.p.p.

estremi di reato
per mancanza di
di querela (art.   c.p.)

Ordina

l'archiviazione degli atti

Genova 31-12-79

Il Pretore   Il Cancelliere

TRANSLATION

GENOA MAGISTRATE'S COURT
The Lower Court Judge
seen the article 74 of the Code of Criminal
lack of criminal evidence
Orders
to dismiss the case
Genoa, December 31, 1979

The Lower Court Judge   The Justice Clerk

203

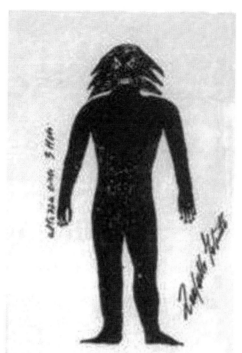

Here is how Zanfretta has graphically reconstructed the image of one of the aliens that kidnapped him.

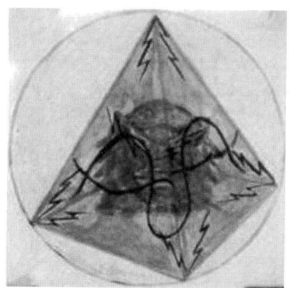

The sphere that the *aliens* allegedly had to deliver to Zanfretta in an artistic reconstruction by painter Giuseppina Stabile.

FOREIGN FORUM

UFO FLAP 1978:

Villa Casa Nostra - the scene of the action - and Fortunato Zanfretta

ITALIAN STYLE

PART TWO: DECEMBER

Last issue, we examined the first three months of the four-month UFO flap in Italy from September through December of 1978. By far, December was the peak month for total number of reports, although many of the ones celebrated in the press - replete with photographs obscured by time exposures and extremely long telephoto lenses - seem to be based on sightings of Venus in the pre-dawn eastern sky. Indeed, Roberto Pinotti informed us that on December 7, at dawn between Caorle and Jesolo, strange craft and beings were seen surfacing from the sea by hundreds of people who had spent the night watching odd lights offshore. It turned out to be an Air-Navy drill with lagoon troops, landing-craft and hovercraft! Still, many people fled from the "invasion". One cartoon in the press had a patient asking a doctor: "I've never seen a UFO... is it serious?".

Nonetheless, the most remarkable claim of the whole flap occurred in December — a repeat abduction with lasting effects:

TYPE: CE III
DATE: Dec. 6
TIME: 11:30 PM
DURATION: unstated
WITNESSES: 1
PLACE: Torriglia, near Genoa
SOURCE: Gente magazine (Jan. 20).
Skywatch: Shado Italy news (Vol. 1, No. 1, 1979)

Fortunato "Pietro" Zanfretta, 26, was on duty as a private security guard just outside a small house (the "Villa Casa Nostra") in Marzano when he saw four lights moving about in the garden about 300 feet away from him. Assuming they were the flashlights of thieves, he tried to radio his headquarters but his car engine, lights and radio had all failed without reason. Ignoring this, he left the car with his gun and flashlight in hand. From the lights, Zanfretta concluded that the thieves were behind the house. He walked through the open gate and got close to a wall in order to surprise them.

Instead, the "thieves" surprised him. Feeling himself touched from behind, he whirled around, levelling his gun and flashlight. Inches away from him was something that made his "skin crawl"... a monstrous being with grey, undulating skin. He had to raise his flashlight beam high to see the creature's "ugly, frightful" face, revealing the height of the being to be no less than ten feet. When he illuminated the being's face, the flashlight also cut off without reason. Terrorized, Zanfretta dropped his flashlight; it lit up again and he grabbed it. The strange giant seemed to have left, so the security guard ran for it.

While running, he became aware of an enormous light behind him. Turning around, he saw a huge, flattened triangular form which was blinding in its brilliance; the guard shielded himself with his arm. The triangle ascended from the back of the villa, bigger than the house itself, with a sibilant sound. A strong heat could also be felt.

Zanfretta made it back into his car and called in (successfully) to his operations center, the Vigilanza Valbisagno in Genoa. One account places the time at 11:50 PM, another at 12:15 AM. The radio operator, Carlo Toccarino, said that the guard was speaking in excited, disconnected phrases:"(He) was constantly saying, 'Mamma mia, is he ugly!'. I then asked if they were assaulting him, and he answered, 'No, they aren't men, they aren't men'. At this point, communications were interrupted and I immediately contacted Lt. Giovanni Cassiba."

Patrol guards Walter Lauria and Raimondo Mascia found Zanfretta in front of the villa around 1:15 AM, laying on the ground. When he saw them, he jumped up, pistol and flashlight at the ready. Bulging-eyed, the guard didn't seem to recognize them, nor to understand when they told him to lower his weapon. They rushed Zanfretta and disarmed him. To their surprise, his clothes felt warm even though it was December-cold outside. The gate was also closed now as normal. Furthermore, they could clearly see landing traces on the ground.

The Carabinieri came out to the site and also witnessed the two 9-foot diameter impressions, shaped like horseshoes in the dew-frosted grass. They expressed open confidence in the case, as did Torriglia station brigadier, Antonio Nocchi: "I've known Zanfretta for many

13

Evidence Supports Man's Amazing Encounters With 10-Foot-Tall Creatures Aboard Spaceship

The greatest blitz of UFOs in history has electrified the world since last fall. The ENQUIRER sent crack teams of reporters to the far corners of the globe to track down the amazing facts about these spectacular and bizarre sightings. Here, in the first of a series of articles, we document for you the details about one of the most incredible — and significant — UFO encounters ever. It is the terrifying story of a security guard's two visits aboard a spaceship with triangular-eyed creatures from outer space.

Shortly after midnight on December 6, an Italian security guard's patrol car mysteriously stopped dead. At the same moment he saw four strange lights and stepped outside to investigate with gun in hand. Suddenly, he was struck from behind.

"I whirled and shined my flashlight and saw this enormous green creature," he recalled.

It is the last thing the guard remembers — in his conscious mind — until 105 minutes later when he found himself stunned by the blinding light and heat of a UFO blasting off into the dark night sky.

Two weeks later, a group of experts listened in amazement as the 26-year-old guard, Fortunato Zanfretta, recounted under deep hypnosis the full details of his incredible UFO encounter. Their conclusion was that he was telling the truth.

And police say they found physical evidence to support the security guard's story — a large horseshoe-shaped burn mark where the spaceship was supposed to be and a 20-inch footprint which "could only have been made by a giant foot," a police spokesman said.

Three days after the hypnosis session, an event occurred that really sets Zanfretta's experience apart from the thousands of other UFO sightings.

He was driving to the same village outside Genoa when a strange force seized control of his patrol car and took him to the same spot where he again saw the four lights. Under hypnosis a second time, he says he was again taken aboard a UFO and was carefully examined by 10 triangular-eyed green creatures.

"I believe 90 percent of what he said was the truth," said Dr. Mauro Moretti, the top medical hypnotist and physician who hypnotized him. "You cannot invent things under hypnosis."

The ENQUIRER has thoroughly investigated Zanfretta's story as part of our worldwide probe of the recent amazing blitz of UFO sightings. Here is a detailed account of this astonishing — and significant — encounter:

Zanfretta, a family man with a reputation for honesty, was making his rounds in the village of Torriglia at about 11:30 p.m. December 6 when he saw strange lights at a client's unoccupied villa.

"As soon as I saw them, the motor, headlights and radio in my car went dead," he recalled.

"I took my gun and flashlight and went to see what was happening. I started to walk around the house. Someone pushed me in the back, like a punch. I whirled around, shined my flashlight and saw this enormous green creature. It is the last thing I remember."

On December 23, Zanfretta

SECURITY GUARD Zanfretta, who says he was examined by 10 triangular-eyed green creatures on spaceship, is seen with wife after his incredible experiences.

MAP SHOWS where Zanfretta was twice taken aboard spaceship.

sought professional help to unlock the secret of what happened from his mind. With Dr. Moretti, a psychotherapist and two parapsychologists present, Zanfretta underwent deep hypnosis and was able to talk about the gap in his memory.

"Zanfretta said the monster was about 10 feet tall, with hairy green skin, yellow triangular eyes and red veins across the forehead. In place of a mouth there was what appeared to be a metallic chain or fence," Dr. Moretti recalled.

"The creature escorted him to a very large, triangular UFO with several portholes and a round or semi-circular base. He said there was brilliant light inside the UFO and it was very hot," Dr. Moretti continued. "There were rows of instruments and control panels.

"Inside, there were about 10 alien beings like the one he had met outside. All the monsters

looked alike and they had fingers like ours."

Though they spoke no Italian or any other human language, Zanfretta said they communicated with him by "light signals and sounds" transmitted through a helmet placed on his head. The helmet was so tight it gave Zanfretta a headache, Dr. Moretti said.

Zanfretta does not need hypnosis to recall what happened when the encounter was over. He recalled: "The next thing I knew, I was standing in the dark, feeling groggy. The creature was gone. I picked up my flashlight from the ground and ran toward my car.

"As I ran, I saw this great, blinding light rise up. It was a UFO. I only saw that it was flat,

UNDER DEEP HYPNOSIS, Fortunato Zanfretta recounts details of encounter with outer space beings to Dr. Mauro Moretti (right) and psychotherapist Angelo Mosca.

triangular and white. It was enormous and it gave off so much light and heat that I couldn't see it clearly."

When the spaceship was gone, Zanfretta glanced at his watch. It was 1:15 a.m. He assumed he had fainted when he saw the monster and had regained consciousness seconds before the UFO took off.

Giovanni Cassibba, another guard, was sent to find out what was wrong and found Zanfretta sitting in his patrol car, looking dazed. "His face was cold but his head felt hot," Cassibba told The ENQUIRER. "He was in a state of shock."

This was confirmed by Dr. Giorgio Gianniotti, a prominent neurologist who examined Zanfretta in Genoa's San Martino Hospital. "The man was in a state of shock," Dr. Gianniotti said, "but he is perfectly sane."

Just three days after Zanfretta had undergone hypnosis, he remembers suddenly feeling faint while driving toward the same village.

"I couldn't keep my eyes open. The car drove itself. We moved so fast I didn't know if I was driving or flying.

"The car stopped suddenly,

the door opened by itself, I saw the same lights as I saw before in the villa. I felt as if one was calling me. After I don't remember what happened."

However, during a second hypnosis session on January, Zanfretta told Dr. Moretti the same creatures took into their ship again and put a helmet on his head.

"This time," the hypnotist continued, "the man examined his pistol and first made him take off his clothes. I took off my clothes. Some kind of ray over his and redressed him.

"He said over and over, 'Have you never seen me before?'

"Police examined the car where Zanfretta said the monster landed.

"They found a horseshoe-shaped imprint between 9 and 10 feet in diameter, burned into the ground. They also found one inch deep.

"It could only have been made by a giant foot," a spokesman said.

"It was raining that night, but other footprints could have been washed out.

The guard's boss, Gian Tulti, said: "I don't believe creatures from other planets, but I do believe in Zanfretta. He wanted publicity, he would have found other ways of getting it.

"I was present at the hypnosis session. When Zanfretta described the creatures he also said they told him the next time they come, take him away."

— PAUL

NEXT WEEK: U.S. Guardsmen tell of what they spotted in the Midwest. One witness describes "a huge cylinder-like object bigger than a B-52, with very bright red lights."

FIRST ENCOUNTER with outer space beings took place outside this villa in Torriglia near Genoa, Italy.

Here is how the American weekly "National Enquirer" presented the Zanfretta case to his readers in the issue of July 6, 1979. Subsequently, the same magazine, published two more articles on the case.

AFTER THE STORY
FROM 1981 TO OUR DAYS

An Endless Story

Over the course of the past few years, I found myself reading and hearing so much nonsense about the Zanfretta case that it left me quite perplexed. Probably because this incredible story of UFOs and the night watchman tends to move so far away from the chronicle of actual facts that it was becoming a kind of urban legend where anyone, arbitrarily and to his own liking, added a few new details.

I must therefore point out to the reader that my job doesn't leave any room for fairy tales and the kind of nonsense that more and more often can be found on Internet sites and in certain publications. Instead, this book, as anyone who has read this far can easily verify, shows in the first part the events that actually took place (the research, the documents, the testimonies) and the texts of the hypnosis sessions concerning the episodes that the security guard, the unwilling protagonist Piero Fortunato Zanfretta, lived through from 1978 to 1980. The extraordinary events are very difficult, if not impossible, to explain.

Essentially there are two reasons that explain why we are witnessing the proliferation of absolutely unsubstantiated news on a case such as this. The first is that the vast majority of those who invent themselves as "journalists" or commentators on a story of this kind often don't know anything about it at all. For example, I remember reading somewhere that the horseshoe-shaped two-by-three meter print that was found on the icy grass where Zanfretta was found for the first time in December 1978 by his colleagues in Marzano of Torriglia, had become "the prints left by a herd of horses which had escaped through a fence." Clearly, the unknown author of this nonsense had taken the restricted spaces of the Liguria Apennines for the boundless prairies of the American West, just because he had heard of that horseshoe-shaped print. And I could go on with hundreds of other examples. It's clear, in fact, that when we are faced with a particularly unusual story that stimulates one's imagination, there is always someone who starts fantasizing about it on his own, without even worrying about having better knowledge of the real outlines of the story itself. Perhaps this was also due to the fact that this book was no longer in circulation. I hope that with the publication of this new edition, the matter of misinformation on the

Zanfretta case can be somewhat curtailed.

However, I must say that Zanfretta indirectly also played his part in spreading certain fictions. And this is the second reason for the account being somewhat penalized. Indeed, since 1980 and more specifically since Dr. Mauro Moretti requested the night watchman in hypnosis to recall all the details of his extraordinary night-time adventures (an instruction that, as we shall see, was almost always disobeyed), Zanfretta went from unwitting victim of inexplicable facts to conscious protagonist of these very episodes. Also because, and I will never tire of saying this, up to that moment, the night watchman hadn't been able to disclose anything about his experiences. If he were asked what had happened, he would reply with a shrug and a laconic "Beats me!"

Now instead, Zanfretta freely tells all his stories, and unfortunately in doing so, he sometimes subjectively reinterprets those distant events. This is understandable in its dynamics. We are talking about a person who, regardless of whatever significance his adventures might have, has been highly traumatized by those episodes. And when years later he was finally able to talk about it, he has done so recalling those moments emotionally rather than with the clarity of events that have just occurred. In his shoes, who on earth would be able to retain a clear and calm recollection of such traumatic experiences?

In the end, to find out more about what happened to him during the years we had lost touch, I decided to contact him. Let me say that we had grown apart when he didn't keep me informed. I guess he feared I would not understand the misfortunes of which he was victim in 1994 that cost him his security guard license. I learned this from other people. I have no reason to doubt, as Zanfretta himself claims, that on that occasion "someone got him involved in order to attribute faults to him that he did not have." But the fact that he hadn't told me had annoyed me.

And so in the end, after several years, we met up again. When he came to see me in the newsroom, he told me that his life had changed completely. To begin with, he had divorced and had a new job working for a Genoese religious institute. The oldest of his four children, Margherita, 32 years old, had also given him two grandchildren. According to his story, after the last "encounter" of August 13, 1980 reported in this book, another five meetings took place, the last of which would have been on August 8, 1981.

However, at this point, it is necessary to spell out that Zanfretta's latest adventures on the Genoese mountains had an aftermath. In June 1985, therefore one year after the publication of the first edition of this book, the former night watchman had visited Dr. Moretti's office twice, telling him that he "wanted to speak to him but that he didn't know what he had to say to him." At that point, Moretti informed me and so one day the three of us met up to discuss that strange urgency. Basically, Zanfretta gave us to understand that maybe it would have been better to put him under hypnosis again "because he had an important message to communicate." This behavior should make us understand that in a state of normal wakefulness, Zanfretta could not speak of his experiences at all. In some way, if we wanted to communicate with him on another level, that is the one that concerned his "contacts" with the alleged aliens, he had to be put under hypnosis. And so it was that we all decided to meet in Dr. Moretti's office the evening of Friday, July 12, 1985. Along with Zanfretta, Moretti and me, there was also Bruno Ferracciolo, the television director who had filmed a two-episodes drama on the story for Rai Tre that was broadcast on December 12 and 18, 1984. The program, produced by Grazia Galardi, was entitled "UFO's in Genoa? Close Encounters of Piero Zanfretta" featuring actors Vanni Valenza (who played Zanfretta) and Mario Marchi (playing the guard's supervisor). It was later confirmed to me by the managers of the Ligurian regional headquarters of RAI that that drama was one of the most in demand from RAI's video library both in Italy and abroad. It is therefore not surprising that Ferracciolo was so passionate about the story and that he followed it with interest.

The session began at exactly 9:15 p.m. and what transpired was really remarkable. In this regard, I must immediately say that over the course of the hypnosis session, Zanfretta changed his tone of voice several times, especially when he claimed he had established contact with the aliens. On those occasions he literally became another person. In fact, during the session his voice was somewhat feeble, almost tired. When the mysterious alien suddenly made his appearance, speaking through him and shadowing his personality, then the voice would became hard, imperious and the language would change as well. As I did previously for the hypnosis sessions, in order to differentiate between his normal tone and the altered one, I will put the latter in bold font. This way the reader will be able to distinguish one from the other and will understand the peculiarity of those events we lived through back then. But let's get to the session.

The Shocking Hypnosis

Moretti, after putting Zanfretta under deep hypnosis, begins to question him.

Doctor Moretti: "You've come to the door of my office twice, now you will also be able to explain why. And then you will tell me everything that you need to tell me. Shortly your mouth will open and you will begin to speak automatically. Just as your arm moved on its own before, so will your voice come out by itself now."

Zanfretta, however, doesn't speak. Moretti persists.

Doctor Moretti: "Why did you come looking for me twice downstairs from my office? Did you need me?"

Zanfretta: "Yes."

Doctor Moretti: "I'm here now, you can speak freely."

Zanfretta: "They want to see you."

Doctor Moretti: "And do you know why? If you can tell us..."

Zanfretta: "No."

Doctor Moretti: "Then you're only a messenger?"

Zanfretta: "Yes."

Doctor Moretti: "Have you been given instructions that I must follow?"

Zanfretta: "They told me to seek you out because they want to contact you."

Doctor Moretti: "All right."

Zanfretta: "I think I also came to see you another time."

Doctor Moretti: "So I don't have to do anything for now?"

Zanfretta: "No, not until I come and get you."

Doctor Moretti: " If you want to, can you establish contact with them at any time?"

Zanfretta: "I don't know."

Doctor Moretti: "For example, if I asked you now, would you be able to do it, if you wanted to?"

Zanfretta: "I don't know."

Doctor Moretti: "It's okay, Piero. I'll ask you something now. So, Piero: I would like that part within you that knows everything, even what you don't know, to tell me everything you can tell me about a particular box. Everything that's written inside you regarding that box."

Zanfretta: "They gave it to me in 1979. At the moment, it is hidden up in the mountains, every twenty days I go and check that everything is OK. I open it and check it."

Doctor Moretti: "Is it full? Is there something inside?"

Zanfretta: "Yes, a sphere with a gold pyramid inside."

Doctor Moretti: "Gold? Did you say gold?"

Zanfretta: "Gold. And every corner of the pyramid discharges electric shocks. On each side of the pyramid there are signs, like one that lights up and turns off. And under the sphere there is a hexagon with twelve buttons with strange signs and every time I open the box, the sphere pulsates with light."

Doctor Moretti: "Now, Piero, listen to me. Now you'll go and check it. Your mind and your spirit are going. And while you're going, you'll describe the road you're taking and everything you see. Because remember that the mind can travel in space, just as it can travel in time. The mind is pure energy. And now your mind leaves this place and travels. And you tell me everything your mind is seeing, until it reaches the precise spot where the box is."

But here comes the surprise. In fact, every time he gets close to the heart of Zanfretta's mystery, the night watchman suddenly splits in two and in his place an unexpected guest steps in: the alien.

Zanfretta: "Negative for this question, tixel."

Doctor Moretti: "Now, it seems that your mind is not obeying what I'm asking because it is controlled and so I ask you: who put these answers inside you? Who put the order inside you not to respond to certain questions? And when did this happen?"

But Zanfretta doesn't reply. Then Moretti tries again.

Doctor Moretti: "Go back in time, if you want to. When were you given the order not to answer some of my questions? A long time ago? Some time ago?"

Zanfretta: "In 1981."

Doctor Moretti: "Did they hypnotize you?"

Zanfretta: "They don't want to."

Doctor Moretti: "Let's see if you can give me an answer to this question. Why do they want to contact me: what's the purpose? Can you imagine why, since you know them? Because it's true: you obey them. But you would never suggest anything that could be dangerous for me: your conscience would prevent it, would it not?"

Zanfretta: "They think that you may..."

Doctor Moretti: "That I can help them?"

Zanfretta: "No. That you might answer certain questions."

Doctor Moretti: "Therefore I'm not in any danger?"

Zanfretta: "No. They know that I am here."

Doctor Moretti: "How do you know that they know this, Piero?"

Zanfretta: "Because they told me yesterday evening."

Doctor Moretti: "Ah, you were in contact yesterday evening?"

Zanfretta: "At a quarter to midnight. They're interested. I went to the window and I felt them calling me."

Doctor Moretti: "Now Piero, we are here and they know this, right?"

Zanfretta: "Yes."

Doctor Moretti: "Can they, if as you say, they know - and I believe you - that we are here, can they give us a sign right now? Any sign, even through you, of course."'

Zanfretta: "I don't know."

Doctor Moretti: "You're lying, Piero. You do know. I would like you to tell me the truth. I know that you care for me, that you respect me, I have always helped you therefore you cannot tell me things that aren't true. Tell me the truth!"

Zanfretta: "What do you want to know?"

Doctor Moretti: "I would like to know if at this moment, through you, they can give us or give me a sign. It's their choice. Therefore, you see, I am very helpful. A sign of their own choosing. Whatever that may be. For example, since they know so many things that maybe you and I don't know, they could perhaps through you say something that we discover is really true, but that you and I didn't know. And so that's their sign. Something like that. Since they want to contact me, there must be willingness from both sides."

But once again Zanfretta remains silent. And so Moretti eggs him on.

Doctor Moretti: " I am using you now as a sort of radio-bridge, because I know that they do the same. Therefore, I am not posing the question to you really."

And it is at this point that, instead of Zanfretta, the mysterious alien replies. The voice changes from feeble and becomes hard and strong, almost bossy. And it speaks in the unknown language first and then it translates into Italian. Of course I'm reporting this language as it sounded.

Zanfretta: "**Selex, selex etel. Lixenar, elixsi sandé**."

Doctor Moretti: "Piero, do you know their language? Can you tell us what they said?"

Zanfretta: "**Earthling, we're listening. Speak.**"

Doctor Moretti: "You asked for my cooperation. Good. May I have a sign which lets me know with certainty, that it is you now, really you, talking through the mind of Piero Zanfretta?"

Zanfretta: "**Chelesens, salex si esel. I repeat: what do you want to know**?"

Doctor Moretti: "Where are you right now?"

Moretti tries therefore to have more precise information, but the answer is always the same and, in this case Zanfretta's voice goes back to being feeble.

Zanfretta: "Negative for this question, tixel."

Doctor Moretti: "Can you tell me right now why you want contact with me?"

Zanfretta: "**Elexen, elax esé. Tilixin alas. We're thinking of taking you to our spaceship and then we can talk. It's no use asking why. Unfortunately, we are still far away. What matters to us is that he doesn't lose the box. Only he knows where it is and nobody can get close to it. If he tries to bring someone, we can't be held responsible. As far as you're concerned, we will call you when the time comes. Don't worry. You will understand very soon. Rest assured, no one is going to harm you. In any case, we will get you ready. Because when you see us... we will be very different from you. Don't worry.**"

Doctor Moretti: "Therefore a kind of friendly and equal collaboration ..."

Zanfretta: "**Telex, tezilex. You do not have to worry. On our command, our friend will bring you to us. Don't be afraid. It will happen in a few moments. When he comes and calls you, go. Without asking questions.**"

The tone is peremptory and allows no discussions. In fact, Moretti reacts.

Doctor Moretti: "And if I refused? Given that you need me and I don't need you, I can set the conditions."

Zanfretta: "**Silex, selex ché. Speak**."

Doctor Moretti: "First of all: I'll come only if I know exactly where the box is. So that I can look after it as well. Second condition: I would like to know what the box is for. If I don't get specific answers on these two matters, I will not collaborate with you at all. This, where we live, is called diktat. Or blackmail."

Zanfretta: "**Exinten lex enagò. Don't worry about the sphere, just trust us. You'll come anyway. Whether you want to or not.**"

Doctor Moretti: "Can I bring one of the people who are here with me now?"

Zanfretta: "**We'll decide this later. We know these people. We are also seeing them now...**"

Doctor Moretti: "You know them?"

Zanfretta: "**Besides, laughing will not solve anything.**"

Doctor Moretti: "Who's laughing?"

Zanfretta: "**One of them laughed. He doesn't know what that means. He may take it as a joke, whatever he wants. However, in time he will not laugh anymore. The one who laughed will come.**"

Actually Ferracciolo did crack a smile, hearing Zanfretta talk like that. But the night watchman, lying on the table with his eyes closed and in deep hypnosis, had apparently noticed it.

Doctor Moretti: "Now I ask you this. You're saying say that you're watching us right now, is that true?"

Zanfretta: "**Silex, elexensen: we are watching you.**"

Doctor Moretti: "Good. Then, if you're watching us, you can tell us what our friend who, as you know, is called Bruno Ferracciolo has in his hand. The one that's sitting on a chair like mine. If you can see, you can clearly see what he has in his right hand. If not, we, I'm sure you understand, have every right to believe these statements to be false."

But the attempt to have a minimum of certainty about what was happening in the office failed once again.

Zanfretta: "**Selex den: do as you like.**"

Doctor Moretti: "Indeed that's what we'll do. Now I would like you to speak freely, everything that you have to say through Piero, say it. We will listen to you with pleasure and with interest."

Zanfretta: "**Teletex elexsen. Now listen to me because I'm not going to speak again: we think we will arrive around the month that you call November. Then we'll call you.**"

Doctor Moretti: "You, the one who's talking, do you have a name?"

Zanfretta: "**I am the prince of the Dargos.**"

Doctor Moretti: "How far away is your planet, in terms of light years?"

Zanfretta: "**We do not intend to reply any further. We'll be in touch again.**"

Doctor Moretti: "One more question, please."

Zanfretta: "**Telexen. Speak.**"

Doctor Moretti:"Since I wasn't looking before, can you tell me who laughed? Because I heard laughing as well and I certainly wasn't at all pleased. You know that I am very serious and concerned about this thing. Can you tell me who, among my friends, laughed?"

The new attempt was obvious: to make the unknown interlocutor who hid behind Zanfretta show that he knew who had laughed. But whoever he was, he certainly wasn't stupid considering that he didn't fall into this verbal trap either.

Zanfretta: "**You said the name before.**"

Doctor Moretti: "Bruno Ferracciolo? I didn't mention any other friend."

Zanfretta: "**You said the name before.**"

Doctor Moretti: "Do you have anything else to communicate?"

Zanfretta: "**Not at the moment: don't worry. We'll be in touch. Big things will happen. We will need lots of help.**"

Doctor Moretti: "In November then..."

Zanfretta goes quiet. Understanding that there's something wrong, Moretti asks him another question.

Doctor Moretti: "Do you want to say something, Piero? Is there something annoying you?"

Zanfretta now goes back to being the person he always was, with his usual feeble voice.

Zanfretta: "I asked them to continue talking, so I'm trying."

Doctor Moretti: "Why, what do you want to know?"

But the answer is disarming.

Zanfretta: "**Negative for this question, tixel.**"

Moretti plays dumb.

Doctor Moretti: "No, you Piero, what did you want to know from them? Why did you want them to keep talking?"

The answer, once again, is the same as before. The message was quite clear: Moretti wasn't allowed to know anything that could be verified, not even what kind of relationship might exist between Zanfretta and his interlocutors.

Zanfretta: "**Negative for this question, tixel.**"

At this point Moretti has an angry outburst.

Doctor Moretti: "This f... negative..."

Then he starts again.

Doctor Moretti: "Listen up, Piero, since you know them: they're a bit disagreeable, tell the truth. They've got that arrogant attitude, haven't they?"

Zanfretta replies normally again.

Zanfretta: "You must know them, see them ..."

217

Doctor Moretti: "Listen: has it been long since you last saw the one with the egg-shaped head?"

Zanfretta: "A month and a half ago."

Doctor Moretti: "But according to you, is he one of them disguised as a man or is it a human being who cooperates with them? What do you reckon?"

The reply comes from 'above'.

Zanfretta: "**His name is Selen, he is one of them.**"

Doctor Moretti: "But he lives here?"

Zanfretta: "**No.**"

Doctor Moretti: "Does he come from the spaceship?"

Zanfretta: "**No. He keeps me under control. He's the one who always takes me there, in the evening.**"

Doctor Moretti: "Is he the one who takes you to the sphere?"

Zanfretta: "**Yes.**"

Doctor Moretti: "Ah, so you don't go alone?"

Zanfretta: "**I took two friends with me, but they have not been able to reach the sphere.**"

Doctor Moretti: "Did they get close?"

Zanfretta: "**Yes, but they were very afraid. And they stopped.**"

Doctor Moretti: "Otherwise you'd have taken them?"

Zanfretta: "**Yes.**"

Doctor Moretti: " Would you take me and some other friend, like Rino, who's not afraid?"

Zanfretta: "**I don't know the consequences ...**"

Doctor Moretti: "And if we take responsibility for it? Would you feel more comfortable?"

Zanfretta: "**They said no and no it is.**"

Doctor Moretti: "But you did with your other friends... why was it OK with them and not with us who are your friends? You could have called us ..."

Zanfretta: "**They wanted to see how brave they were. Instead, they got very scared. They weren't brave enough to come.**"

Doctor Moretti: "How far away from the sphere did they stop? A few meters?"

Zanfretta: "**About 400 meters.**"

Doctor Moretti: "They were close, then."

Zanfrella: "**There's a lot of walking to do...**"

I wanted to know more, so I approached Moretti and whispered a few words. He then addressed the night watchman.

Doctor Moretti: "Have you heard the question?"

Zanfretta: "**No**."

Doctor Moretti: "Rino was asking what the sphere is for? Do you know?"

Zanfretta: "**Before they arrive, the sphere needs to be activated. It prepares a large ray where they will be able to land**."

Basically, Zanfretta still speaking in a hard tone says that the sphere is a sort of beacon radio.

Doctor Moretti: "I understand. Therefore, if, for instance nobody turns it on, they cannot land."

Zanfretta: "**That's not a problem**."

Moretti: "And have they never thought that you could be busy, that you've been held up, that perhaps you may feel ill, have the flu, be in bed. In other words, something happens and you can't go and turn it on."

Zanfretta: "**The day it happens I will be in perfect health. And even if I couldn't, I would go anyway. Because it has been said so ...**"

Doctor Moretti: "Rino is asking what your role is. Is it to monitor it or to use it...."

Zanfretta: "**I just have to monitor it**."

Doctor Moretti: "That it's still there?"

Zanfretta: "**That it's there and that it's in working order**."

If we wanted to joke, it would seem that Zanfretta was also working as a night watchman for the aliens.

Doctor Moretti: "Are you tired or do you feel like answering a few more questions that our friend Rino would like to ask you? Will you reply sincerely, like you do with me..."

The one who replies is Piero Zanfretta again.

"Of course, Rino is my friend."

Doctor Moretti: "Good."

Thanks to Zanfretta's willingness, I took the opportunity to find out if he knew whether anyone of us had been contacted by his "friends." I knew for sure that I hadn't and so did Moretti and Ferracciolo. Thus, if he had answered 'yes,' we would have doubted his statements. But it wasn't easy to make him contradict himself.

Di Stefano: "Piero, a question. As far as you know has anyone of us here present ever been contacted in some way, or followed, by these people?"

Zanfretta: "I don't know."

Di Stefano: "Can you ask them? You're able to do it now."

Zanfretta: "No."

Di Stefano: "Piero, tell me the truth. You said that you don't know if they have ever contacted anyone here, but instead you do know..."

Doctor Moretti: "We're appealing to friendship, eh?"

Zanfretta: "I can't answer the question, Rino."

Di Stefano: "Why?"

Zanfretta: "They don't want me to."

Di Stefano: "For what reason? I mean, what's wrong in admitting that some of the people present were in some way followed or contacted by them? By contacted I mean followed, that's it."

Zanfretta: "It could be who might be coming with Moretti. And this will happen at the last moment."

Di Stefano: "You're saying that one of the two people here, and not Dr. Moretti, has already been, shall we say, checked by these people?"

Zanfretta: "They've already decided."

Di Stefano: "They have already decided? And do you know the reason?"

Zanfretta: "No."

Di Stefano: "Tell me: what would happen to these people who are contacted by them and that, one way or another, are part of their plans?"

Zanfretta: "I can't understand."

Di Stefano: "The people who will be contacted by them, what role should they play here on earth?"

Zanfretta: "This will be decided by them. It's not up to me."

Di Stefano: "Listen, can you tell me when one of these two people who are present here was followed?"

What I wanted to ascertain with that question was what kind of control these alleged entities might be able to exercise and especially how. But the reply was appropriate.

Zanfretta: "**Negative for the question**."

Di Stefano: "Why?"

Given that Zanfretta had gone quiet, I asked him the question again.

Di Stefano: "Piero, I'll ask you this question again: when was the last time that these people were, or one of these people was, visually contacted?"

Even in this instance, the reply came from 'space'.

Zanfretta: "**Selex chenà. Try to disconnect. Insisting is useless, you** won't do anything else anyway. **The connection is closed**."

Di Stefano: "Can I ask you another question?"

Zanfretta: "**Ilixix là, speak**."

Di Stefano: "How many people do you think are of interest for your projects? People who have been directly or indirectly involved in this affair."

Zanfretta: "**About your number twenty. When we arrive, the others will arrive too, whether they want to or not**."

Di Stefano: "So, can I ask you if I have ever seen you personally, under any shape or form?"

The purpose of my question was to ascertain if I had ever came into contact with someone else, other than Zanfretta, who was involved in that affair. But I wasn't dealing with someone stupid: Zanfretta or someone else smelled the trap. And he didn't answer. So I egged him on.

Di Stefano: "I would appreciate an answer."

Zanfretta: "**Selex, delixten tà: negative for this question, tixel**."

Ultimately there was really nothing to do. And so I let Moretti take over again.

Doctor Moretti: "Piero, it's Dr. Moretti again, I would like to ask you a question. When Rino or I ask you a question you cannot answer, what do you feel inside? What is the difference between the Piero who usually listens to all my questions and who is in hypnosis, and the Piero who at some point cannot answer some of the questions? I mean, what do you feel inside?"

It's clear that Moretti is sniffing around the mechanism that kicks in when Zanfretta is under hypnosis. A mechanism, I must very clearly say, that is absolutely anomalous at a scientific level. In fact, we were watching a hypnotized human being that went absolutely beyond his hypnotizer's control. Such a situation never occurs in the course of a normal session of hypnosis. Literally, it was as if there was a third party that crept into the relationship between hypnotized and hypnotizer, taking the place of the former. And this time Zanfretta replies normally.

Zanfretta: "I feel that everything becomes dark and they make me say those words."

Doctor Moretti: "At the end of the day, it's just as though someone had hypnotized you before me, and had told you something, had given you instructions."

Zanfretta:"**Selex, delexen: do not insist. We would cause harm. We**

repeat: do not insist. We would cause harm. Closing connection."

Doctor Moretti: "To whom? To Piero or to us?"

But the 'alien' decided on his own, and whenever he wanted, whether he would reply or not. Therefore this time, it was Zanfretta's turn to speak even though he was still in a stupor.

Zanfretta: "What? Ah, I understand..."

Doctor Moretti: "Are you're talking to me, Piero?"

Zanfretta: "Yes, I didn't understand..."

Doctor Moretti: "They said that if we insist they will cause harm. And I asked them: to whom? Piero or us?"

Zanfretta: "I didn't hear anything ..."

Doctor Moretti: "What's the last thing you heard?"

Zanfretta: "Rino's question, if he was contacted."

Doctor Moretti: "So the last thing you heard was Rino's question, if he was contacted ..."

Zanfretta: "Yes, he has asked me this question."

Doctor Moretti: "Yes. Then, nothing?"

Zanfretta: "Darkness ..."

Doctor Moretti: "Don't you remember that a moment ago I asked you what happens inside you when you're not able to answer and you told me 'everything becomes dark'. Do you remember this?"

The answer, in some way, is chilling:

Zanfretta: "No."

Doctor Moretti: "Now I ask you one thing: have you formed a personal opinion of these, these beings, from when you first saw them up until now? Your opinion...or maybe at the beginning you had a certain opinion and then you changed it ... Therefore just your own personal opinion of these beings."

Zanfretta: "Yes, I think they need a lot of help... and I don't know how to give it to them..."

Doctor Moretti: "Have you suggested to them somehow the possibility that we, your friends, might cooperate in order to help you."

Zanfretta: "No, they decided it."

Doctor Moretti: "I get it."

Zanfretta: "You told them, one day."

Doctor Moretti: "Uhm, who did?"

Zanfretta: " You told them, one day."

At that point Moretti remembers that during one of the earlier hypnoses, a few years before, he had been accommodating towards the alleged aliens and had offered to help, if needed.

Doctor Moretti: "Ah, yes, yes, yes, I remember, that's true."

Zanfretta. "They thought of you, as well as the other three people."

Doctor Moretti: "Yes, yes, I remember, it's true. So in any case you haven't formed, shall we say, a bad opinion eh? Notwithstanding the fright, apart from all these things..."

But who replies is not the same Zanfretta as before. The voice is again a little altered, hard again.

Zanfretta: "**No**."

Doctor Moretti: "So you're not afraid anymore?"

Zanfretta: "**No, because I'll be back on the mountain**..."

And Moretti points out the change to him.

Doctor Moretti: "Have you noticed that, compared to a couple of minutes ago, you changed your tone of voice?"

Zanfretta: "No."

Doctor Moretti: "You were talking very quietly before and now you've changed your tone of voice ..."

And once again he goes back to being the same Piero as before.

Zanfretta: "I only heard Rino and you. That's all..."

Doctor Moretti: "Now you are talking with your normal voice again."

Zanfretta: "Yes."

Doctor Moretti: "In November, when they want to take Rino and me, you'll come with us, right? Because, in other words, we would feel safer, you understand..."

Moretti tries once again to make Zanfretta fall into a trap by adding me to the alien list. But, whoever is using Zanfretta's voice, doesn't fall for it.

Zanfretta: "**Telexselen**..."

Doctor Moretti: "I think there's an interference ..."

Zanfretta: "**We repeat: we're interested in you for now. The other person will arrive as well at the right time. This is the last time**."

Doctor Moretti: "But you are from Dargon, we are Italian. We immediately understood it was Rino. Eh! We understood. Therefore it is useless to beat around the bush, to talk. We understood and we can say it without hesitation. You cannot ask for trust without giving trust. You must stop having this overbearing tone. No, if we are to collaborate, the relationship must be one of trust and mutual respect. Between us there should be the same relationship of trust, friendship, etc. as there is, I don't know, between Piero and us. And it should be the same with you. So you should change your attitude, you should change your tone, you should change this way of doing things and your behavior. If you want our collaboration, you must also 'get used to' our ways..."

But the alien interrupts Moretti while he's speaking.

Zanfretta: "**Selex**..."

Doctor Moretti: " ... and our way of thinking."

Zanfretta: "**You're going too fast. Everything in due course, this is what you say. Don't worry...**"

Doctor Moretti: "Well, I see that the tone is already a little more polite and less imperious. And I'm pleased about that..."

Zanfretta: "**The connection is over. Closed. Anyway we'll be in touch again, when you least expect it.**"

Doctor Moretti: "Still through Piero?"

But Zanfretta is back to being himself, with a blank expression.

Zanfretta: "What?"

Moretti is a little confused because he no longer knows when it is Zanfretta replying or when the third party makes his appearance.

Doctor Moretti: "Are you listening to me, Piero?"

Zanfretta: "Yes."

Doctor Moretti: "They said they will be back in touch with me when I least expect it. Since you're experienced in these things by now, how do you think that will happen with me? Like they have done with you? Just your opinion..."

Zanfretta: "You will have strong headaches. And when you do, I will, too. I will come looking for you and you'll be forced to come with me. Because your mind will not be in control anymore..."

Doctor Moretti: "Well, it's not a very pleasant prospect..."

Zanfretta: "I know, it happened to me, too."

Doctor Moretti: "And you keep having those headaches every time, even now?"

Zanfretta: "No. Only when they call."

Doctor Moretti: "So you were telling me that you had strong headaches initially. I remember, you told me. And this is what will happen when you and I have to go up: you have a headache, I have a headache. You'll come and get me and we'll go. OK."

Zanfretta: "You'll be behind me... you'll see."

Doctor Moretti: "Well, of course, a new experience. They must know that I am curious... Eh?"

Zanfretta: "And then you can ask them these questions..."

Doctor Moretti: "Well, I asked you because, unfortunately, we have to say that after so many times, you're experienced in all this. You can understand that one is a little worried the first time, really."

Zanfretta: "Of course ..."

Doctor Moretti: "Perhaps even you the first times: the doubts, the questions, the fears, eh?"

Zanfretta: "Of course, it was very unpleasant for me but it will be different for you..."

Moretti: "Less unpleasant... all right, I certainly believe you, Piero."

Zanfretta: "You're not subjected to me only, I submit to somebody else."

Doctor Moretti: "I understand. So what you're telling me is that the relationship between me and them will be on equal terms, right?"

In some way, Moretti seeks to be reassured, and Zanfretta or whoever on his behalf, goes along with him. But in actual fact, we had an inkling that we weren't talking about a relationship as equals but rather a relationship where one would give orders and the other would obey. With no objections.

Zanfretta: "Yes, the difference is that you will not have problems..."

Doctor Moretti: "Yes."

Zanfretta: "With the police or with the Government. It's your problem, yours and that's it."

Doctor Moretti: "Sure. You, on the other hand, I know, have had so many problems, so much hassle. We all know."

Zanfretta: "When you tell what you have seen, the same thing that happened to me will happen to you. Even if you are a doctor."

Doctor Moretti: "Ah, I've no doubt about it. I've no doubt about it. But maybe we'll keep it to ourselves, won't we?"

Zanfretta: "You won't be able to, this thing is too big. However there will be another eighteen people with you and me."

Doctor Moretti: " Ah well, you're presenting me with a fascinating experience."

Zanfretta: "There will also be two Carabinieri, a policeman, me, you and other important people."

Doctor Moretti: "Based on your experience, when they have a commitment, are they punctual? They said November this time. I mean, if it's November, November it is. Have they always been accurate, punctual when it comes to this? About what they said?"

But Zanfretta has once again lost contact and replies normally.

Zanfretta: "I don't know. I just get the headache. And then I know that I have to go up there."

Doctor Moretti: "Has it ever happened that they told you in advance? Something like that had come out once, they said something about the 'great cold'. Do you remember?"

Zanfretta: "Yes. Wait and see."

Doctor Moretti: "Are you allowed to mention two or three names among these eighteen people? If you know them and if you're are allowed to say it, of course. It's just curiosity. Not that we want to push you."

Zanfretta: "One should be a friend of mine. And he still doesn't know. His name is Antonino Monteleone, he's a Carabiniere."

Doctor Moretti: "Do you have to contact them all, like you did with me?"

Zanfretta: "No. Eight already know."

Doctor Moretti: "Piero, Rino here is extremely curious. He's asking me lots of questions. But I'm afraid that you cannot answer many of these questions. Shall I get him to ask you all the same?"

As a matter of fact I wanted to learn more, especially regarding the names of the "players." But I knew that the chances of getting an answer were very small, almost non-existent.

Zanfretta: "I don't know..."

Doctor Moretti: "I'll get him to ask you. If you can answer, do so, OK?"

Zanfretta: "All right."

Doctor Moretti: "Listen to Rino, then. To what he's asking."

Di Stefano: "Who are the eight people that have already been contacted?"

And right on cue, we get the same answer.

Zanfretta: "**Selex... I will not repeat myself anymore now: we will hurt the earthling. Too bad for you. Connection closed.**"

Insisting was useless. Also because we were running the risk that something could really happen to Zanfretta. Moretti couldn't understand how, since a normal state of hypnosis doesn't harm a person in any way. But was what we were witnessing a "normal session of hypnosis"? Perhaps the answer wasn't certain. However, Moretti took charge of the situation again. It was time to stop.

Doctor Moretti: "Okay, quiet now, there's no problem. Now, Piero, don't think about anything anymore. Sleep deeply, quietly, have a nice restful sleep. Without thinking about anything. Sleep deeply, quietly. When I wake you up you'll be in a state of wellbeing, tranquility and serenity. Nothing will bother you and you will rest until I, and only I, wake you up."

Of course it was essential that Zanfretta rest before being awakened. And that is why after only twelve minutes, Moretti began the final phase of the hypnosis, the awakening.

Doctor Moretti: "Now, Piero, I'm going to count from ten to zero. At the word zero you will open your eyes and you'll be in a state of perfect wellbeing, peace, tranquility and serenity. Ten, nine, eight, seven, six, five, four, three, two, one, zero."

The Strange Awakening

At this point as a routine matter, the hypnotized person should awaken as ordered by the hypnotizer. This, at least, is what normally happens. But as it happened, this was not a session like the others. Given that the tape recorder kept going even after the hypnosis session had ended, today we have evidence that Zanfretta didn't awaken normally at all. In fact, as he told us immediately, he couldn't see properly. "I see everything white, you're all white," he was saying, "and I've got such a headache, my head feels heavy..."

Not even Moretti could explain why this was happening. It really was as if Zanfretta had made an enormous effort during the session and that his brain had been affected. But what kind of effort could it have been? Should we believe that he had really been in radio contact, as it seemed, with his friends the aliens? And how? Only with his head? How are we able to comprehend something like that?

In any case, this recording was kept safe and completely unedited until today. I can only say that, at least as far as I know, Moretti was never contacted. Nor was anyone else as far as I know. But as I write, I have to admit that I'm not reliable because in that period, and subsequently as well, we didn't have the any substantial basis for investigating Zanfretta's mysterious activities. We can only acknowledge what he was saying under hypnosis and at a later stage, at a conscious level.

But in this regard, it must be noted that at the end of that session in 1985, after he had woken up, he denied what he had declared under hypnosis, saying that he knew absolutely nothing about what we were telling him. Nor did it seem that he had any knowledge of all those details. In short, the person talking under hypnosis was another

Zanfretta.

Instead, what was left inside of him, and certainly very well, was his role as guardian of the famous sphere. Later in this chapter, we will see the interest that this mysterious object provoked on an international level.

A Normal Life

As far as things go, Zanfretta's life was no longer subject to any serious trauma. He says his life is on track and normal. He often speaks of his story with friends and acquaintances who make it a topic of conversation, often spiced up with irony and jokes. Just think of the movie "Invaxon" (to be read *Invasciun*, in Genoese dialect), completely based on a joke that he filmed in 2004 with the band Buio Pesto. "I don't care if they believe me or not," he replies. "I personally lived through this story and that's enough for me."

And he doesn't feel like adding anything else. His character has acquired by now the blurred traits of a legend and he often has fun listening to people speak about him without revealing his true identity. In Torriglia for example, the town that can be regarded as the center most frequented by UFOs in the region of Liguria, there is nobody who is not familiar with his adventures, but very few could recognize him. After all, as happens to everyone, he suffered considerable physical changes over time and it would be difficult to recognize in the present-day middle-aged gentleman the former young night watchman whose story made its way around the world.

The UFO of Mount Prelà

Aside from Zanfretta, something mysterious happened exactly in Torriglia long after the night watchman's encounters were over.

It was 1988 and for a whole eight months, a large luminous object of oval or triangular shape, depending on the points of view, created a new UFO-based-psychosis in Torriglia. The incident was seen by dozens of people, and was taking place virtually at any time of the day and night, at the foot of Mount Prelà (1406 meters above sea level), and exactly in the spot called "altitude one thousand." We are talking about the area between Torriglia and Propata, right in the middle of the Apennines. This involves a large expanse comprising a dozen villages whose cottages overlook the lake of Brugneto. The only means of communication is the provincial road which, starting from Torriglia goes through Garaventa, Bavastri, Bavastrelli and Propata.

For several months, the locals saw a mysterious bright UFO circling and landing but considered it nothing more than a curious phenomenon. Then, on Sunday, September 18, 1988, someone went to the Carabinieri to report the fact.

"Sunday evening," Flavio Cardinale, a male nurse at San Martino Hospital of Genoa, said at the time, "two guys that had stopped on the road to see if anything was happening. They saw a bright mass moving in their direction. It was 9:30 p.m. and these two, scared to death, immediately ran away to inform the Carabinieri. I only know that they were two Genoese on holiday and one of them is named Luigi Garbarino."

The pair that took off told Brigadier Gaetano Maresca, Commander of the station of Torriglia, that in fact there were four of them and that about that time, they suddenly saw a large bright flying saucer that initially descended on the summit of Mount Prelà, then slowly flew toward them as they had pulled up on the provincial road at the time. At that point, terrified, the four fled, two in the car and one on a motorbike. The fourth guy, who had arrived on the spot sitting on the rear seat of the same bike, was literally left behind and he started running, screaming to the others to wait for him.

Brigadier Maresca admitted having listened to many witnesses who claimed to have seen the mysterious flying light near the mountain in question.

"The first time it happened to me," said Flavio Cardinale "was Sunday, September 11, five minutes after midnight. My mother and I were coming from Garaventa, where we have several friends. Immediately after the bend, halfway up the mountain, we saw an immense deep blue light, almost fluorescent oval shape in front of us. My mother was frightened and wanted to go, but I wanted to stay. Other cars arrived and we all stood there stunned, watching. Also because on that mountain there is absolutely nothing. Then I went back with other people on Wednesday the 14th and we saw that strange light this time as well, though smaller and with a color that changed to green."

But male nurse Cardinale was not the only one to witness the maneuvers and the landing of the UFO. Mr. Renato Avanzino, secretary of the Regional Vocational Center and councilman of the Municipality of Torriglia, said: "I saw that light the evening of Friday, September 16th. It was around 9:30 p.m. and I was with my wife and two children, intrigued by what I had heard in the village. I went up there in the cold of night for a second time. There were also many other people, of course. Well, at some point at the top of Mount Prelà we distinctly noticed a large triangular light of about 15 meters by 10 meters, which changed its color between white and yellow and that very slowly dropped down to settle three quarters of the way up the mountain. This appearance only lasted a few minutes, and we all saw it clearly."

As the news of the UFO of Mount Prelà spread through Torriglia and surrounding areas, the fear of ridicule that has always kept silent any potential witnesses to UFO phenomena was decreasing. And someone acknowledged that that UFO had been flying around in the area for months. "I've been seeing that big very bright oval since this winter," admitted Elio Dondero, a worker who lives in Garaventa but works near Torriglia. "Passing through here all the time, I used to see it half way up the mountain, in any weather condition. Even rain or fog. It shines with a dull light, very intense and with its outlines clearly defined, but it's as if it didn't light anything up around it. Once I also noticed human shadows, or so it seemed, walk in front of that thing. But what should I have done? Who was I supposed to tell? Perhaps they would have said I hit the bottle too much... And so I chose to keep quiet. Except now there are really a lot of people who have seen it. I'm no longer the only witness..."

Exactly like it had arrived in the first harsh winter months of 1988, the UFO of Mount Prelà disappeared completely. Brigadier Maresca, mindful of what had happened when Brigadier Nucchi was Commander of the station of Torriglia, never wanted to release any statement on investigations he was forced carry out, seeing the fuss that the new UFO had created. But the report on that investigation was never disclosed, nor did the Carabinieri command want to comment on what had happened.

Zanfretta in Tucson

Although I hadn't dealt with the Zanfretta case for years, and my profession had taken me in many directions other than UFO-related events, one day in 1991, I received a letter from the United States. Lieutenant Colonel Wendell C. Stevens, retired officer of the Intelligence Services of the United States Air Force and later publisher and media producer, was inviting me to the first World Congress of Ufology to be held in Tucson, Arizona, from May 3 to 7, 1991. I had met Stevens some years before when he had come to Genoa from Los Angeles with a television crew to interview me on the Zanfretta case. Now he very kindly was asking me to submit a report that would outline to an audience of world experts the details about what I had written in this book. And not only that. He also asked if I could possibly take Zanfretta with me so that the experts could speak to him.

I don't know how Stevens had heard of the book and who had talked to him about me and my American experiences. I assume, however, that this news is also part of the worldwide publicity that Piero Zanfretta's adventures had in the '80s.

During my four years of study in the United States I had never been to Arizona, and I was curious to see a convention of that kind. I asked the editor in chief of my newspaper, who at the time was Indro Montanelli, if he'd let me go as a correspondent. He said yes. At that point, I extended the invitation to Zanfretta, pointing out to him that the American organizers would cover all expenses. He managed to get time off from his employer and so we left.

Among other things, the journey was pleasant, also because Roberto Pinotti, president of the National Ufologic Center and top Italian expert on ufology, came with us as well, as he was also invited to the convention. I first met Pinotti in 1984 when he and his team had organized the first Italian Congress of Ufology held at Genoa's Trade and Convention Centre. We had become friends. Pinotti, who speaks good English, has an encyclopedic knowledge on UFO-related phenomena and is the author of several books, as well as being director of the official magazine of the National Ufologic Center. In other words, he could be considered a world expert in the field of ufology and he would surely have made a good impression.

Just to give the reader an idea of the convention, suffice to say that it was held at the Hilton Hotel in Tucson, and in addition to the Americans, experts from Japan, Russia, Spain, Puerto Rico, England, Canada, Mexico, Peru, Venezuela, Iran, Chile, Brazil and Hungary participated. The quality was high, considering that among others there were people like Dr. Marina Popovich, one of the most well known astronauts of the Russian space program, and Sergeant Major Robert O. Dean, retired from the United States Air Force, NCO of NATO Supreme Headquarters and former colleague of Stevens in U.S. military intelligence.

Moreover, the presence of the Secret Service at that convention was 'in the air'. So much so that in his introduction, Dean blatantly addressed the alleged secret agents that were there, thanking them for their presence. Obviously, I don't know if the greeting was ironic, as it seemed to me, or if Dean was really aware of the presence of Secret Service agents among the audience. However, what happened afterwards made me think pretty hard about the presence of people who perhaps weren't what they seemed.

I will not describe what went on at the convention because on Friday, May 17, 1991, I published a lengthy article in the national edition of *Il Giornale* (which can be read on my website), and also because it would be far from the Zanfretta case. Instead, what I find important was the meeting I had with two Americans immediately after my speech on the stage of the convention. After I read my report, which I had illustrated with a long series of slides that were projected on a screen above my head, that same afternoon I was contacted by a couple of Americans. Brian P. Myers and Tina P. Choate were respectively president and CEO of the International Center for UFO Research, Inc. (ICUFOR) of Scottsdale, Arizona.

The first thing they said to me was that they wanted to speak only with me and Zanfretta. Since Zanfretta didn't speak English, they asked if I could possibly translate for him. They explained that they would rather keep Pinotti out of the meeting, also because "he knew nothing about the deal" that they wanted to propose to us. However, the group of Italians always went everywhere together, so I would have to find an excuse with Pinotti and the situation was embarrassing. Fortunately, though, Pinotti had joined a group that wanted to go to Roswell, in the desert of New Mexico, where in 1947 a flying saucer had presumably fallen, so we were able meet the two Americans without any problems.

When we sat down in the lobby of the Hilton, the pair introduced themselves saying that they were the spiritual heirs of Professor Joseph Allen Hynek, the famous astrophysicist considered to be the most famous ufologist in the world, in the sense that they had inherited his archives and continued his work after he was struck by a brain tumor in 1986. In fact, Hynek had moved with his wife from Chicago to Scottsdale, a pleasant tourist town just outside Phoenix. That's where they had met him and had begun working with him. As I had the opportunity to ascertain later on, things hadn't gone exactly that way, but at the time that was the version I was given. And they came to the point: Myers and Choate said they believed Zanfretta and were convinced that he had really received that famous sphere from the aliens. And not just that. They stated that there were two other cases similar to Zanfretta's in the world and that on both occasions the people "kidnapped" had been given similar spheres. They claimed that they were able to come into possession of those two spheres, but that a third one was missing to carry out a project on a global scale.

You can imagine what went through my mind hearing those statements. To begin with, I was bewildered. Since there was no certain evidence concerning Zanfretta's whole story, how would I ever be able to have taken the sphere seriously? And now two strangers were telling me it was all true, and that that very object would allow us to carry out a very ambitious project. So I asked for some clarification.

They replied saying that ICUFOR was part of a group, the Space Science Center Authority Ltd. in Scottsdale, which was building a city of the future with a level of technology never seen before, and that it was to become the largest tourist attraction in Arizona. The area had already been purchased. This mega project began in 1990 and was called "A Vision of the Future." Involved in it were also a few international corporations that I would rather not mention here, since I was never able to verify and confirm all the information I was given. However, I can testify that I was delivered a comprehensive report on this project, which I still have, and from which I was able to gather that there was an operational involvement of both the American public authorities and well-known, very large global privately-owned companies.

However this project, which cost several billion dollars, was not only a huge business deal in the tourism industry. At least as far as ICUFOR was concerned, it had a second purpose: to get hold of the third sphere, the one they claimed Zanfretta had, to bring to fruition a not-too-well-specified project within the Space Science Center.

As Brian and Tina spoke, I translated everything to Zanfretta. Looking at him, it seemed to me that he was the first who could not believe his ears. Even though you could read satisfaction on his face

233

because finally someone was saying they believed him. But even he wasn't able to come to any sort of decision right there and then. After all, what did we have to agree on? Exactly what did those two want? And how were he and I supposed to commit? But, above all, what guarantees would we have for that not-too-well-defined commitment?

Furthermore, the convention would end the next day and we had to go back home. We needed time to talk among ourselves before deciding on what to do. I also felt out of place because I saw myself in a role that was not my usual one. I am a journalist and I had dealt with Zanfretta's unfortunate adventures as part of my job; I never would have imagined I'd be involved in a situation like that. To cut a long story short, we said goodbye and they promised that they would come to Genoa as soon as possible so that we could get to know each other better and discuss the details of the transaction.

That same evening, Zanfretta and I talked at length about the strange proposal. For the first time, he mentioned that maybe he would put the sphere at their disposal if he could maintain control over it. After all, they had given it to him to deliver it to Hynek and those two were his heirs. I must say, though, that Professor Hynek had already been to Genoa in 1984 when he was a guest of the first Italian Convention of Ufology. And on that occasion, when he could be easily reached, Zanfretta hadn't given anything to him. Therefore, still assuming that he really had the sphere, it is likely that he felt he was the only guardian and didn't intend to share it with anyone.

In any case, we noticed that we were being spied upon up to the moment of our departure from the airport in Tucson. Somebody took pictures of us even while we were on the plane shortly before the doors were closed. But that vague sense of being observed went away as soon as we set foot in Genoa and resumed our normal lives.

The Americans in Genoa

As promised, a short time later we heard from Tina and Brian who announced their imminent arrival in Genoa. That meeting at the Hilton, therefore, was not limited to a simple chat. Those two were really coming from the United States to negotiate with Zanfretta and me about who knows what business transaction.

They arrived at Milan Linate airport and Zanfretta and I went to pick them up with my Volvo. Thinking that they wished to take advantage of their holiday to do a bit of sightseeing, I found them a hotel in Santa Margherita . But after a few days, I had them move to a hotel near where I live because they wanted to be closer to me. But the purpose of their journey was not tourism: they simply wanted to talk business and make an agreement with Zanfretta to have at their disposal the mysterious services that the sphere might have granted.

Thus, so that they would understand what had happened, Zanfretta and I took them to the places where the encounters with the alleged aliens took place. Among other things, when we arrived near the village of Rossi, and when I explained to them that the UFO described by Zanfretta had allegedly hidden in that valley, Brian put his hands in front of his face as if in prayer, closed his eyes and concentrated like some oriental holy men do. He stood like that for a few minutes while Zanfretta and I looked at each other not understanding the reason for that behavior. Tina, on the other hand, was looking at him seriously not saying a word.

The next day Brian and Tina outlined for us the terms of the proposed agreement. The pair wanted Zanfretta and me to move to the United States for a period of time, and more specifically to Arizona, where we were supposed to bring the mysterious sphere. For this purpose they would send a private plane that would pick us up at Genoa's Colombus airport and take us to Phoenix, via Chicago. The agreement was more than anything else with Zanfretta, I would have to translate for him as his trusted person. Once we arrived in the United States, Zanfretta would make the sphere available (in fact, according to what he said, he was the only one who could open the box containing it). At this point, once the sphere was united with the other two (although I haven't the faintest idea of how this could be done technically), it would reveal that hidden message that the aliens ultimately wanted to communicate. Brian and Tina didn't dwell on any explanation concerning the essence of this message, but it didn't take me long to gather that it would probably reveal a form of energy that would revolutionize human knowledge with unimaginable consequences on the world economy. Basically it was energy that didn't need combustion, although presumably it must have been radioactive, since the sphere had to be transported in a box made of lead. And therefore it would be a discovery that would provide unlimited wealth to those who were able to exploit this science-fictional force.

To me, what those two were talking about really did seem like science fiction. To begin with, they told Zanfretta that "for the rest of his life he wouldn't have to worry about financial problems again." Basically, they would grant him a substantial settlement that would allow him and his family to live in comfort forever. As far as I was concerned, they had prepared a contract that would establish an Italian-American joint-venture of which I would be the biggest beneficiary for the income from rights deriving from the publication of my book on the Zanfretta case in English in the world market. Included in the agreement were the rights to the immediate making of a movie by Paramount in Arizona (but in an American version that still followed the thread of events that happened in Genoa and surrounding areas), as if Zanfretta's night time adventures had had an American backdrop and local characters.

The only problem was that Zanfretta had to produce the sphere from wherever he had hidden it.

For my part, I said that I had to think about it, considering that concluding the deal successfully didn't depend on me. Zanfretta, albeit happy about how things were turning out (he saw himself in Hollywood already), substantially said the same, but something in his eyes didn't convince me entirely. To be clear, I had the feeling that what he meant, although he did not explicitly state it, was "I'd like to but I can't."

The Hypnosis of Truth

At this point we looked for the truth in hypnosis once again. As a matter of fact, the pair did ask Zanfretta to be put under hypnosis again to see if subconsciously as well, he really meant to work with them. Piero didn't look like he was that enthusiastic about the idea, but he said yes all the same. The hypnosis session therefore took place the evening of Monday, October 7, 1991, in Dr. Moretti's office, in the presence of the American couple and myself. But right from the very beginning, we knew that something was not right. In fact, Moretti instructed Zanfretta to mechanically raise his right arm every time he lied. By connecting the question to the sudden lifting of the arm, we realized that Zanfretta not only had no intention of lending his sphere to the Americans, but he didn't trust them. And, unlike what had happened during the hypnosis session of 1985, the alleged aliens were nowhere to be found. It was as if the interference,

236

as Moretti had called it, had completely disappeared. So let's see the full report of that session.

The Subconscious Speaks

Doctor Moretti: "It has been a long time since we last were in touch, since we last spoke. In all these years, have you had any further contact with those beings?"

Zanfretta: "Yes."

Doctor Moretti: "Did they treat you well?"

Zanfretta: "Yes."

Doctor Moretti: "Would you be able to contact them as you did in the past? To see if they use your voice? Do you think it's possible?"

Zanfretta: "No."

Doctor Moretti: "Piero, the contact you've had during this time, in these recent years, did it have to do with the sphere?"

Zanfretta: "Yes."

Doctor Moretti: "You've never wanted to talk about the sphere in the past. You weren't allowed. And, by the way, what was the name of the people you were in contact with? Do you remember?"

Zanfretta: "The Dargos."

Doctor Moretti: "Have they ever told you where they came from? I mean, if they came from planets, constellations ..."

Moretti, therefore tries once again to "extort" some information from the night watchman. But to no avail.

Zanfretta: "No."

Doctor Moretti: "Now, listen closely. Trust me. Now in front of you there is a large clock, but the hands of this clock spin back in time, they go backwards. And this clock will take you to the moment of your last contact. And you will tell me, and only me, you will relive, will relate everything that's happening. Quietly and calmly. There: step back in time, Piero, back, back, the past becomes the present."

Zanfretta: "I have to go, now. It's twenty to. Good, no one is following me. Impossible... how do I get off? It's impossible... how can I walk on the beam? I'm scared of falling... How strange: it looks as if it's marble ... and the light goes on by itself, and takes me down. Yes, you will come back... huh? You told me I shouldn't... Will you take me away?.... He doesn't know what it's for... Why are you putting your hand in the glass? He was screaming... But it's blinding...

It's wonderful... what do I have to do? Ah... but what do I have to do? Just look after it and wait for your return... Why was it better to open it?... I understand... When will you be back?... But I want to know... What insomnia? It helps me to understand... I would give it another month, I don't care... All right I will be your guardian for the box ... All right... But you can't hurt me... Bye...

I have to get back on the beam..."

From this series of choppy sentences we gather that Zanfretta at some point during his nighttime walk finds himself on the mountain where the cave containing the sphere is. However the road is steep and below there is only emptiness. At that point, he is afraid of falling and the aliens then suggest that he climb onto a kind of "ray of light" which turns out to be as solid as a rock. This "light" takes him down to the cave and here he meets someone with whom he speaks of the famous sphere. Or rather, this person explains to him how it works and he thinks it's "wonderful." At that point, he learns what his duties will be and asks when they would be returning, but they don't tell him. He wants to know though that they will not hurt him. Then, worried, he returns to the "ray of light" that should take him back to the mountaintop.

Doctor Moretti: "When did this contact take place? What day are we talking about?"

Zanfretta: "Saturday, half past midnight ..."

Doctor Moretti: "Of which month?"

Zanfretta: "March."

Doctor Moretti: "Of what year?"

Zanfretta: "1982."

Doctor Moretti: "Do you know which day?"

Zanfretta: "The second week ... "

We would only need this reference to 1982 to understand that what Zanfretta says while he's awake, that is that the last meeting he had was in 1981, doesn't match his reports under hypnosis. Meanwhile Moretti continues.

Doctor Moretti: "Have you heard from them since then?"

Zanfretta: "They will arrive..."

Doctor Moretti: "Do you still have the sphere?"

Zanfretta: "Yes."

Doctor Moretti: "It seems to me that something has changed inside you with respect to the sphere: has it not?"

Zanfretta: "Yes."

Doctor Moretti: "Maybe you're tired of keeping it to yourself, to be the only one to bear this responsibility."

Zanfretta: "Yes."

Doctor Moretti: "Of course you would need people that you can absolutely trust, right?"

Zanfretta: "Yes."

Doctor Moretti: "Why have you changed your mind regarding the sphere? You didn't want anyone to have it before and now you have this new compulsion. Did they give you permission?"

Zanfretta: "I don't know..."

Doctor Moretti: "Is it something that comes from within?"

Zanfretta: "Yes."

Doctor Moretti: "Would you like to share your secret with a friend? Someone you can trust?"

Moretti is attempting to see how open Zanfretta really is, considering that with this deal with the Americans on the table, we had to verify whether Zanfretta really intended to collaborate or not. We were all wasting a lot of time without even knowing for sure if the person concerned actually agreed. And the reply was the usual one, delivered with a much harsher and harder voice than the one he had used up to that moment.

Zanfretta: "**Negative for this question, tixel.**"

Doctor Moretti: "A little while ago you told me that you felt the need to no longer be the only one dealing with the sphere. Did I understand correctly?"

Zanfretta: "Yes."

Doctor Moretti: "But you're not sure: perhaps something else is stopping you from doing so, right?"

Zanfretta: "Yes."

Doctor Moretti: "What's stopping you? Can you try and describe it for me?"

Zanfretta: "They told me to wait for their arrival..."

Doctor Moretti: "You know when they arrive."

Zanfretta: "Yes."

Doctor Moretti: "Can you tell me?"

Zanfretta: "Between mid-March and mid-April 1992."

Doctor Moretti: "And until then you can't decide what to do about the sphere as you'd like to... Correct?"

Zanfretta: "Yes."

Doctor Moretti: "Listen, we'll take another small journey in time and space now. With your mind you are now inside the spaceship. When you are inside and can see it perfectly, once you're inside, I would like you to raise your right hand to let me know."

And Zanfretta from his table, raises his hand.

Doctor Moretti: "Good, thank you Piero. OK, now you're there. They are giving you the sphere, right at this moment. You hold it between your hands, you hold it in your hands, right now. Now, since I was left outside and I can't see, show me how you hold it, how big is it? Can you touch it?"

Zanfretta: "Yes."

Doctor Moretti: "Have you got it with both hands, or just one? What color is it Piero?"

Zanfretta: "It's all metal..."

Doctor Moretti: "Is the sphere inside a box or is it, you know, in your hand?"

Zanfretta: "It's inside a box..."

Doctor Moretti: "Are you holding the box now?"

Zanfretta: "Yes."

Doctor Moretti: "Would you feel like opening the box?"

Zanfretta: "Yes."

Doctor Moretti: "Open it, please: I am outside and I cannot see."

Zanfretta: "I must put it down..."

Doctor Moretti: "Yes, put it down and open it. So you can see what's inside ... maybe it's empty... maybe it's empty..."

Zanfretta: "It doesn't open..."

Doctor Moretti: "It doesn't open?"

Zanfretta: "It opens... it lights all up..."

Doctor Moretti: "And what's inside the box?"

Zanfretta: "A glass sphere, with a gold pyramid, there's a lot of light... the sphere...turns and discharges shocks... I can't do it..."

Doctor Moretti: "I wonder what it's for. Do you know?"

Zanfretta: "No."

Doctor Moretti: "No one told you?"

Zanfretta: "No."

Doctor Moretti: "Piero, can you see who gave you the box? The being that gave you the box with the sphere inside?"

Zanfretta: "Yes."

Doctor Moretti: "You can describe him?"

Zanfretta: "Yes. They are tall, in the front, on the head, they have something like red hair: the blood flows fast. And on the sides they have large spikes. The eyes are triangular and have holes..."

Doctor Moretti: "Are you afraid of them?"

Zanfretta: "No."

Doctor Moretti: "Listen, are they in front of you now?"

Zanfretta: "Yes."

Doctor Moretti: "Through you, can we communicate with them?"

Zanfretta: "Negative for this question, tixel."

Doctor Moretti: "Piero, but you're just a means of transmission. Don't worry about anything. Let them use your mouth to speak, even to speak as they want. It doesn't matter."

But the attempt fails. The day wasn't right.

Zanfretta: "They don't want to..."

Doctor Moretti: "Is there is a reason?"

Zanfretta: "They have little time available."

Doctor Moretti: "So they haven't told you anything about the sphere... or do you know something? What use could it have here on earth, I mean why does it have to be kept here on earth until their arrival."

But the answer is exasperating.

Zanfretta: "I don't know. They only told me to look after it."

Doctor Moretti: "Listen, Piero, do those beings and you too know our American friends who have come here?"

Zanfretta: "No."

Doctor Moretti: "Do you know them?"

Zanfretta: "Yes, a little."

Doctor Moretti: "Looking after the sphere whether here or in Arizona, wouldn't it be the same thing?"

The question was relevant in trying to understand how agreeable Zanfretta was to work with the Americans, but he didn't get the result he hoped for.

Zanfretta: "I don't know..."

Doctor Moretti: "There may even be a safer place than here, a place where scientists, people that can be trusted, could keep it... Do you know, have you ever heard of Dr. Hynek?"

Obviously in this way Moretti wanted to smoke Zanfretta out, considering that as we had seen in previous hypnosis sessions, Zanfretta had already repeatedly mentioned Hynek.

Zanfretta: "Yeees."

Doctor Moretti: "Good, these people are Dr. Hynek's scientific heirs following his death."

Zanfretta: "Dr. Hynek died?"

Doctor Moretti: "Yes, Dr. Hynek is dead. However, these people are the ones Dr. Hynek told to continue his work. That's why they're interested in you, in the sphere and they want to help you. Do you understand?"

Zanfretta: "At the moment, I can't give it to anyone. That's what I was told."

Doctor Moretti: "Of course, I don't mean hand over, Piero, sure. But you could keep it in another place, for example."

Zanfretta: "I have to wait for their return. If I get the sphere out before time, they will hurt me. I'd like to pull it out, but I can't."

Doctor Moretti: "I understand Piero, yes, of course. And nobody wants anything to happen to you. Listen, what will happen when they return? What do you think? Do you have any idea?"

Zanfretta: "I don't know. I'm waiting, but that day seems so far away..."

Doctor Moretti: "Piero, can I ask you something else?"

Zanfretta: "Yes."

Doctor Moretti: "Listen, do you remember saying that you need a box made of lead to carry the sphere?"

Zanfretta: "Yes."

Doctor Moretti: "And how do you know that?"

Zanfretta: "They told me."

Doctor Moretti: "Ah..."

Zanfretta: "It is very important that it doesn't open and make contact with light. It must be enclosed and sealed in a box made of lead."

Doctor Moretti: "So, listen Piero. When they come, you know who they are, right?"

Zanfretta: "Yes."

Doctor Moretti: "Ok, do you think that this sphere could be transported by a private plane from Genoa to Chicago?"

Zanfretta: "Yes, what's important is that I'm there."

Doctor Moretti: "Sure. And what danger could there be, if the sphere comes into contact with any light?"

Zanfretta: "I don't know."

Doctor Moretti: "But they told you that it's very important that this does not happen..."

Zanfretta: "Yes."

Doctor Moretti: "It is difficult for you now of course, isn't it?

Because you'd like to hand over this sphere but at the same time you are afraid of them, and you can't, right?"

Zanfretta: "Yes."

Doctor Moretti: "This is part of our problem, isn't it?"

Zanfretta: "Yes."

Doctor Moretti: "Can you tell me, you can tell me this, the dimensions of the box? More or less, as you might guess it."

Zanfretta: "Forty by forty. I measured it..."

Doctor Moretti: "Do you happen to know how thick the lead should be? Did they tell you this?"

Had he replied yes, it would have been possible to guess how much radiation the mysterious object might give off. But, as usual, he didn't provide any precise indication.

Zanfretta: "No."

Doctor Moretti: "Piero, perhaps you can tell me this. In the past, before they gave it to you, had this sphere ever been here on earth other times?"

The purpose of the question was to ascertain whether Zanfretta was aware, as the Americans had said, of other spheres that had been given to other earthlings over the years. Also because the Americans claimed to have found another two. But, thinking about it, what could poor Piero know anything about that?

Zanfretta: "I don't know."

Doctor Moretti: " Piero, they talked with you many times. Did they ever mention whether in addition to yourself they had been in contact with any other people, here on earth?"

Zanfretta: "I don't know."

Doctor Moretti: "Listen, Piero, you trust me, don't you?"

Zanfretta: "Yes."

Doctor Moretti: "Well, I want to ask you now: would you like to work with these American friends? They are people I completely trust."

Zanfretta: "I don't yet..."

Doctor Moretti: "Why?"

Zanfretta: "I don't know them well enough..."

Doctor Moretti: "What would you like to have so you could get to know them better and have full confidence in them. Because they are the disciples... you do know whose, don't you?"

Zanfretta: "Yes, Hynek..."

Doctor Moretti: "Ok, what would you need in order to trust them?"

Zanfretta: "I don't know, I don't know them well enough..."

Doctor Moretti: "Fine, fine..."

Zanfretta: "I am sorry..."

Doctor Moretti: "No, don't worry. What you're saying is right, I understand..."

Zanfretta: "I'd like to..."

Doctor Moretti: "You'd like to, but?"

Zanfretta: " ...my friend Rino that..."

Doctor Moretti: "Excuse me, I didn't understand: can you repeat?"

Zanfretta: "My friend Rino..."

Doctor Moretti: "Of course, of course: but Rino is with them..."

Zanfretta: "I am sorry, but I can't help it..."

Doctor Moretti: "So that's not your deep desire? There's more: you can tell me..."

Zanfretta: "Maybe later on... I'd like to know them better: you can't get to know people in only three or four days..."

Doctor Moretti: "Of course..."

Zanfretta: "It seems strange to me that good people... I don't know what to do about it."

Doctor Moretti: "Sure, I understand. After all this is too important, isn't it? I perfectly understand."

Zanfretta: "When I saw them the first time, they didn't inspire much confidence in me."

Doctor Moretti: "Why?"

Zanfretta: "Because it all happened so quickly and then, at the airport, I changed my mind. I like them now. But it's too early to trust them. I am sorry..."

Doctor Moretti: "But, even the day that you do finally trust them, sadly, what are we going to do with the sphere? Even if you trust them, from what I understand, there's little to be done...Or there could be a compromise. I'm not saying now, right? The day that you trust them completely wouldn't it be possible to contact these beings and see if there's any way they'll let you keep the sphere. Keep it, but together with other people you trust, and in a different place. Do you think that they, through you, can hear my question now? Do you think that they have this kind of power or not, that special conditions are needed? You, let's say in your own mind, would you like that?"

Zanfretta: "Yes, I told them that in time I would introduce them. And they told me they weren't... And I said that I don't know if they had seen them, that they're ugly... they're horrible... that they're so

244

tall...Fine by me..."

Doctor Moretti: "So they were ready to do what? To give the sphere to other people in addition to you?

Zanfretta: "No."

Doctor Moretti: "Ready for what?"

Zanfretta: "Our American friends are ready..."

Doctor Moretti: "Ah, they're your friends then?"

Zanfretta: "Yes."

Doctor Moretti: "Your American friends are ready. Are you?"

Zanfretta: "I don't have a problem with them, I saw them..."

Doctor Moretti: "What are your problems then?"

Zanfretta: "For them, they've never seen them..."

Doctor Moretti:."Ahhh ... I'll ask you something. You'll answer me sincerely, as you always do. However, if some part deep within you is of a different opinion from what your mouth says, then this arm will rise. Are you ready to answer?"

In this way, Moretti wanted to check if there was a latent conflict in Zanfretta's head or not. As if on that table there were two separate people and not just one.

Zanfretta: "Yes."

Doctor Moretti: "Good. Would you, when the time comes, go willingly to the United States and go with these friends to see the places where what is expected to take place does take place when the moment arrives?

Zanfretta: "Yes."

But the arm slowly rises.

Doctor Moretti: "You give your approval and your collaboration because a book could be written, translated into English for the United States, about your story and the movie, too. You give your approval, through Rino, of course .. "

Zanfretta: "Yes."

Doctor Moretti: "These friends want you to know something very important. Something that, if you are contacted, you are also able to convey to someone. In this Space Center, which is in Arizona, a custom-made structure will be made to accommodate the sphere. This is a piece of information that you should have. Therefore, it's something very important that's already been organized while we wait for the right time. Did you get my message?"

Zanfretta: "Yes."

Doctor Moretti: "Are you happy about this?"

Zanfretta: "Yes."

But once again, the arm slowly rises.

Doctor Moretti: "I know that you're happy about it, but you're also a little sorry that this thing, that there are so many new people involved, maybe it was better when it was something just between us, right?"

Zanfretta: "Yes."

The time had come to stop the session. Basically we had seen and heard that Zanfretta would have wanted to hand over the sphere and in doing so could considerably improve his life. But he could not do this. And that's not all. He didn't trust the Americans and the thought of taking the sphere to the United States didn't appeal to him in the least. So it was that the two Americans heard everything, since I had translated everything for them as we went along. What else should we have asked? And so the session ended.

Doctor Moretti: "Now, Piero, rest. Have a nice deep sleep, forget all this and don't think about anything anymore. Sleep deeply. A heavy, restorative sleep. When I wake you up, you will feel just as if you've had a good night's sleep. And you'll wake up feeling fit."

Moretti lets Zanfretta rest for ten minutes, then continues.

Doctor Moretti: "Now, Piero, it's 9:45 p.m. on October 7, 1991. You've slept soundly, you're feeling very well, you're feeling fully fit. Even though you slept very well, you'll sleep well tonight once more. Now I'm going to count from ten to zero. Slowly you'll come out of hypnosis. When I say the word zero, your eyes will open, your body will be strong, your mind will be serene and fresh just like someone who has just had a deep, restful sleep. You'll be in good spirits and also a bit euphoric. Ten, nine, eight, seven, six, five, four, three, two, one, zero."

Zanfretta opens his eyes again, smiles, looks around and sits up. He is doing well and, as usual he remembers absolutely nothing of what he said.

Return to the United States

I don't know what impression our Americans guests had from that hypnosis. Perhaps it wasn't the best. In any case, in the end, after a two-week stay in Liguria, Tina P. Choate and Brian P. Myers went back to Arizona. Since there was nothing in writing, I remained

246

skeptical. But I had to change my mind when on January 20, 1992, I received a 3-page fax from Chicago Attorney at law Nicholas J, Constantine. It was a contract listing 17 points (which I still have) where I was really being asked to form that company that Tina and Brian had previously spoken about. There was a problem, though: the contract stated that the agreement would be governed by the laws of the State of Arizona (that no one knows in Italy) and that I would be responsible with 50 per cent ownership, while Tina and Brian had operational management with 25 per cent each. In other words, they would run the show, but if something went wrong I would be liable.

After showing the contract to a professor of International Law at the University of Genoa (who told me that if I signed it, I would no longer be able to sleep at night), I decided that I would write to Mr. Constantine asking that a few ground rules that guaranteed my safety be included in it. Meanwhile, the pair of them kept calling me at home at all hours, including in the middle of the night, trying to convince me to sign and "that everything would be all right."

However, I still had my reservations. Also because they never wanted to tell me who would pay for all those expenses, like our flights from Italy to the United States and back. In any case, I spoke with Zanfretta asking him what he intended to do. It was also for this reason that one day, it was Monday, January 20, 1992, Piero Zanfretta went to lie down once again on Dr. Moretti's table, and this is what he said.

The Enlightening Hypnosis

Doctor Moretti: "Piero, the Americans are not here now. I know that you needed to talk freely with Rino and me. Now you have the chance to do so, to talk about everything you had inside before and could not talk about then... When I say the word three you can speak with the deepest and most unprotected part of yourself. One, two, three: we're listening to you with complete trust and respect."

However, despite these nice words, Zanfretta remains silent. And so Moretti steps in again.

Doctor Moretti: "Is there something in particular that you wanted to tell us and that you didn't want the Americans to hear? Would you prefer Rino to ask you the questions now that it's just between ourselves?"

247

Zanfretta: "Yes."

Doctor Moretti: "In that case I hand the session over to Rino and you will answer Rino's voice as if it were my own."

Rino: "Piero, when do you think they will allow you to hand over the sphere?"

Zanfretta: "I don't know..."

Rino: "Can you contact them, now?"

Zanfretta: "No."

Rino: "Why not?"

Zanfretta: "They are too far away."

Rino: "And when are they going to approach us? Isn't there a precise date that you had to remember?"

Zanfretta: "No."

However, given that when he was awake, Zanfretta had projected that his alleged "encounter" would take place in the spring, I asked him a more specific question.

Rino: "Does a date between March 15 and April 15 of this year mean anything to you?"

Zanfretta: "Yes."

Rino: "And what does it mean?"

Zanfretta: "They will come..."

Rino: "Did they tell you that they will arrive between March 15 and April 15?"

Zanfretta: "Yes."

Rino: "And what else did they say?"

Zanfretta says something incomprehensible and as a precaution, Moretti takes charge of the session again.

Doctor Moretti: "Now Piero, you can recognize my voice and for now I'm taking charge of the session again. Listen closely: we will go on a trip back in time. Imagine a large white clock with black hands. This clock runs in the opposite direction. Backward, backward, backward: you're surrounded by a thick fog. A fog that takes you outside time and space. Thought has no boundaries. The fog is thick, very thick. Now the clock-hands stop: we are at the exact moment when you last spoke with them. And I'm listening to you speak with them. I'm listening to your words and their words, which you are translating. Do you know what day it is?"

Zanfretta: "No."

Doctor Moretti: "It doesn't matter... you will tell me now everything that happens. Now you're inside the spaceship and you tell me everything that is happening. Inside the spaceship: the conversations and the particulars..."

Zanfretta: "How does it open? From there? Look at that... How many lights, they hurt my eyes. Yes, I'll open it... But what's it for? But it is like now... What do I need it for? OK, it is only ready for a moment. When will you return? It's been a long time..."

The conversation is confused, the recording of the session is also technically faulty. However, it is clear that Zanfretta is relating a conversation with someone who is giving him instructions.

Doctor Moretti: "When are they coming back? What did they tell you?"

Zanfretta: "They'll be back in 1992."

Doctor Moretti: "Ask him if in 1992 they'll give you permission to take the box away or show it. You can ask them that. Or if they're coming back for other reasons..."

But Zanfretta doesn't answer for a few minutes. Then he resumes.

Zanfretta: "What is it used for? I'd like to know now..."

Doctor Moretti: "Why are you coming back in April? Why are you coming back? Why? To release the box or not? To release the box from the cave or not? Say it..."

Zanfretta: "To release the box from the cave or not? And do I have to wait this long?"

At this point, Zanfretta mutters something incomprehensible. Every so often he utters a few words, but we can't understand him.

Doctor Moretti: "They didn't want to tell you anything about their return in April? Whether they'll release the box? Whether in April you'll be able to take it or if instead it will stay where it is? Did they give you an idea about anything, Piero?"

Zanfretta: "No, but they didn't reply..."

Doctor Moretti: "Now I will ask you a very important question and you will answer with the truth as you know it. According to you, when they come back in April and make contact with you, is it possible that nothing will happen? They might just check the box and leave it there for who knows how long..."

Zanfretta: "I don't know... I will be there waiting..."

Doctor Moretti: "Now Piero, I will ask you something and you'll answer me. Many times things might have gone in a certain way and we might have stored them differently in our mind. In perfectly good faith. Now, I will ask you something and you'll tell me. But if by chance, without meaning to, you make a mistake in telling the story, just your right hand will rise. Now, completely forget the order I gave you, forget it completely. Sleep, forget what I said..."

Moretti's attempt is obvious. Basically he's doing the same thing he had instructed Zanfretta to do during the hypnosis with the Americans: he is putting Zanfretta in the condition to reveal by himself when he's forced to say something whether he wants to or not. In a sense, it is a stratagem to free him from the conditioning which the mysterious aliens have imposed on him.

Doctor Moretti: "Have you ever been followed into the cave?"

Zanfretta: "No."

Doctor Moretti: "Have you ever suspected that you were being followed?"

Zanfretta: "Never."

Doctor Moretti: "Have there ever been incidents or strange circumstances while you were going to inspect the cave?"

Zanfretta: "Yes, one night I was hit by something at the bottom of the cave. I went to have a look. I thought someone was there... But it was a hare."

In this regard Zanfretta claims that one evening a hare had gotten into the cave while he was there. At that point, the sphere allegedly struck the animal with a large ray of light killing it on the spot. When he went to look, he found the animal cut exactly in two, lengthwise. One part was incinerated, the other vitrified.

Doctor Moretti: "Are there buttons under the sphere?"

Zanfretta: "Yes."

Doctor Moretti: "Do you know how to use them?"

Zanfretta: "No."

Doctor Moretti: "You know what they're for?"

Zanfretta: "They just flash. On the top as well..."

Doctor Moretti: "Do you think it's dangerous to touch them?"

Zanfretta: "I don't know..."

Doctor Moretti: " Now I'll temporarily hand the session over to Rino's voice. You will answer Rino's voice exactly as if it were my voice."

Di Stefano: "Piero, listen. Are you convinced that you want to go to the United States, if they let you? If they give you permission to use the sphere and establish a relationship with those Americans to find out what the sphere is for?"

Zanfretta: "Yes."

Di Stefano: "Piero, tell me the truth. If those gentlemen, those entities, allowed you to use the sphere, what would you want to do with it?"

Zanfretta: "Solution three."

Di Stefano: "What is solution three?"

But Zanfretta doesn't explain and doesn't reply. And so I persist.

Di Stefano: "Piero, to find out what the sphere is for, what do you think we need to do?"

But Zanfretta continues to remain silent. So I start again.

Di Stefano: "Let's put it another way. Are you willing to look for someone you can work with to find out what the sphere is for? If they give you permission, of course. What attributes should these people have to be able to work with them?"

But Zanfretta continues to remain silent.

Di Stefano: "I'll ask you another question then. Do you want to come with me to the United States to see if these people are genuine or not? If they deserve your trust or not?"

But Zanfretta doesn't reply. His mental conditioning is more than obvious.

Di Stefano: "Listen Piero, what is it you don't like about the Americans? Not just those two that came here but in general?"

Zanfretta: "I don't know..."

Di Stefano: "Listen Piero, do you think that those beings who gave you the sphere have friends or someone in the United States?"

Zanfretta: "I don't know."

Di Stefano: "Piero, based on how you see things, why is it that you don't you want to go to the United States? What is it you don't like about going there?"

Zanfretta: "They're too sure of themselves..."

Di Stefano: "What do you mean? What makes you think that these people don't deserve to be trusted?"

Zanfretta: "I don't know..."

Di Stefano: "But, do you think it's worthwhile going there to see whether you can maybe get in touch with someone other than them? I mean go to the United States?"

The question is clear, but once again Zanfretta answers in the same way.

Zanfretta: "I don't know."

Di Stefano: "Would you like to try, though..."

Zanfretta: "Yes."

Di Stefano : "Piero, listen up. From what you remember of the past, these people, the ones who gave you the sphere, do they have someone here among us? Do they know someone else other than you? Do they have one of them around us? ".

Zanfretta: "No, they only know me..."

Di Stefano: "On the spaceship have you ever seen a register, something with some photographs, with people you knew?"

Zanfretta: "Yes."

Di Stefano: "And do you remember who these people were?"

Zanfretta: "I did know someone..."

Di Stefano: "And of those you knew, can you name a few? Even if you know them by name only. Perhaps you can just recognize the photograph."

Zanfretta: "No."

Di Stefano: "Not even one?"

But Zanfretta doesn't respond.

Di Stefano: "Listen Piero, tell me in all honesty: do you feel like going on in this venture in which you and I, but not just us, Dr. Moretti as well, are involved? Hoping that when these individuals, these entities return, they'll let us study the sphere?"

Zanfretta: "Yes."

Di Stefano: "Do you think it's right to do so?"

Zanfretta: "Yes."

Di Stefano: "Piero, when you don't answer certain questions, is it the fear of someone or something that prevents you from answering? Of the consequences that your answer might have? Or is it that you just don't know?"

But even this small attempt to learn more about what was happening inside Zanfretta during those hypnosis sessions, ended miserably. In fact, the former night watchman was silent, leaving us to struggle with our doubts. And so Moretti took charge of the situation again.

Doctor Moretti: "Piero, it's Dr. Moretti. Are you afraid inside yourself that someone else beside us who know each other might put the sphere to bad use?"

Zanfretta: "Yes."

Doctor Moretti: "And if someone used it in a bad way, would it mean danger? Would you feel somehow responsible for it?"

Zanfretta: "Yes."

Doctor Moretti: "So, tell me if what I'm saying to you is true: that in reality, if it was your choice, you would not want to go to the United

States, and that you would not give the sphere to the Americans because you feel morally responsible for it and would not want to be guilty of handing it over to someone you thought might use it in the wrong way. Is what I'm saying correct?"

Zanfretta: "Yes."

At that point, the matter was crystal clear. Zanfretta in his heart had no intention of handing over "his" sphere, much less showing it to anyone. Unless he was commanded to do so by his alien "superiors."

Doctor Moretti: "So answer this question as well. Is it true that you would even sacrifice the financial aspect of this, and even a lot of money, because you feel a bit like its guardian, the one morally responsible for the sphere? And even if the extra-terrestrials said 'You can freely give it away,' you might even turn down a lot of money, but you wouldn't give it to people that you are afraid might use it badly. Is what I am saying true or not?"

Zanfretta: "It's true."

Basically, Moretti had perfectly understood the individual and now he knew that all other consideration aside, Zanfretta would never give that sphere away.

Doctor Moretti: "Because, let's admit it, after so many years now, the sphere is not only theirs, in the end it's also a bit yours, isn't it?"

Zanfretta: "Yes, it's mine."

Doctor Moretti: "And therefore it's fair that when they give you permission, if they set you free you, you'll use it only as you see fit. Is that right, Piero?"

Zanfretta: "Yes, it was entrusted to me. "

Doctor Moretti: "And you want to be doubly sure about this. Otherwise if you're not, no amount of money would be enough for you to give it to anyone else. Is what I'm saying true?"

Zanfretta: "Yes."

Doctor Moretti: "Tell me honestly, I'm the only one listening to you now: would you give it to Rino if you suspected that Rino, perhaps out of naivety might give it to the Americans? If you thought this, would you give it to Rino? Answer me, honestly."

Zanfretta: "No."

Doctor Moretti: " So one thing is clear to me. The moral aspect of all this is the real and most important factor for your decision on who might or might be the right one to receive this sphere. Is that right, Piero?"

Zanfretta: "Yes."

Doctor Moretti: "Good, I thank you for these answers. And now, for your safety and protection, I will give you a hypnotic order. An order that will automatically work within you forever. Listen to my words closely. From now on, Piero, nobody except me, Dr. Moretti, I repeat nobody, no voice in the world will be able to put you under hypnosis because you know that they would do it to misuse the sphere. I repeat: except for Dr. Moretti, except for my voice, you will not let yourself be put under hypnosis, you will not go under hypnosis with any other voice because you would run the risk of being hypnotized to use the sphere the wrong way. And you will prevent it. You'll prevent it. You'll prevent it by not going under hypnosis. Now Piero, don't think about it anymore, sleep a deep and quiet sleep and when I wake you up, you shall feel perfectly refreshed and rested and you'll feel very well. Truly comforted. Sleep, sleep and don't think about anything anymore. Now I'll count from ten to zero. As I count, you'll very easily come out of hypnosis progressively. When I say the word zero and you open your eyes, you'll be in a state of perfect mental clarity, fresh, rested. Without any kind of discomfort or ailment, you will feel very well straight away. Ten, nine, eight: the sleep becomes lighter. Seven: very light. Six: hypnosis is extremely light. Five: you begin to loosen up your muscles. Four: lighter and lighter. Three, two, one, zero.

Zanfretta was awake. And Moretti, being the excellent psychologist that he was, had managed to clarify all his doubts and concerns.

The Deal Goes Awry

It was at that point, when I came to the realization that my fears regarding Zanfretta, his sphere and his behavior had every good reason to exist (he didn't intend to show it to anyone), that I wrote to the two Americans telling them that I didn't want to be involved any further in a deal that did not convince me in the least.

And so Zanfretta's American story was unsuccessful, to mutual disappointment on both sides of the Atlantic.

For the record, at the end of 1992, the movie "Fire in the Sky" came out in cinemas worldwide (the title of the first edition of my book was "Lights in the Night" which I then changed because a novel by Simenon had the same name). The film was based on the abduction of the logger Travis Walton, in Oregon, by a UFOs: a story which was somewhat less compelling than Zanfretta's. The film was produced by Paramount and Walton was the only person who Tina and Brian allowed to see their archive.

The Archive Mystery

Only later, with some targeted research, did I learn Tina P. Choate and Brian P. Myers' official story. It all began in 1952 when Jim Lorenzen, an electronics engineer at the observatory of Kitt Peak in Tucson, and his wife Coral, a science journalist, founded The Arial Phenomena Research Organisation (APRO) in Arizona. The pair wrote to the most committed UFO researchers in the world and soon managed to put together a rich archive of thousands of cases, with photographs and testimonials.

When in 1984 Professor Joseph Allen Hynek, founder of the already well-known Center for UFO Research (CUFOS), moved to Scottsdale with his wife, he met two people, Brian P. Myers and Tina P. Choate, who introduced him to a wealthy millionaire who was passionate about the study of UFOs and who offered to finance the illustrious academic's studies. At that point, the three opened an office in Scottsdale, but pretty soon Hynek clashed with the two partners, believing he couldn't trust them any further. And he sent them away. Among other things, during that time Hynek became ill with a brain tumor and in 1986 he died. We don't know why Hynek didn't trust the pair anymore, but we can assume that the disagreement had to do with his highly-documented archive that somehow, and this is what the parties concerned have claimed, ended up in Tina and Brian's hands.

Two years later, in 1988, Jim Lorenzen also passed away and his family, his wife Coral and son Larry, were left with the house completely full of filing cabinets overflowing with news on UFO sightings from all over the world. For the record, there were eighteen large office cabinets with something like 15,000 documented cases. Having heard about the death of Mr. Lorenzen, Mark Rodeghier, president of the CUFOS of Chicago, the organization founded by Hynek, offered to buy the archive just as he had done with that of the NICAP, an organization of the same kind.

But at this point, something happened that is still unclear today. In fact, Brian P. Myers and Tina P. Choate re-emerge from the shadows. In the interim they had founded the International Center for UFO Research (ICUFOR), which still exists today in Scottsdale. The pair managed to convince Larry Lorenzen, we don't know at what price, to sell his father's impressive archive to them and one day they turn up with a big truck in front of the Lorenzen house, load all the files and take them somewhere, the location of which no one has ever learned the whereabouts. Someone said that the files ended up in a garage, but it is only guesswork. In fact, today, Brian P. Myers, aged 57 and Tina P. Choate, 61 years old, possess the largest UFO document archive in the world and have prohibited access to everyone except Travis Walton. After that, they went back into the shadows and gave no cause to talk about themselves again. There are no biographies, no recent news or photographs of them anywhere.

I have the only ones that show them in Genoa with Zanfretta and me.

The Secret Project

It is therefore possible that the couple's strange behavior and the enormous financial availability that they flaunted was really due to the presence of a mysterious millionaire (Brian and Tina always refused to identify their backer) who has already used large sums to implement a plan which will be brought to fruition when a mysterious new sphere turns up somewhere in the world. Attention had probably been focused on Zanfretta because the organization that the American couple owned was convinced that he truly had it. Then, when they saw that the former night watchman wasn't closing the deal, they dropped him. And it wouldn't be too incredible to think that these two people studied all the cases in their rich archive to see if, in fact, among the many testimonies from people who claim to have been abducted by UFOs, there is one that can lead them to the famous third sphere.

We know for sure that not even the project of the Space Science Center Authority Limited has been completed. Therefore we can assume that there were business-related problems that in some way have delayed its development.

The research, therefore, continues. And I'm not ruling out the possibility that Tina and Brian throughout these years have already been in some other remote part of the world looking for a trace that can lead them to the sphere. However, we need to be sure of one thing: no American millionaire, as eccentric or fixated as he may be, throws his money away on some idle research. He surely must have some shred of evidence that leads him to step in and to invest capital in such an ephemeral direction... And so, while Zanfretta keeps repeating to the four winds that he really does have that sphere, there is indeed someone who is seriously looking for it, and who knows at what cost.

The Sphere Enigma

Nevertheless, in those days there really was a feeling that that sphere could pop up at any moment. One afternoon, Bruno Ferracciolo and I even went up to the mountains near Rossi to see if we could get closer to the bottom of the valley where Zanfretta's mysterious flying saucer allegedly hid. It is in fact around that area that the former night watchman goes every twenty days to check on his sphere.

But we were forced to give up after a few hundred meters. The terrain in that area is too rough to be able examine it without suitable climbing equipment. Between one escarpment and the other, there are differences in height of even ten meters, and one false step would be enough to fall into ravines where you can't even see the bottom. We might think that if the aliens really existed, there would be no doubt that they would have chosen the right place to make their appearances. In fact, as we have already seen throughout the progression of this book, 14 kilometers of practically uninhabited Apennines with the exception of a few tiny rural villages extend from those heights before reaching the province of Alessandria. Only very narrow trails join one hamlet to the next and a provincial road that climbs up among the hills is the only accessible way. That is Zanfretta's kingdom. A kingdom which he has shown he knows only too well, and in which he moves with a truly enviable self-confidence.

As if all this weren't enough, it must be said that the former night watchman kept saying that the sphere really existed and that under certain conditions he meant to show it. Actually this was never so, but as we have seen once before already, he said that he took two of his friends up on the mountains to show them this extraordinary object, but they got scared just before reaching the site. If we put it this way, the story could also lend itself to easy irony but let's try to imagine the scene. We're talking about a narrow mountain road with absolutely no lighting, around midnight or shortly after. It's freezing and Zanfretta invites his friends to get out of the car and venture out with him on the crest of an escarpment, in complete darkness. And he, unconcerned about the dangers, advances surefooted in the night. Can we blame those two if, at a certain point, they said to him, "No, thanks, we're going back home?"

In actual fact, imagination aside, the story didn't go exactly like this. But let's hear how things really went from the voice of one of the protagonists of that evening. Giorgio Valle, 60 years old, retired security guard and Zanfretta's former colleague and friend: "In that period," Valle says, "Zanfretta told us that those people, the alleged aliens, needed help. In other words, they were looking for someone. Among other things, he claimed that the aliens had photographs of us all: Tutti, Cassiba and me as well. He explained to me that someone had taken a picture of me while I was sitting in the car in Piazza della Vittoria. So, more out of curiosity than anything else, Mino Ferri, an engineer who worked with us at the Val Bisagno Institute, and I offered to go with him one night to meet with these beings. We decided on one evening, but that time Ferri found an excuse and said he couldn't come. Therefore only Zanfretta and I went. The appointment was in Piazza della Vittoria. I can't remember the year or the day. Even though we were in the '90s. I'd say it was in early autumn, it wasn't very cold yet. We went with my car and I drove. While we were starting the climb that goes to Rossi, at some point Piero told me that they were behind us, that a red light was following us. I looked in the rearview mirror, and if I have to tell the truth, I never saw that red light. In any case we got to the top and he said that they were around there. He could feel their presence. I looked at the sky, but frankly I couldn't see anything. It was between 11:30 p.m. and midnight. He told me to wait for him in the car because he 'had to go where he had to go.' There was no light and the silence was absolute. I don't deny that in my heart I was afraid. I was comforted by the fact that I had the gun with me. As a security guard, I could also go around armed. But what would a gun do against those creatures? So I sat there, without moving in the driver's seat, for about half an hour. Then Zanfretta came back. He told me that everything was all right, that he had seen them and we could go back. They had decided not to do anything for that evening. Even though, according to him, we had to be introduced to those people. So we went back

258

and it ended there. In fact there should have been a second evening, but Ferri once again categorically refused. He'd had second thoughts about it and didn't want to get involved in that story: he was afraid. Therefore we didn't pursue it. So, my adventure ends here. Since that day I haven't had a chance to go up to the mountains with Zanfretta again."

From Valle's story we can understand that, actually Zanfretta had no intention of showing the sphere to his friend and that night excursion had just been, in the end, a night-time stroll in the mountains.

It was precisely because of all of these reasons that in the end, at Zanfretta's suggestion, we all went back to Dr. Moretti's office. This will be the last time. By now we were all a little tired of this dilly-dallying. The question was: does the sphere really exist? And if the answer was yes, did Zanfretta really mean to make it available, under the right conditions? The session took place the evening of Friday, April 24, 1992, i.e. after that April 7, 1992, which was supposed to be the date of the last appointment with the alleged 'aliens'.

The Final Hypnosis

Doctor Moretti: "The clock keeps ticking. The hands will stop just before one in the morning between April 7 and 8, 1992. When the clock stops, the fog will disappear. And you will not be here any longer, you will be there at that moment. And you will describe for me everything that is happening to you. Everything that is happening. Moreover, if whatever you say doesn't correspond exactly to what has actually happened, your right arm will rise, without your being aware of it. Everything you say that doesn't match with the absolute truth will make your right arm rise. Now, forget this order. The last order I have given you. Forget, forget. Now, Piero, return to your travel in time. Find that moment again and live through it again as if it were here right now: one o'clock in the morning during the night between April 7 and 8. You can speak in a loud and strong voice, even If you're in deep hypnosis."

Zanfretta: "I cannot answer..."

Doctor Moretti: "You don't remember it?"

Zanfretta: "No, doctor Moretti told me that he was the only one who could speak to me."

Zanfretta, therefore, mindful of the instruction he had received from Moretti himself during the previous hypnosis, was reacting as if his interlocutor wasn't the same doctor.

Doctor Moretti: "Excuse me? Can you speak up a bit, please?"

Zanfretta: "Doctor Moretti..."

Doctor Moretti: "Yes..."

Zanfretta: " ...requested that he be the only one who can speak to me. And he gave me an order of silence."

Doctor Moretti: "I gave you an order of silence. Who gave you an order of silence?"

Zanfretta: "Doctor Moretti."

Doctor Moretti: "Sure, but I am Dr. Moretti. Do you recognize my voice now?"

Zanfretta: "Yes."

Doctor Moretti: "I'm giving you permission to speak now."

Zanfretta: "I'm going to see the box. Who knows what all those words are..."

Doctor Moretti: "What words, Piero?"

Zanfretta: "In the strange language. I want to get down. I'm parking the car. No one is there. I must be careful. Away with the beam. Box of .... , why are you pulsing like this? No, no... I'll come back tomorrow. Not tonight, I'll come back tomorrow. Why is it casting so much light? No, I'll come back tomorrow. Gave...to concentrate... The pen, a leaflet...writing... in Rino's sheet...Yes... what? slowly...yes, I'm writing...all right...No, this is not possible...okay...now I'm going home, quickly... Good God..."

Doctor Moretti: "What are you saying?"

Zanfretta: "What they told me... Now the light of the sphere is back to normal...and I wrote what I heard repeating... in my head."

Doctor Moretti: "And do you know what you were hearing?"

Zanfretta: "Yes, earthly friend, we haven't been in touch with you for a long time. But we weren't receiving any answers. Do you still have the light?"

Doctor Moretti: "Why are you worried about what they said?"

Zanfretta: "Because it makes no sense."

Doctor Moretti: "What doesn't make sense?"

Zanfretta: "To keep something for so long and then be told that they will return in my time to take the box back. And now they'll have to think about the damage they have done to me..."

Doctor Moretti: "I'd like to ask you one thing now since you might have the experience to be able to reply. At first, remember? They wanted to give it to Hynek, and now they say that they want to take it back, don't you find it strange?"

Zanfretta: "That's what I asked them too, but they haven't given me an answer. They only said: wait for our return. The light is back to normal, they have cautioned me about the danger that it can bring. All right: I'll do as you say."

Doctor Moretti: "What are they saying?"

Zanfretta: "That I don't have to worry about anything and that I have to wait a while longer..."

Doctor Moretti: "Did they tell you how long you have to wait?"

Zanfretta: "No, I insisted and they sent an electric shock to my head."

Doctor Moretti: "Do you remember, Piero, that strange message they gave you in that language? Did you write it down?"

Zanfretta: "Yes."

Doctor Moretti: "You have it in front of your eyes now, try to read it."

Zanfretta: "I can't..."

Doctor Moretti: "You can't understand it?"

Zanfretta: "No."

Doctor Moretti: "But you know you can do it..."

Zanfretta: " No."

Doctor Moretti: "And isn't it strange that they gave you something you don't know how to read?"

Zanfretta: "They asked me to. I only know that they'll be in touch soon..."

Doctor Moretti: "Piero, have you ever tried to photograph the sphere?"

Zanfretta: "Yes, some time ago. Rino had given me the camera..."

Doctor Moretti: "And do you remember how you took the photo? With the flash, without..."

Zanfretta: "I took a dozen external photos and a dozen internal photos."

Doctor Moretti: "Meaning inside the cave?"

Zanfretta: "Yes."

Doctor Moretti: "And did you take the internal ones with the flash?"

Zanfretta: "Yes, four one way, and four the other way. And while it was opening."

Doctor Moretti: "Did they come out well?"

Zanfretta: "Well, I took them..."

Doctor Moretti: "Where did you take the external shots from?"

Zanfretta: "I took one picture where the road splits, four from the top toward the tree. A tree where there is a point of reference. And four more from the opposite side. The other ones inside the cave."

Doctor Moretti: "And why did you think of taking these four?"

Zanfretta: "Because Rino asked me. He told me to take some pictures and I did..."

At this point I have to add a clarification. I once gave Zanfretta a camera with fixed focus lens, equipped with flash and loaded with a 36 shots 110 ASA roll, asking him to take photos outside and inside of the cave, in addition to the sphere itself. The external photos, once developed, showed the profile of the mountains, while the internal ones were all completely burned. As if the film had been subjected to a strong light source or radiation. There was only one very strange thing in those photos: in one of the shots it looked as if a flow of energy had become impressed in it and it went from the bottom upwards forming a whole series of dots with a small sphere in the center. I have shown the film and photos to several professional photographers and none of them have been able to explain to me what that strange phenomenon that had been photographed could be. So that readers can understand what I am talking about, I am publishing that photo in this book for the first time.

Doctor Moretti: "No-one followed you?"

Zanfretta: "Yes, an Alpha 33 with two people inside followed me."

Doctor Moretti: "Did you see them?"

Zanfretta: "I did a U-turn. When I went back they ducked. I couldn't even take down the number plate: there was too much traffic..."

And here a new event comes into play. In fact, who were those people following Zanfretta? Who could still be interested in following him? Let's keep in mind that when he said those things he was still in deep hypnosis therefore the degree of reliability is pretty high.

Doctor Moretti: "Instead of the camera, would you be willing to bring a video camera with you to film the cave, to film everything?"

Zanfretta: "But nothing comes out... I don't know..."

Doctor Moretti: "Why? Because it is dark?"

Zanfretta: "No, when I open the box there is so much light..."

Doctor Moretti: "And could you film the outside? Like you did with the photographs, the cave and all the rest?"

Zanfretta: "Yes."

Doctor Moretti: "How is it going with Rino? Do you still have a good relationship?"

Zanfretta: "Well, sort of..."

Doctor Moretti: "What happened? You can tell me."

Zanfretta: "He wants us to go down there, that we film the outside. And I try to make him understand that it's very dangerous, and that I don't want to have people on my conscience for nothing..."

Doctor Moretti: "Because the road to get there is dangerous?"

Zanfretta: "No, you can get there no problem. It's when you're close to the cave that it's dangerous. Besides, I can't show him the exact spot. It's very dangerous, I'd like him to understand..."

Doctor Moretti: "Well, you know, maybe with all instructions and countermands that have been given lately, mind you, it's not your fault, it's possible that there are uncertainties, you know..."

Zanfretta: "I can understand that. But what can I do about it?"

Doctor Moretti: "Not so much for the person involved, but due to a whole series of situations that you're aware of. Do you understand what I mean?"

Zanfretta: "Yes."

Doctor Moretti: "Anyhow, this is not important. What do we have to do now, Piero?"

Zanfretta: "About the sphere? We wait for them to call..."

Doctor Moretti: "Can you get in touch with them?"

Zanfretta: "No, not yet. They will call me..."

Doctor Moretti: "And they will tell you when they are coming? To pick it up or are there other options?"

Zanfretta: "I don't know."

Doctor Moretti: "They told you they're coming to tell you what exactly?"

Zanfretta: "They're coming to pick up the box..."

Doctor Moretti: "They're coming straight to take the box... and there's nothing you can do...?"

Zanfretta: "But I can't take it away before then: I want an explanation. I can't take it away, I want an explanation first..."

Doctor Moretti: "And if they take it and say nothing to you?"

Zanfretta: "That remains to be seen..."

Doctor Moretti: "In any case, considering how they have behaved up until now, anything can happen..."

Zanfretta: "They can't do whatever they want, after all these years...

I want to bring them to the point of showing themselves. I want the others to see it."

Moretti: "In any case it's difficult for me to imagine that these beings suddenly behave differently from how they have done up to now...!

Zanfretta: "I will try, I have to find a solution..."

In the end, it is with these words that Moretti terminates this short hypnosis session. The conversation had reached a dead end. Zanfretta wanted satisfaction from his alien interlocutors, but on the other hand they had him act as they wanted and had no intention of treating him as a partner. Indeed, we can safely say that they saw him no more no less than a servant at their bidding. Proof of this is that if he simply dared to insist or behave differently from how he had been ordered to, he was immediately punished "with electrical shocks inside his head."

The Mystery Continues

At this point, some reflection on this whole incredible story is required. The questions that would need an answer are at least two. To begin with, how much is actually true in the story about the aliens? We have seen that there have been numerous witnesses who confirmed the presence of a big flying saucer in the area where Zanfretta was at that precise moment. Also, the investigation that was carried out on site confirmed what Zanfretta said under hypnosis. But nothing else gives us concrete proof of the existence of these alleged aliens.

Moreover, the logic of events must be examined. Let's think about a far-fetched situation: that is, let's take for granted a reality that in actual fact we know nothing about. Let's admit that the aliens exist, that they have kidnapped Zanfretta making him the guardian of their sphere and that, at some point after several years, they told him: "We're coming back now and we're taking our sphere back, thank you for looking after it all this time." What sense would all this make? The first one to wonder about this was Zanfretta himself who, thinking about it, found such behavior inexplicable. In fact, why leave a device of that type hidden in a cave on the Liguria mountains for years, complete with a private security guard to then simply take it back? For over thirty years, who was that sphere for and what was it for?

Clearly, if we are unable to answer this question the entire story seems absurd and meaningless.

And let's not take into account the final result, that is, the disastrous consequences that this affair has had on the life of the individual concerned, meaning Zanfretta. Therefore, it is not a coincidence that he now wants some satisfaction from his mysterious interlocutors.

And that is what Zanfretta and I were discussing the evening of Saturday, October 28, 2006, when he came to see me in the newsroom after work. The conversation turned to the clinical tests that the Security and Patrol Institute "Val Bisagno" repeatedly had him take. "One day," he told me, "from the head X-rays they had taken, they saw a foreign object, right here, inside the nape of the neck." And he brought the index finger of his right hand behind his head, turning it to the left for me to see. "The professor who was visiting me, an elderly specialist, told me that I had this foreign object inside the bone, but there was no scar tissue. And he asked what I had done. I replied that I knew nothing about it and that perhaps it had been those beings to put that implant there, also because it is actually from that spot that I receive the orders and the electrical shocks, too. So he replied that they had to briefly operate to remove it, but I refused. The head is my own, as if I'd let anyone touch me. The professor insisted, saying that they could even force me to do it, but I didn't want to listen and so I left. The last thing I'd let them do is operate on my head. Are we mad or something?"

To be honest it's hard to blame him for that. However, this whole story made something inside me click. I had in fact kept the entire original dossier of the clinical examinations which Zanfretta was subjected to in 1979; among the tests, there are also the X-rays of his skull. At the time, Zanfretta himself had handed the file to me (with his employers' consent) because he wanted me to publish the results in this book, as I eventually did. That year the radiological examinations were carried out not once but twice in two different laboratories in Genoa.

The first time was at the Istituto Radiologico Colombo (a radiological institute owned by Dr. Vittorio Turtulici, specialist in Medical Radiology and physical therapy) located in via Colombo 11/10. It was August 7, 1979, and the radiology report was: "Hypo-development of the frontal sinus and normal transparency of the maxillary sinuses. Hypertrophy of the left nasal turbinate. Regular amplitude and morphology of the Sella turcica."

The second set of tests were carried out on December 13, and 18, 1979 at the Radiologia Medica -Fisioterapia (Medical Radiology and Physiotherapy owned by professor Pierfausto Antonietti, lecturer in Medical Radiology at the University of Genoa), located in via Caesarea 2/41. In this case, the report says: "Nothing in particular on the crown, Sella turcica of regular shape and amplitude. Congenital malformation of the frontal sinus. Slight haze on the right ethmoidal and moderate deviation of the nasal septum toward the right." In other words, in both radiological examinations, nothing odd was found in Zanfretta's skull. Just to be sure, on the morning of Tuesday, October 31, 2006 I showed all the X-rays of Zanfretta's skull to a well-known doctor, Enrico Bartolini, Specialist in Radiology and President of the provincial Medical Association as well as owner of the analysis lab, Istituto Salus located in Piazza Dante 9 in Genoa.

Dr. Bartolini, after carefully examining all the X-rays said he didn't see anything peculiar in that skull and his opinion was further confirmed by one of his collaborators, Dr. Rolla, who among other things, remembered Zanfretta's story well.

Have we explained everything, then? Can we conclude by arguing that perhaps the ex-night watchman imagined it all and everything in his skull is in order? I wish it were so simple: the thing is that the Security and Patrol Institute "Val Bisagno" made Zanfretta undergo repeated radiological examinations to the head, at least five more times over the years, and the last one was a little before 1990. This is what the person concerned claims and what I personally could ascertain by listening to the testimony of his former colleagues. The question is: why? Why did Zanfretta's employers deem it necessary to have continual X-rays of their employee's skull? What were they looking for? Or are we correct in thinking that, after 1980 the exams actually confirmed that there was indeed something there and they wanted to learn more about it by monitoring the nature of that "foreign object"?

"All I can say," Zanfretta replies, "is that every so often I was ordered to go to some laboratory to have X-rays to the head done and afterwards they wouldn't tell me anything. I have never seen the result of a single exam. On the other hand at that time, I did everything I was ordered and that's it. However I remember that I've had radiological examinations more than once at San Martino Hospital, in a laboratory on via XX Settembre and once again at Galliera Hospital. I've not had any more since I quarreled with the professor that wanted to operate on me."

So who was this doctor? Zanfretta claims that he doesn't remember his name, but that everything he was told took place during a visit to the clinic Villa Serena in piazza Leopardi 18, in the suburb of Albaro, where he was undergoing one of the frequent check-ups at the time. This, at least, is what he says. But how can we verify if those tests were normal clinical investigations, perhaps made for professional reasons (for example, when police headquarters revoked his gun license) or "secret" studies to check the conditions that would lead to surgery to the head in order to "remove a foreign object"?

Once again, too many questions remain unanswered. First of all, where are all the clinical documents concerning Zanfretta? Unfortunately ownership of the Security and Patrol Institute "Val Bisagno" has changed and we know nothing about the previous managers. Some of them, like Colonel Luigi Cereda for example, have died. Gianfranco Tutti, the director, I was told, has retired somewhere.

And in any case it is perhaps no coincidence that today, among all the people who in those years had something to do with the Zanfretta case, we cannot find a single name in the phone book. And privacy is sacred, obviously....

In other words, as far as the past is concerned we can at this point consider the clinical documentation lost, unless any "coups de scène" should occur in the near future. All that's left to prove is whether that "foreign object" really was there in his head. And it's for this reason that on May 10, 2007, Piero Zanfretta turned up at the Genoese headquarters of the Istituto Salus (medical analysis, radiology, instrumental medical diagnostics and imaging) to undergo a CAT scan of the skull. The examination was carried out by Professor Giorgio Ramella with multilayer technique, using contiguous axial layers of 5mm thickness. This is the report of the exam:

"No parenchymal sensitometric alterations centers and no particular supra and subtentorial sensitometric alterations are determined as the outcomes of vascular lesions.

There are no masses or groupings occupying space, intra-and extra-axial.

Symmetrical ventricular cavities of normal size and morphology, regularly aligned with the Sagittal plane.

Cortex furrows and cisterns of the base are regularly represented, no evident endocranial vascular and parenchymal calcification."

Simply put, there is nothing irregular in Zanfretta's skull. The only anomaly, even if clinically it cannot be defined as such, is an abnormal enlargement of the bone at the base of the nape of the neck. It is as if at that point, which is usually concave toward the base of the neck, there was a kind of large cyst that in the CAT scan appears of the same consistency of the bone. We cannot to know if this protrusion was present before 1978, the year of his first alleged encounter, as there are no X-rays of his skull before that date. Therefore, after so much going back and forth and so much talk, we're back to square one.

What is left of the Zanfretta case then? Above all, the great mystery that our man continues to hold inside him. He tells everyone that he really does have the sphere but now, no one takes any notice of him anymore and takes this affirmation as a something weird and with no substance. At least to all appearances. Because we have to wonder who, even in recent times, goes to the trouble of following him up to the mountains at night, trying to steal his secret. And what if, contrary to the way things seem, there really is someone taking him seriously and who believes that the sphere actually exists? After all, the Americans did and that's not to say that someone else in Italy is not secretly doing the same. And what would happen, I wonder, if something happened to Zanfretta? What would happen to the sphere in the cave? And what could happen, assuming that this thing does exist, if one day a hiker casually discovered the cave and went inside?

Questions that are not to be taken for granted given that in September of 2012, Zanfretta suffered a brain aneurysm and after spending a few days in intensive care, the doctors of the Department of Neurosurgery of San Martino Hospital in Genoa managed to save his life by cauterizing the vein that had caused the cerebral hemorrhage. It took him over six months of rehabilitation to get back to his normal life. Today, Pier Fortunato Zanfretta is a pensioner who supplements the low monthly salary the State gives him by continuing to work as a night watchman for the religious institute where he has been working for years. Every so often, when someone reminds him that he is a well-known personality in the world he shrugs and smiles. He rarely talks of his adventures and he only regrets the fact that some still don't believe him. "It's all true," he keeps repeating. "One day you'll see..." Then, tired of the sniggering and the ironic wisecracks, he turns around and leaves with a tired and heavy step, hanging his head. He knows, after all, that the Zanfretta case is and will remain, despite everything, an open case...

The administrative office of the first World Congress of Ufology held at the Hilton Hotel in Tucson, Arizona.

Pier Fortunato Zanfretta in front of the notice board of the Holiday Inn where he was staying during the first World Congress of Ufology.

Rino Di Stefano in front of the Hilton in Tucson where the first World Congress of Ufology was held.

Group photo with the Italian, Russian and Spanish delegations. From the left, standing: Valery Uvarov, Pier Fortunato Zanfretta, Rino Di Stefano, Viktor Kostrykin, Wendell C. Stevens, Marina Popovich, Antonio Ribera and, kneeling, Roberto Pinotti.

From the left: Brian P. Myers, Tina P. Choate, Pier Fotunato Zanfretta and Rino Di Stefano in a club on the Eastern Riviera of Liguria.

The photo taken by Zanfretta of the mountains near Rossi.

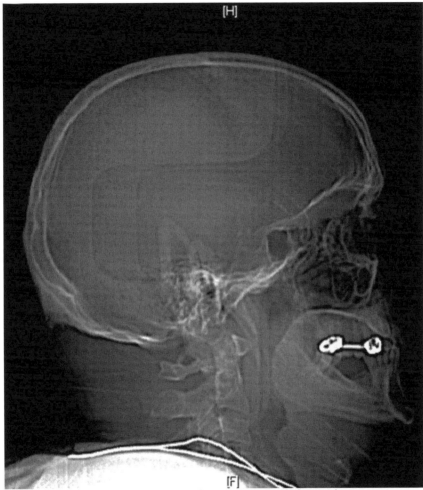

The Zanfretta's skull as it appears in the CAT scan made by Zanfretta on May 10, 2007 at the Salus Institute in Genoa, Italy. The medical report, signed by professor Giorgio Ramella, was: *absolutely normal.*

About the Author

Biographer, columnist and fiction writer Rino Di Stefano was a deputy editor in chief of the Italian national newspaper, *Il Giornale*. Recently retired, he continues his professional activity of investigative journalist. He is the author of five books: *The Zanfretta Case*, in its sixth edition of which a television adaptation was broadcast; *Alcibiades*, translated from English to Italian of the work of professor Walter M. Ellis of Loyola Marymount University of Los Angeles; *"My dear Marion..."*, an historical essay about past Italian president Sandro Pertini; *Over the Horizon*, a collection of political essays about the life of Italian minister Claudio Scajola; *The Viral Solution*, a novel about the spread of AIDS in the USA (this book has been awarded both in Italy and in the States); *The Orchid Shadow*, a novel about the role of a mysterious Italian immigrant in the Teapot Dome Scandal in Washington D.C.; *The Return of the Prince*, a novel about the paranormal presence of Raimondo de Sangro, Prince of San Severo and one of the most interesting personality of the European XVIII century, in today Naples. In 2014 RSI, the Swiss Radiotelevision, broadcast the movie *The Machine Coming From The Future* by Victor Tognola, a documentary about the Di Stefano's report published on *Il Giornale*. Di Stefano received the Italian National Award Chronicle of Mystery 2014. One year later, Di Stefano also received the Italian National Journalistic Award Joseph Allen Hynek 2015. He lives in Genoa, Italy.

61690318R00155

Made in the USA
Middletown, DE
13 January 2018